Michael Hart

4.

The

Party

And Econ

1945-1983

THE BRITISH PARTY SYSTEM AND ECONOMIC POLICY

1945-1983

Studies in Adversary Politics

A. M. GAMBLE
and
S. A. WALKLAND

With a foreword by
J. E. S. HAYWARD

CLARENDON PRESS · OXFORD
1984

Oxford University Press, Walton Street, Oxford OX2 6DP
London New York Toronto
Delhi Bombay Calcutta Madras Karachi
Kuala Lumpur Singapore Hong Kong Tokyo
Nairobi Dar es Salaam Cape Town
Melbourne Auckland

and associated companies in
Beirut Berlin Ibadan Mexico City Nicosia

Oxford is a trade mark of Oxford University Press

Published in the United States
by Oxford University Press, New York

British Library Cataloguing in Publication Data

Gamble, Andrew
The British party system and economic policy 1945–1983.
1. Political parties–Great Britain–History 20th century 2. Great Britain–Economic policy–1945-
I. Title II. Walkland, S.A.
330.941'085 HC256.5

ISBN 0-19-876174-0
ISBN 0-19-876173-2 Pbk

Set in Press Roman by Rod-Art, Abingdon, Oxon.
and printed in Great Britain by
Biddles Limited, Guildford

FOREWORD

In a pluralist political system, such as that of the United Kingdom, there are always a great many actors in the policy process. They vary in importance according to the type of issue considered. In the case of economic policy, if one initially excludes the crucial foreign actors, at least six clusters of domestic decision-makers are involved. The partisan heads of the national government – the Prime Minister, the Chancellor of the Exchequer, the Chief Secretary to the Treasury, the Secretary of State for Trade and Industry, and so forth – are the formal political decision-makers and in some cases may have played an active part in actually making the policy choices. Next the senior civil service officials on the Prime Minister's staff, in the Cabinet Office, and in the economic ministries will play an important part in identifying economic policy issues, preparing the decisions and then implementing them, in conjunction with their political 'masters' and the other actors. Thirdly, the heads of public financial and industrial corporations, who are responsible for public economic management, will play a particularly important part in making and carrying out some of the major economic policy decisions. Fourthly – moving out of the public into the private sector– there are those responsible for private economic management: the leaders of the major financial, industrial, and agricultural firms, as well as of the trade associations and peak employer organizations, notably the Confederation of British Industry. Fifthly, the leaders of the major trade unions – whose role had often been greatly exaggerated though not in this book – and of the Trades Union Congress have frequently played a part in the economic policy process. Finally, there are the institutions of democratic mobilization, communication, and legitimation, notable the political parties and Parliament. The principal question raised by this book is whether the main responsibility for British economic decline can be laid at the door of the political parties, understood to include the partisan heads of the national government.

It is unfortunate that the policy role of the political parties has in recent years been identified so closely with the model of adversary politics. This usually Right–Centre view is at one extreme of the conspectus of possible views and attributes an exaggerated importance to the alternation of political parties in power and in the process of economic decision-making and policy application. At the other extreme, there is the usually Leftist view that in terms of economic policy actually carried out in office, the Conservative and Labour parties have been virtually indistinguishable. The two authors of this volume eschew these extreme positions but the reader may gain the impression that they lean in opposite directions. Andrew Gamble dismisses adversary politics in Britain as so often a 'sham' offer of 'imaginary choices', while Stuart Walkland asserts that 'on a deeper level the adversarial thesis is amply justified'. Gamble seems sensibly to have given up the search for an new scapegoat on which to pin the responsibility for Britain's economic failures. As he circumspectly writes in his conclusion, 'The adversary politics thesis in its well-known version exaggerates the role of parties in policy formulation and implementation and underplays the role of other bodies and institutions, and still more the constraints which circumstances, administration procedures, events, and outside forces impose on any government.' Earlier, he hammers home an implication of the same point when he criticizes both the monetarist and Keynesian accounts of British economic stabilization policy for attributing a decisive influence to the national government over events. Party politicians are all too inclined to adopt the flattering standpoint that the British government has sovereign power in economic policy matters, whereas it has only limited discretion in trying to adapt the national economy to meet the exigencies of the United States-dominated international economy.

Now a problem with Gamble's approach is that it seems to encourage a rather fatalistic attitude towards Britain's slide into economic failure, and some of Stuart Walkland's vehemence stems from his reluctance to adopt the quietist attitude of a non-prescriptive analyst. However, while he is right to claim that 'analysis is easier than prescription', even if the latter is grounded upon a correct analysis of the ailment to be cured, he castigates both those analyses that are barren of prescription and the many panaceas that have been boldly propounded, only to be expeditiously consigned to the dustbin, an awful set of warnings to the injudicious prescriber of quack remedies. The authors of this book clearly do not regard party differences and changes of policy direction as having been mainly responsible for Britain's economic predicament. The differences have generally been over secondary issues while on fundamental matters like foreign economic policy, the parties have been in agreement. One of the most controversial issues between the parties has been nationalization, with the prospect of privatization and renationalization. The two main British parties seem self-indulgently and intransigently divided on this issue, with a necrophiliac Labour party, committed to giving the kiss of life to dying as well as lame ducks, and a body-snatching Conservative party, hell-bent on scouring Britain's industrial graveyards to see what can be profitably retrieved for privatization. Both authors agree that quarrelling over the private–public sector boundary may be ideologically important but has little to offer as a solution to Britain's economic difficulties. They regard the main problem as being the shared and unchallenged assumptions underlying the 'bogus adversary politics' of both parties which have prevented the application of the radical remedies required.

The reader will have to form his own judgement about whether the constitutional and electoral reforms that the authors succinctly outline are equal to this ambitious task. For what it is worth, I have taken the view (leaving aside the crucial cultural and international constraints, about which little can be done in the short run) that the major source of Britain's difficulties is to be located among the non-state actors and in particular in the failure of both private and public *enterprise* to live up to that proud name, recalling past exploits. With the best will in the world, the efficacy of a subsidiary state intervention cannot be great when industrial firms, banks, and trade unions – who are directly involved in economic activity and *decide* in a more direct sense than do British governments – are unable to invest, produce, and sell efficiently the goods and services on which the competitiveness of the economy depends. Politicians in power prate and posture, taking the credit and the blame for the diverse fortunes that ensue from the interplay of international market and institutional forces, without – in any country – usually being genuinely responsible for either the good or the bad results. That this presents problems in a democracy is clear but one should not necessarily conclude that the remedy is to make changes in the political processes themselves.

I would like to end on a personal note. Having commenced my career as a university teacher at Sheffield, it is a particular pleasure to see that the ambiance of forceful argumentation and scrupulous scholarship that I well remember continues to animate members of its Politics

Department. I have much sympathy with the view that those who study politics as an academic discipline should do all they can to suggest improvements in their own country's system of government, even if most politicians usually do not appear to be unduly interested in our findings. As this book focuses attention on the British parties themselves, I trust they will respond by showing some interest in its arguments and its proposals for improving Britain's economic performance.

JACK HAYWARD
Professor of Politics
University of Hull

PREFACE

At first sight this book might appear as an exercise in reductionism, to take its place alongside other studies which have sought mono-causal explanations for Britain's economic decline. Such explanations have been many, ranging through deficiencies in the theory or application of economic doctrine, the influence of institutions, to national cultural characteristics. The list of causes is long, and all have either been disputed or had their relative importance queried.[1] The studies collected here do not offer another all-embracing explantion. They concentrate on post-1945 fiscal and monetary policy and economic planning, and are preliminary and incomplete. Many areas of economic policy are not explored – labour supply and wages (except in so far as the latter come under demand management), and welfare and regional policy, for example, although some of these have been strongly influenced by adversary politics. One justification for this book, however, is not only that such a study has not been attempted in any extended form, but also that its focus, the party system, is of especial importance since it relates generally to many of the factors, social, industrial, administrative, and constitutional, which form the basis of other explanations.

The authors differ in their political beliefs, but this has not proved the obstacle to collaboration which it might be thought to constitute. They would agree that every political society, to exist at all, needs some degree of consensus, more often than not based on myth, and fortified by ritual. As Pareto observed, both ritual and myth play a fundamental role in legitimation. But the myths produced by the post-war British system have been economically damaging and have impeded the development of the conditions needed for economic growth. As Professor S. E. Finer has pointed out, many of the myths have arisen from the operation of a representative political system in which the choices which voters have to make between candidates, leaders, and policies have become increasingly ritualistic and a denial of any effective democratic participation by the electorate. He observes that the actual way

British government functions bears little relation either to traditional theories of the constitution or to popular notions about how British democracy works.[2] The rituals of the British two-party adversary system have contributed to the political failure to reverse or arrest relative economic decline. This failure has produced both rationalizations and scape goats, few of them convincing. But it is also producing, so far in characteristically mild British fashion, a gradual breakdown of the post-war political structure.

The authors believe that this process should be accelerated, by constitutional changes, in particular electoral reform, in order to extend the constricted boundaries of current political consciousness, to formulate a new political agenda, and to produce wider political debate than the post-war political system has been able to secure.

This series of studies was made possible by a grant from the Social Science Research Council, which we would like to thank. This enabled us to use the skilled services of Mr Brian Duncan as research assistant on the project. We are grateful to the members of the Faculty of Social Sciences at Sheffield University who contributed to early discussion of the project, and for the help of Mr Ivon Asquith and Mr Andrew Schuller of the Oxford University Press. Mrs Elizabeth Dawson typed the book with her customary efficiency.

A. M. G.
S. A. W

Department of Political Theory and Institutions
University of Sheffield
August 1983

CONTENTS

1

ECONOMIC POLICY AND THE BRITISH POLITICAL SYSTEM

The adversary politics thesis is concerned with the relationship between the state and the economy. It argues that the way in which the political system works and the kind of public choices that emerge from it in the form of government economic policies have had significant and harmful effects on the overall performance of the economy. This book attempts to evaluate some of the evidence for and against this proposition. But before looking in more detail at the adversary politics thesis itself it is necessary to say something about the nature of the political system and of economic policy in Britain.

Why governments need an economic policy

One way of approaching the complex relationship between state and economy is to ask, why do governments need an economic policy at all? Why has the political process become so involved with questions of economic performance and organization?

There are two complementary answers to these questions. In the first place all governments need an economic policy because state and economy are so interdependent. There never has been a state existing independently outside a self-sufficient economy. The modern industrial economy has always required extensive involvement by public agencies in order for it to exist and to function. Three ways in which state and economy are interrrelated and interdependent are central to any understanding of economic policy. Firstly the national economy is part of a wider world economy. The British economy since the sixteenth century, and on an increasing scale since the middle of the nineteenth, has been progressively integrated into an ever widening and more specialized world division of labour. The development of a system of world production and world trade, however, has not been matched by a parallel evolution of world political authority. Instead the political conditions which allow international economic activity to proceed have to be negotiated between nation states claiming sovereignty over their own territories and their own peoples. But the prosperity and even the physical survival of these populations has come to depend on the maintenance of international flows of trade and capital and labour. It follows that every such national government must have a policy for dealing with the relations of its own economy to the world economy. Such a *foreign economic policy* must embrace the degree of freedom to be allowed the movement of goods, of capital, and of labour; the question of the relation of the national currency to other currencies; and the problem of security – the enforceability of contracts and the safety of property outside national frontiers.

Secondly an industrial economy organized on capitalist rather than collectivist lines requires an elaborate system of markets. There is nothing natural or spontaneous about such markets. If they are to exist and function properly certain requirements have to be guaranteed by a force outside the market agents themselves. These include the security of property, the enforceability of contracts, the independence of agents, and the stability of the medium of exchange. The market order requires constant public involvement and intervention if a system of free markets – principally financial markets, commercial and industrial markets, and labour markets – is to become established and maintained. At a minimum, public policy has to ensure that all the commodities required for modern industrial production to take place are freely available in sufficient quantity. Governments are involved in maintaining the market order in the passive sense that without the provision of a legal framework markets could not function properly, but also in an active sense because public agencies necessarily become involved in removing market rigidities (due, for example, to monopoly over the supply of a particular good), or remedying market failures (where resources of the right type or right quality are not produced by the market spontaneously).

The third reason why governments need an economic policy is the most clear-cut of all. The government has direct responsibility for the public sector of the economy, those goods and services which are provided by public agencies or financed from public funds. Every government is obliged to find a means of funding its own activities and those of the wider public sector. Then it must borrow, from its citizens or from foreigners; or it must collect taxes from its citizens; or it must draw on the financial surpluses of public corporations or simply print money. All four of these play a part in public finance but much the greatest role is played by taxation. Every government must therefore maintain a coercive tax-gathering machinery and must develop a fiscal policy determining what kind of taxes are to be levied, on whom, and at what rate. These are intensely political questions but fiscal policy has a wider significance because of the different effect of particular taxes upon the economy. At the same time, to the extent that the public finances rely on borrowing from the financial markets or on exploiting the government's right to issue legal money by printing new money, the government is obliged to have a monetary policy as well. The growth of the public sector, the increase in taxes, and the increase in borrowing have forced governments to acknowledge that the financing of the 'public household' cannot be considered in isolation. Whatever monetary policy or fiscal policy is adopted will have consequences for the rest of the economy. If it influences the performance of the economy it will have consequences for future public finances, for example by raising or lowering the tax yield. The existence of a substantial sector of the economy which is publicly managed and publicly financed means that the government must develop a *stabilization policy*, trying to use monetary and fiscal measures both to raise the necessary public finance for state activities and promote a stable environment that encourages expansion and minimizes disruption.

Governments therefore need an economic policy because of the interdependence of state and economy, and this economic policy has three main divisions – *a foreign economic policy*, an *industrial and commercial policy*, and a *stabilization policy*. But there is another way of answering the question why do governments need an economic policy – by examining the sequence of unique historical events by which public responsibilities have gradually been extended. All governments may need a foreign economic policy, but which policy is a matter for political argument and conflict between opposing interests and ideas organized and expressed through institutions of various kinds. Public responsibilities have expanded because of the scale and complexity of economic activity in an industrial society and the constant emergence of new social needs, which range from education, health, and sanitation to roads, ports, and technological research, and which private agencies have either been unwilling or unable to provide. The identification of such costs and such needs has been piecemeal but cumulative, and has meant an enormous enlargement of the public sector in both economy and society. A further reason for public involvement has been the need to regulate and contain social conflict, particularly between labour and capital. These two processes and the pressure groups associated with them have shaped British party politics in the last hundred years. There have been constant conflicts between the major parties over where the boundary between the public and private sectors should lie, over the extent of public responsibilities for welfare services, over the rights of trade unions, and over policy on trade, foreign investment, and immigration.

During the last hundred years there have been unmistakable trends towards a more collectivist society on the one hand and a more market-orientated society on the other. The public sector has been enormously enlarged and the extent of government monitoring and regulation of all aspects of the economy greatly increased. This has led not unnaturally to a much larger bureaucratic machine, and a growing awareness both among politicians and the electorate of the government's powers and ability to influence the economy. The experience of organizing the economy for war between 1940 and 1945 was particularly important. The ease with which full employment was achieved and the resources of the whole economy mobilized for a total war effort contrasted vividly with the persistent failure to eradicate unemployment throughout the 1920s and 1930s. After 1945 the government was expected to have solutions to economic problems, an expectation which politicians of all parties were ready to encourage. Only since the second half of the 1970s have determined efforts been made to play down the efficacy of government and to disclaim government responsibility for what happens in the economy.

The steady progress of collectivism has received enormous attention in writing on British politics. But the penetration of market relationships into every sphere of British society is no less significant. The changes in the organization of the family, the entry of women into the labour force, and the development of a mass consumer society are important aspects of this. Hence the paradox; Britain is both a more collectivist and a more market-orientated society in the 1980s than in the 1880s. This has important political consequences, not always fully appreciated.

The British political inheritance

For one hundred years the British political system with its ancient institutions and rituals has been gradually adapted to the very different pressures and demands of mass democracy. This has been achieved without sacrificing continuity and with only marginal institutional changes – the most important being the curtailment (but not removal) of the legislative powers of the House of Lords. The rise of the Labour party and the stresses of two world wars have brought remarkably few changes in outward institutional forms and procedures of British politics. This contrasts with the enormous changes in both British society and the British economy over the same period.

The singular nature of the structure of British representational politics has seldom been noted. But it has quite astonishing characteristics, especially when compared with those of other West European states. Almost uniquely in Europe, until the founding of the Social Democratic Party, which has still to locate itself securely in the British political spectrum, all three main British political parties have their roots firmly in the nineteenth and early twentieth centuries, and in the case of the Conservative party, even earlier. They carry with them, inevitably, a baggage of assumptions, attitudes, and basic predispositions which developed in their formative periods. Unlike most other major West European states, in Britain the vast changes in the social and economic environment which the twentieth century has seen have had to be accommodated by developments and reactions within the traditional parties, and have not given place, as has been common in countries of the West which do not share the British political inheritance, to new parties and political groupings. Admittedly many issues which have activated continental politics in the post-1945 period have had few if any counterparts in Britain – the continuing lay/clerical struggle is one prominent example. But largely due to the discontinuities which resulted from different experiences of war and occupation, and also as a result of new constitutional imperatives, European political structures have become more diverse and sophisticated, and more responsive than their British counterparts to complex social and economic evolution.

Political culture is an imprecise but useful concept, if it is taken to mean the dominating strands of thought and experience which condition political and intellectual responses in a particular historical period. Victorian liberalism is one such culture, and, as numerous commentators have pointed out, it has had continuing effects into the twentieth century which the political and economic philosophers who called it into being could hardly have foreseen. It is, and this is of primary significance for some analyses deployed in this volume, an inheritance of thought and feeling which instinctively separates politics from economics, an intellectual disjunction which has had profound political and institutional repercussions on twentieth-century Britain. This persistent tradition has many more minor facets – in particular a strict conceptual division between public and private powers, and an emphasis on individualism in politics and law which has found it difficult adequately to recognize or legally define corporate institutions, let alone provide a framework of public law for relating them to the state. It is also a strong tradition of limited government – limited in the post-1945 period not in the range of activities undertaken by government, but in a reluctance to use public power. It is as a result an intellectual inheritance which elevates the political process and stresses the constant need for political consensus. There is in Britain no main source of formal political power outside the representative political process – no powerful and independent bureaucracy, a state within the state, as in France; no strong body of public law which regulates the organization of parties and political groups, and which is shaped and implemented by a powerful judiciary, as in West Germany. The so-called British constitution, neither codified, detailed, nor entrenched, is little except what politicians can agree upon as the conditions for the exercise of political authority.

With its ingrained fear of institutionalized power, there is very little in liberal theory concerning the role or even the concept of the state. In Britain the state has no legal existence. There is the Crown, government departments, public corporations, local authorities – all have legal personalities. But there is no legal organization in Britain called the state. The operation of government, the relationships between its parts which determine its fuctioning, are not defined in terms of an all-embracing legal framework, but largely in terms of the political process within which, and only within which does British government take on meaning. Constitution-making has not been a major feature of the politics of Britain, and has received little practical or academic attention. What is meant by the constitution in Britain is really a reflection of political practice and a description of existing institutions. Perhaps this decidedly British emphasis is changing, as economic failure and political change slowly force British politicians, and students of government, back to some basic constitutional considerations. But constitutional reform is still generally regarded in pragmatic terms, rather than in terms of formal legal principles.

The ideology of liberal democracy essentially views the state as a neutral complex of political institutions, encompassing only a part of social existence. Society and the economy exist independently of the state. In liberalism, paradoxically enough, this independence from the state is guaranteed by the state. The rights of individuals are underwritten by law, in particular the rights to private ownership in the sphere of civil society. The framing of general rules by Acts of Parliament guaranteeing and extending civil, political, and social rights was the characteristic activity of nineteenth-century reforming governments. In so far as liberals had any concept of sovereignty, this came to be located in Parliament, and in particular in a House of Commons increasingly representative of the whole adult population. Parliament was the main limitation on government – not the government itself, but the institution which incorporated popular sovereignty and mediated between citizen and executive authority. Even when early utilitarian liberalism gave way to the more sophisticated doctrines of J. S. Mill, and the New Liberalism at the turn of the century, the positive state action needed to alleviate the injustices of a *laissez-faire* economy could still be undertaken through the Parliamentary system without shedding a basic preference for limited government and individual rights. It was a development which found a sympathetic response in some sections of the Conservative party, with its older, more paternalistic traditions. The apparent contradiction between limited government and positive state action was solved through the concept of voluntarism – the calling into play of group and individual responsibility. This came to extend into most fields of government activity, from education to social policy and economic regulation. Few polities outside Britain have such a widespread and varied record of the use of private organizations and individuals in the processes of both the formulation and implementation of public policy. Some aspects of this tendency in the economic sphere will be analysed later in this volume.

This characteristic style of government in Britain has become known in much recent academic discussion as *corporatism.* What the term corporatist here signifies is not bureaucratic, centralized domination of the economy and society by the state, but the sharing of state authority with major corporate pressure groups, the most important of which have become as a result 'governing institutions'. As Alan Cawson has expressed it 'In a corporatist model of policy-making, representation (of demands) and implementation (of policies) are fused within a mutually dependent bargaining relationship in which favourable policy outcomes are traded for co-operation and expertise. The groups which have entered into such relationships are those which have a degree of independent power arising from their structural location in the division of labour'.[1]

The development of 'corporate bias' in Britain has involved the fragmentation rather than the consolidation of the authority of the state. It has greatly narrowed the scope and range of the issues that are directly settled through Parliament, and has reinforced the necessity for consensus and the management of public opinion. The liberal order in Britain has preserved itself by co-opting every important interest into the process of policy formulation and implementation, while maintaining a highly centralized machinery for actually taking decisions. The result has been a deadlocked state or 'pluralistic stagnation'. Institutional continuity and civil strife have been avoided by at the expense of inertia at all levels of British government. British governments have often been too weak to carry through any substantial measures of reform.

Apart from the liberal inheritance two other inheritances, the aristocratic and the radical, are important for understanding this peculiar character of British government and politics. As Tom Nairn in particular has insisted,[2] what is so special about British government and political institutions is that so many of them originated before the modern era and have stubbornly resisted many attempts to reform them. The absence of any true political revolution in Britain since the seventeenth century decisively shaped the kind of liberalism Britain acquired in the nineteenth century. It was a liberalism which took full account of the organization of civil society in Britain, with its elaborate network of guilds, associations, and corporate bodies. No atomized free market society of competitive, self-reliant individuals ever arose in Britain. The continuing social power of the Land, the Church, the Crown, the aristocracy, the Universities, the learned professions, and the armed services not only provided a secure institutional base for the survival, and ultimately revival, of the Conservative party. It also ensured that the effect of liberal ideas would be to consolidate rather than to challenge the existing order.

To the aristocratic inheritance can be traced many features of British political institutions; the patterns of recruitment to jobs throughout the public service; the emphasis upon community, loyalty, and trust; the small number of participants in policy-making; the degree of secrecy; the prevalence of amateurism as an ideal throughout the public service; the persistent evidence of disdain for industry and of preference for commerce, finance, and the professions among the British upper classes; the great gulf in status and life-styles between manual and non-manual occupations in Britain, on which foreign observers so often remark; finally, to which all the foregoing contribute, the cohesiveness and effectiveness of the British Establishment, whose members share or have acquired a common background, a common outlook, and a common appreciation of how things work in Britain and how things should be done.

The emphasis on liberty and tradition are distinguishing characteristics of British political institutions. But there has always been as well an important radical inheritance, which although never dominant, has always supplied movements and institutions of opposition to the dominant political order. The development of such institutions and movements – a free press, chartism, trade unions, women's votes and women's rights, non-conformist churches, and nationalist movements have repeatedly challenged the closed and exclusive character of Westminster politics. Sometimes the challenges were met by concessions which defused the challenge and widened the basis of British democracy. In a few cases, Ireland is the most prominent example, the challenge could not be handled and secession resulted. But at no time was there a major remaking of British political institutions. New interests were appeased and co-opted within the liberal order, so increasing the pluralism of British civil society, while blunting the pressure for a more effective democracy.

A party system

The way in which these different inheritances have shaped British politics has long been reinforced by the British two-party system which itself owes its continued existence to the nature of the electoral system. The simple plurality voting system makes the survival of third party parliamentary representation difficult, it ensures that most governments win parliamentary majorities on electoral minorities; and it obliges the two main parties to become broad coalitions in pursuit of government office.

Two mass parties become the main channel by which popular participation in policy-making is secured. Party leaders seek to balance what is electorally 'popular', what is 'popular' within their parties, what is 'popular' with the opinion formers of the media, and what is 'popular' with foreign governments, civil servants, corporate interests, and the multitude of individual agents in the financial, commercial, and labour markets, both domestically and internationally. In this process the independence of each party leadership to determine policy is essential. This is codified in the doctrines of parliamentary sovereignty and the autonomy of members of Parliament. That is why ideas of making MPs delegates of their parties or obliging party leaders to adhere to a manifesto drawn up by the party strike at the heart of the British notion of parliamentary government and are so fiercely resisted.

The British two-party system exists alongside the constitutional notion of Crown-in-Parliament, of unfettered parliamentary sovereignty. In order for this to ensure political order rather than disorder it is obviously essential that there should be fundamental agreement between the party leaderships on the principles of parliamentary government and on the unwritten constraints on the exercise of executive power. In the era of mass democracy the constitutional orthodoxy of the Labour party has been largely beyond question although recently under increasing strain. The only serious breakdown in the two-party system occurred between 1910 and 1914, when the Conservatives disputed the constitutionality of the Liberal Government's Irish policy and were prepared to support armed action against it. By contrast the understanding between the Conservative and Labour parties has rarely been broken. The most conservative and laudatory account of British parliamentary government still remains *Government and Parliament* by Lord Morrison.[3] In this recollection by an ex-Labour Cabinet Minister there is no breath of criticism of any of the institutions of British central government, nor any trace of the forebodings of many pre-war Labour intellectuals, such as Harold Laski, who argued after the events of 1931 that no Labour government would ever be allowed by either the government machine or the financial markets to implement a radical socialist programme.

Labourism, with its emphasis on parliamentarism and constitutional propriety, has always been the dominant outlook of the Labour leadership. Until the 1970s the leaderships of both major parties tended in practice to play a similar role in the formulation and implementation of policy. But it is also true as other observers have noted that, especially in the sphere of economic policy, there has been an essential and enduring disparity in the aims, the doctrines, and the ethos of the two main parties during the past sixty years. The attachment of Labour to parliamentary forms has tended to obscure these differences.

The reaction against *laissez-faire* in the late nineteenth century brought important currents of opinion in both the Liberal and the Conservative parties close to the ideas of social democracy developed within the Labour Fabian tradition. All emphasized the educational and responsible properties of representative government and the civic values of government by consent. All emphasized also the need for greatly enlarged functions for the state in economic management and the provision of welfare. The Fabian socialists, like many of the Social Imperialists in the Conservative party, wanted an efficient industrial society and envisaged both an active legislative role for Parliament in order to transform capitalist society and a greatly enlarged bureaucracy to administer the new public sector.

In common with other European social democratic movements they believed that Parliament and other institutions of the state were capable of being used to build socialism, just as the Social Imperialists, and many later Tory radicals, believed that the same institutions could be used to modernize British society. Because popular sovereignty resides in Parliament this has blinded reformers in all parties to the degree to which power is shared in Britain among a great variety of corporate interests. Capturing a parliamentary majority appears to give political power to the government party. But in Britain this formal power is heavily circumscribed by the bargains government has struck with producer interests and market agents, throughout the public and private sectors. The British state displays at one and the same time a highly centralized policy-making machine and a highly fragmented political authority.

This paradox of British political experience can be traced within both major parties. It is clearest in the Labour party where there is a marked tension between the collectivist economic goals of the party enshrined in its constitution and the central role in policy-making and finance played by the trade unions – one of the principal corporate interests of civil society, and as such fundamentally opposed to measures of planning, such as compulsory wage control or direction of labour, which threaten its position. Labour's collectivist ideology has generally been anti-markets and pro-planning, but the trade unions as far as their own direct interests are concerned have always been pro-markets (in the sense of free collective bargaining) and anti-planning. Only very reluctantly have union leaderships acquiesced in incomes policies, and when they have, they have often suffered eventual repudiation by their own members.

The tension is less marked in the Conservative party but it is still present. It arises because of the periodic need felt by the leadership of the Conservative party to advocate interventionist measures to rescue the national economy. However, what Conservative modernizers from Joseph Chamberlain and the Social Imperialists to Harold Macmillan and Edward Heath have always discovered is the deep conflict with the principle of voluntarism and the autonomy of corporate interests which any serious programme of modernization encounters. Collectivism in whatever guise has always required new institutions and new procedures for formulating and implementing policy, but it is precisely institutional reform which has proved so elusive.

A major reason for this is the way in which the two-party system operates. The two major producer interests in the economy are extremely closely identified with the two major parties. The bulk of the central funds of each party come from its main corporate supporter.[4] In the case of the Labour party this funding has given the trade unions a position of immense power in the internal structure of the party. There is no such formal representation of business in the Conservative party, but the Conservative party has acted as the umbrella party for all sections of property since at least the 1920s and the links between the party leadership and the business establishment, particularly the City of London, have always been extremely close.

The mirroring of the industrial divide between capital and labour in the party structure is much more marked than the class basis of electoral behaviour. The Conservatives have been the dominant party throughout the last one hundred years except for brief periods between 1906–16, 1945–50, and 1966–76. To remain so they have always had to attract working-class votes. In the electoral sense they have always been therefore a working-class party – at least half their votes must come from working-class electors. They have built their dominance not on ideology or any particular set of principles, though despite protestation to the contrary they are not short of either, but on presenting themselves as the natural party of government, the party most securely identified with the central institutions and the symbols of both the liberal and aristocratic political inheritance. The party leadership has always seen its role as defending the existing distribution of social power and privilege in civil society and constructing an electoral majority to ensure the formation of a Conservative administration. During the past sixty years the two-party adversary conflict with the Labour party has been very important in mobilizing an anti-Labour and therefore pro-Conservative electoral majority. At the same time the risks of such a polarization have been limited by the practical incorporation of the Labour movement into the mechanisms of British government and civil society and the acceptance by the Labour leadership of informal constitutional conventions. Only in recent years have the Conservatives begun to abandon this strategy, and have launched instead an onslaught against 'collectivism' in general and the political and economic power of trade unions in particular.

The obstacles in the way of a modernization programme for the

British economy were disguised by the partial triumph of collectivist ideas about economic management and welfare. An all-party consensus appeared to have emerged in the 1940s which supported the measures of public ownership and more comprehensive welfare services carried through by the first majority Labour government. Yet the new style of economic management found favour precisely because it was not collectivist. It allowed the dismantling of wartime controls and led to the abandonment of attempts to plan the economy. It reintroduced the liberal preference for indirect regulation of the conditions under which individual agents pursued their interests and made their choices, rather than attempting to intervene directly in the choices themselves. Keynesianism as practised in Britain allowed the financial markets fairly quickly to regain their traditional influence over economic policy, and reinforced the position and influence of the major producer interests throughout the economy.

The manner in which adversary two-party politics in Britain reflects and reinforces the divide between capital and labour in industry has increasingly been recognized as a major problem of the British polity, particularly by the Tory Right, the Labour Left, as well as by all third parties. The most important third party has been the Liberal party, which in 1981 formed an alliance with the newly formed Social Democratic party (SDP). The Liberals were traditionally the party of free trade and *laissez-faire* while the Tories inclined to protection and state intervention. But the New Liberalism with its notion of positive state action to remedy inequality of opportunities and actively promote prosperity, made increasing headway. Lloyd George's programme to conquer unemployment broke new ground in 1929, and both Keynes and Beveridge, whose ideas became so influential in the 1940s, were prominent Liberals. Liberals were in general enthusiastic supporters of the reforms of the 1940s and under Jo Grimond's leadership were active campaigners for the modernization programmes of the 1960s.[5] Despite its small parliamentary size the Liberal party has maintained itself with progressive and radical reform. But increasingly the party has come to stress that no significant modernization of British economy and society is possible until the system of adversary politics is ended and major constitutional changes are introduced. For the Liberals one of the chief failings of the British political system is that is has permitted the emergence of a class-based system which mirrors the class divide in industry. The two-party system is blamed for causing policy to ossify, and for the constant sacrifice of the interests of the national economy, consumers, and domestic industry in order to placate the financial markets and the major producer interests in both public and private sectors. When modernization programmes have failed, both the major parties have retired to the safety of their respective ideological fall-out shelters – one proclaiming collectivism and planning, the other the free market. Liberals argue that since there is no popular support for collectivizing British society and since most markets in Britain are dominated by powerful corporate interests, the adversary rhetoric of the two-party battle conceals the stalemate at the heart of economic policy. It offers no way of finding lasting solutions to the actual problems of the British economy.

This analysis is particularly critical of the manner in which unions have been incorporated into national politics in recent years. Union leaders were imported into the heart of government when Labour was in office, which inevitably produced hostility in other parts of the polity, preventing rather than facilitating the integration of the unions into the formulation and execution of economic and industrial policies on a permanent basis. On this view only a new party political context will be able to alter what has become as essentially dysfunctional and debilitating relationship. The adversary two-party system both expresses and reinforces the characteristic distribution of power through the central institutions of civil society. A different electoral system along with other major constitutional changes, it is argued, would not abolish producer interests or corporate power but by enhancing the authority and independence of central government would allow a virtuous circle of change, reform, and co-operation to become established.

The academic debate on British politics

Following the establishment of post-war inter-party agreement on Keynesian principles of economic management the potential clash between the party of capitalism and the party of socialism appeared to have been averted and the way opened for the continuation of the broad consensus on economic policy which was so evident a factor in the nineteenth century when the forms of modern British government were established. This 'consensus' has been the starting-point for studying British politics for a generation of political scientists and commentators. The workings of British two-party politics have rarely been criticized. As Keith Middlemas has observed[6] in his acute analysis of the politics and government of British industrial society, a nineteenth-century conception of British history survived unquestioned well into the twentieth century. This suggested that a state of political equilibrium was natural to society, which could only be lost by incompetence or mismanagement on the part of the formal institutions of the state. Questions about the actual distribution and use of political power in contemporary society were on the whole not asked or answered. As Middlemas remarks: Anyone interested in asking 'questions about the actual distribution and use of political power in contemporary society, would have been hard put to pierce through the formal descriptive screen of Crown and Parliament, legislature, executive and judiciary'.[7] Middlemas set himself the task to offset this liberal concept of history, by a massive account of the positive efforts to incorporate the unions into the polity in the pre-war period, which, in his view, avoided civil strife and guaranteed a minimum of political and social stability. Middlemas argues that what is missing from so many accounts of British politics is any understanding of the power which has been acquired by corporate interests, which exists alongside the formal parliamentary process and sets limits to it.

But even when more realistic attempts have been made to take account of the existence of corporate interests in a behavioural way, as, for example, in the many studies of pressure group politics, they have in their turn not been able to escape the influence of liberal ideology. In so far as the studies contribute to practical evidence of social and economic conflict they are to be valued. But the dominant theory associated with this type of political enquiry has been that of democratic pluralism and as a result they have missed some of the key conditioning factors of post-war British politics. The theory of groups competing for resources according to a model of perfect political competition is in essence a variation of nineteenth-century liberal theory, with groups taking the place of individuals and with government acting as neutral broker, maximizing benefits in much the same way as the 'invisible hand' of nineteenth-century economic theory. As such, it has tended to miss the essentially skewed nature of the process, brought about by the close relationship of powerful economic groups with the governing political parties.

The intimate relationship between the political parties and their respective clienteles in some areas of post-war public policy is one of the subjects of this book. There has been of late much examination of particular British political parties, but few studies of their interaction in fields of public concern. Political parties do not exist in isolation – they are shaped by their relationships with their political opponents, relationships which in the strict two-party system which has characterized post-war Britain can fairly be described as symbiotic. There has been a marked reluctance amongst political scientists and, with some exceptions, political economists, to study the policy processess of British government which emerge from party interaction. But the relations of parties whose doctrines and aims are so different deserve careful study, especially since in some areas the result has been bipartisan consensus and in others adversary conflict.

Studies of the relationship between the party system and economic policy-making have passed through several phases. Two of the most influential writers on British politics in the 1950s and 1960s, Samuel Beer and Bob McKenzie, both emphasized the achievement of consensus between the parties although they disagreed on how real this consensus was. McKenzie argued that the workings of the two-party system had forced the two main parties to evolve a similar structure of leadership and similar policies although the two parties started from very different values and historical origins. The pressures of parliamentary government and electoral competition continually forced the parties to resemble each other more and more in their internal structure if they remained serious about holding government office. He wrote in 1957: 'The Cabinet and parliamentary system of government requires that the parliamentary leaders of any party must bear the prime responsibility for decision-making on major matters of policy.'[8] In a radio debate with Samuel Beer in 1966 he stated that if Labour had been 'in power for four-fifths of the time as the Conservative party had been in the last fifty years, I strongly suggest to you that then you would see where power really resides in the Labour party.'[9]

Beer, however, while agreeing that in practice there was a convergence in policies, continued to argue that there was a deep division in social purpose between the parties, and the the role of the trade unions in the Labour party was unlike that found in any other party. But he had no criticisms to make of the way the two-party system operated at that time. As for most observers the uncanny symmetry in the electoral support for the two parties which persisted between 1950 and 1974, combined with the degree of practical consensus between them, suggested a harmonious political order which was managing to reconcile the most important antagonisms in society and to provide a framework for successful management of the economy.

Both Beer and McKenzie were reflecting on a political period when the sharp and apparently irreconcilable political polarization of the

1930s had given place to a remarkable degree of stability and consensus, the emergence of new 'progressive' and 'revisionist' leaderships in both major parties, and an apparent withering of the parties' ideologies. This period was to be short-lived and was succeeded in the 1960s by a spate of writing on the reasons for the relative decline of the British economy and on the need for a new programme of modernization.

Much of this writing detected weaknesses in British institutions and particularly in the relationship of government to the major corporate interests, but the remedy for this was sought in the vigorous pursuit of policies to maximize efficiency and growth. Many hopes were pinned on the Labour government elected in 1964 with very broad-based support for its programme for a *New Britain*. The remedy for Britain's economic problem it was thought, could be applied with only minor reforms to the existing institutional framework. The major target singled out for reform was Parliament, but most of the reform plans did not question the existing party or electoral system. What they sought instead was a more active role for Parliament in scrutinizing legislation and monitoring the executive as part of a general drive to increase the effectiveness of government. Similar minor institutional reform was involved in the Treasury.

Some of the analyses as to why Britain needed modernization began however to probe more deeply. Much the most important of these, although it barely entered mainstream academic debate, was the historical analysis of the origins of Britain's crisis in the 1960s which was begun by Perry Anderson and Tom Nairn in a series of essays in the early 1960s and continued in Tom Nairn's later book *The Breakup of Britain*.[10] What is noteworthy about this writing is that it was the first to ask whether there was not something fundamentally wrong with the British political system which could not be put right by a change of government or a new set of policies, and whether the way in which the consensus was organized in Britain made the political system a major obstacle to social and economic modernization. This analysis pointed to the organization of relations between state and economy in Britain as the key to understanding why the intentions and plans of so many 'modernizers' in twentieth-century British politics had been frustrated.

The writing of the 1970s, of which the adversary politics thesis forms a part, was extremely diverse, but common to much of it was the perception that the intractable nature of British economic problems had to be traced to the structure of relationships between state and economy in Britain. The mood of optimism of the 1950s had evaporated and there was a new readiness on every side to contemplate sweeping constitutional changes. This book is concerned with only one aspect of this literature, the relationship between the party system and economic policy, and it is to the writing on this theme that we now turn.

2

THEORIES OF ADVERSARY POLITICS

Adversary Politics and Economic Decline

In recent years there has been increasing discussion of the relationship between the poor performance of the British economy and certain features of British political institutions. The background to this debate has been the persistent failure of the economic policies of successive governments to arrest the relative decline of the British economy. This failure has been associated with a marked weakening of support for the two major political parties. With the diminution of Britain's world role, the arrival of mass democracy, and the growth of government involvement in the economy, economic conditions have become the major determinant of electoral choice and the focus of competition between the parties. Yet despite repeated attempts between 1959 and 1983, the British political leadership was unable to improve economic performance significantly. Indeed in certain respects the performance grew worse.

The conventional targets of Keynesian demand management were full employment, economic growth (measured by increases in output, productivity, and living standards), stable prices, and a surplus on the balance of payments. It was always assumed that there were trade-offs – particularly between unemployment and the rate of inflation and between growth and the balance of payments. In the 1950s and 1960s these were mild enough and the British economy performed better than at any time since the middle of the nineteenth century. But in relative terms the British performance was poor and the judgements on British policy became increasingly adverse. In 1969 the Bank of England and the Treasury declared: 'economic policy may be said quite simply to have failed, in that none of the major economic problems facing the UK in 1959 can be said to have been solved and some of the most important of them have become more severe.'[1]

This judgement could be repeated with emphasis at the end of the 1970s. Recorded unemployment began rising after 1966, doubled to 1½ million in 1974–5 and then doubled again in 1980–1. Inflation, far from moderating, accelerated, touching 26 per cent in 1975 and 21 per cent in 1980. Only in 1978 did it dip below 10 per cent. Meanwhile output stagnated after the sudden acceleration in 1973. Even more telling are the figures for manufacturing output when oil production from the North Sea is excluded. They show that the level of output barely rose at all over the decade. The inability of manufacturing output to expand was reflected in the unemployment figures and in the dramatic increase in the penetration of the UK market by foreign manufactures. In the 1970s the balance of payments moved from massive deficit to massive surplus, but the change had more to do with oil and recession than with any permanent reversal of the trends towards a shrinking manufacturing base and a shrinking share of world trade.[2]

There is a considerable contrast between the promises and programmes for the economy that regularly emerged through the competitive bidding for electoral support by the political parties, and the actual results which governments of either party delivered. This eroded the legitimacy of both major parties. Between 1959 and 1983 no party won re-election after serving a full term in office. It also undermined the two-party system – there is considerable evidence that voters became less partisan in this period, and individual membership of parties declined.[3] The electorate became more volatile and less attached in its loyalties, and large movements of opinion at by-elections and local elections became common.

Within the two major parties the legitimacy and influence of party leaderships at times appeared weak. After 1959 electoral defeat meant a prolonged period of internal party conflict for both parties. This produced an increased ideological polarization of British politics and a growing rejection of the consensus on policy between the political parties which existed in the 1940s and 1950s. Radicalization of the mass party was most evident in the Labour party, although it was Conservative governments (in 1970 and 1979) which went furthest in embarking on radical experiments in policy.

The growing turmoil in British politics, the prospects for a major realignment of political parties, and for significant constitutional changes, were closely associated with the repeated failure of all governments to manage the economy to the satisfaction either of themselves or the electorate. The proportions and consequences of this failure to arrest decline increased dramatically after the onset of recession and stagnation in the Western capitalist economy. In the best traditions of adversary politics both parties blamed the performance of the economy on the world recession when they were in government and on the government when they were in opposition. Britain's weakness, however, long predated the 1974 recession. Unemployment had already begun to rise, inflation to accelerate, and manufacturing output to stagnate. Looked at from the standpoint of the world economy the British economy has been in relative decline for one hundred years.[4] As a part of this world economy Britain suffered the effects of the recession but these were more severe because of accumulated weaknesses.

One persistent theme in writing on Britain's economic decline has been the need for modernization and the obstinate failure of modernization programmes to work. Much attention has come to be focused on the shortcomings of British political institutions and the harmful effects they have had on economic policy. The strongest criticism has been aimed at the adversary style of electoral and parliamentary politics. Finer has argued that adversary politics – 'a stand-up fight between two adversaries for the favour of the lookers-on' – has serious disadvantages for effective policymaking.[5] Under an adversary system the government is unduly influenced by the 'extremists' in its party organization. He claims the 'off-centre' policy has never been supported by a majority of the electorate. Left-of-centre policies alternate with right-of-centre policies, and a climate of general uncertainty is created, inimical to the development of long-term policy and to business confidence. Nevil Johnson has also condemned adversary politics, which he defines as:

> the maintenance of relationships of political competition through a mode of argument which assumes that political questions can best be resolved if expressed in terms of two and only two contrasting alternatives . . . voiced by two competing groups of politicians.[6]

This leads he argues to irresponsible competition between the parties. Conflict is manufactured, issues are oversimplified, and consensus is made much harder to achieve. Over time, adversary politics tends to produce a condition of ungovernability because it destroys belief in the existence of those common interests and values without which a political community cannot survive.

Such outright condemnation of British political institutions might make us forget that it is not very long since these same institutions were widely regarded as the best that frail human intelligence could devise. In the 1950s the adversary system was not thought to manufacture conflict but consensus and stability. As late as 1965, Samuel Beer, discussing the impact of the parties' different programmes and ideologies on policy could argue: 'when we make an overall assessment . . . it is the massive continuity that stands out'.[7] and produced a comfortable picture of a stable two-party system, based on permanent class orientations, enveloping a variety of interest groups, and constituting an enviable mechanism of plural and responsive social choice. Sartori in his comprehensive study of parties contrasted British political institutions favourably with those in existence elsewhere, and similarly argued that simple two-party pluralism

> benefits from the reasonable stimulation provided by alternative government and responsible oppostition, and it obliges the parties to perform an integrative and aggregative function; while on the other hand it discourages the growth of a highly ideologized policy orientation and the polarization of the party system.[8]

This ability of the British party system to make government legitimate and at the same time to permit the representation of demands and interests was always regarded as the special achievement of British institutions. A two-party system was seen as the ideal means of representing opinion and making government accountable given the centralized administrative structure of British government and the homogeneity of the British electorate. The justification for an adversary system was to dramatize alternatives and to permit experiments in policy, so encouraging extensive participation in decision-making and reconciling every interest and every section of opinion to the state through their representation by one of the parties. But, as Beer himself has belatedly recognized, there were always other possibilities in a system in which political attitudes and loyalties were derived from a fundamental class polarization. As Ghita Ionescu has recently noted, 'the class ideology of political representation forms a vicious circle with the adversary British system of politics, thus aggravating its on–off rhythm, which, in turn is one of the causes of the instability of the British policy-making processes'.[9]

The problem was that such as adversary politics was only stable if it was conducted within certain limits. The emphasis on conflict and institutionalized opposition had to be matched by a consensus on fundamentals and the acceptance in practice of a number of constitutional conventions – for instance the neutrality and anonymity of the civil service, hence the need for secrecy in policy-making; the acceptance of the major measures of previous administrations; the pragmatic recognition of the constraints on government, hence the narrow scope for major policy innovation. A gulf became established between the parties as electoral machines and as instruments of government; between politicians in their role as tribunes of the popular will and as adjuncts of the permanent bureaucracy. The conflict between them was ritualized and the impact of popular demands on policy continually muted. In the Conservative party this used to be reflected in its ethos of pragmatism and flexibility, the distrust of ideology and dogma, and the inclination of the leadership to view most questions of policy in terms of what was politically practicable rather than ideologically desirable. In the Labour party, which originated as a mass party outside Parliament, the struggle over what kind of party it was to be was protracted, but a parliamentary leadership gradually emerged that dominated the parliamentary party and the party organization and adhered to the conventions of British parliamentary democracy. The convergence of the parties in practice, despite their adversary rhetoric, was the central theme of McKenzie's study of British political parties in the 1950s.[10]

A political system which appeared to ensure such a high degree of agreement amongst political leaders about the rules of government and the need to insulate policy-making from electoral pressures or ideological demands, and which guaranteed a very high level of support for the political system, through the two parties winning over 90 per cent of the votes, at one time seemed indestructible, and was much admired. The reason why it came to be so criticized can be traced directly to the unsuccessful attempts that successive British governments made to solve the problems confronting the economy. This failure destabilized political institutions and showed a new side to adversary politics, its destructive potential, especially its capacity to destroy continuity in policy and to threaten the constitution.

At its simplest the critics of adversary politics argued that the adversary system exacerbated the problems of creating and sustaining policies that might improve the economy. Few would claim today that the parties performed their 'integrative' and 'aggregative' functions very successfully or that adversary politics did not assist a marked polarization of positions and beliefs within and between the political parties. But there are still many who deny the substance of the adversary politics thesis, who deny in Richard Rose's words that parties do 'make a difference' or much difference to the formulation and implementation of policies. Rose has recently produced a mass of evidence to show that parties are only one (and a relatively minor) input into the policy-making process and that most of the observable discontinuities in British economic policy flow not from adversary politics but from secular trends which governments and parties are powerless to control.[11]

This chapter attempts to unravel some of these issues and to form a preliminary judgement as to the impact of adversary politics. First it is necessary to explore in greater detail three different formulations of the adversary politics thesis. They frequently overlap but for purposes of analysis need to be distinguished.

Three Variants of the Adversary Politics Thesis

The first and most widely known variant of the adversary politics thesis is that the workings of the adversary system in Britain have been the cause of significant and frequent reversals in economic policy.[12] Great weight is attached to the parties themselves and their influence over policy-making. But this influence is not necessarily harmful if adversary politics is conducted within narrow limits, for then both party leaderships could pursue pragmatic policies in office and indulge in ideological politics only in opposition. The centralization of power in the political parties and in the structure of government allows party leaders to reconcile what they see as the realities of power with the requirements of maintaining political support. But if the parliamentary leaderships should ever lose their relative independence from their electors and their parties, then the same adversary style of politics that promoted stability and continuity could promote instability and discontinuity.

This is alleged to have occurred in the 1960s and 1970s. Party leaders suffered a significant loss of autonomy and accepted policies in opposition which marked a sharp break both with the policies the other party was pursuing in government and often with the policies the party had itself pursued when last in office. The result was that each election that resulted in a change of the party in government inaugurated a period of 'manifesto madness', lasting eighteen months to two years during which the party repealed many measures of its predecessor and attempted to implement its own new radical measures. The counterproductive and disappointing results then led to a 'U-turn' and the adoption of sensible pragmatic policies at the instigation of the civil service and under pressures from outside interests, particularly the financial markets. The government pursued these sound policies for the remainder of its term of office but just as they were bearing fruit there was a general election which it lost, and its adversary then returned to office with its own new radical manifesto. So the cycle began again. The main casuality was business confidence and the main consequence a deteriorating economic performance.

This variant of the adversary politics thesis appears to rest on a number of assumptions, the most important being that at any given time there do exist correct economic policies which will work and are therefore pragmatic and embody common sense, in contrast to policies which will not work and are therefore ideological and unsound. Policies are defined as correct either on technical grounds (no other alternatives are feasible) or on electoral grounds (these are the policies desired by 80 per cent of the population). The adversary system is condemned because under certain conditions it allows ideology to distort the policy-making process away from what is technically feasible and from what the mass of voters want. Over a period it destroys consensus by institutionalizing opposition and preventing the articulation of common interests. The remedy emerges smoothly from the diagnosis. The electoral system needs reforming in such a way that an adversary contest between two centralized parties is abolished, the independence of Parliament is restored, and government is carried on by coalitions of centre parties which can ensure continuity in policy formation and the building of a positive consensus. In this way ideological extremes can be prevented from participating directly in government and are confined to an oppositional role without prospect of power. The legitimation of government is to occur henceforward through the exclusion of certain interests rather than through the attempted inclusion of all interests.

The second variant of the adversary politics thesis puts major emphasis on the constraints which the political market places on policy-making. The harmful effects of the adversary system are perceived to lie less in the opportunity it supplies for ideologically motivated policies, and more in the compulsion each party feels to pursue policies and adopt programmes that maximize votes. These policies and programmes are often ruinous for the economy. Competition between the parties generates excessive expectations in the electorate about the government's ability to control the economy and distribute a 'dividend' in excess of national output. Parties in government attempt to manipulate the economy by spending their way out of recession to bring down unemployment, and by engineering booms and rises in take-home pay before elections. The result is that in addition to the ordinary business cycle modern economies are subject to a political business cycle which is geared to the dates of elections and is extremely destabilizing. In particular it is argued that it has led in Britain and other countries to an accelerating inflation and eventually to a far worse slump and level of unemployment than would otherwise have been necessary to restructure the economy. The remedy it is suggested is for economic policy to be shielded from democratic pressures, and the grounds that the management of the economy is too complex to be a matter of political bargaining and competitive vote bidding. The main reason is the inherent instability of democratic politics with its tendency to generate demands without consideration of their true cost; voters have no budget constraint the way that consumers do, so they have no incentive to limit their demands on politicians, since the costs of meeting them will be borne not individually but collectively.

One of the earliest versions of this model was formulated by Schumpeter. He reluctantly conceded the inevitability of socialism (collectivist management of the economy) and also conceded that it could be efficient, but only if its management was effectively insulated from the pressures of democracy. This theme, stressing the perils which the workings of democracy present to economic management, has become standard amongst advocates of a social market economy.[13]

In all these accounts the British adversary system is not condemned in itself but as an expression of the negative features of democratic politics, particularly the generation of ideologically motivated policies and competitive bidding. Hence the carrying of proportional representation (PR) is not seen as a sufficient remedy. It has to be accompanied by other constitutional changes which will significantly limit the powers of any democratically elected government to shape economic policy. The British adversary system is regarded as so pernicious because it is allied to a highly centralized system of government in which the powers of the executive are not restrained by a written constitution or bill of rights of public law, but only by the need to secure majorities in the House of Commons. The scope for damage to the delicate mechanism of the market order is correspondingly enormous.

The two variants of the adversary politics thesis so far considered both emphasize the need to modify two-party democracy, either by reforming the electoral system to make possible a different kind of government, or by insulating the conduct of economic policy from day-to-day political pressures. But a third variant can be distinguished, one that is less technocratic or elitist in its assumptions and does see a positive role for party politics. This is the argument that adversary politics is a symptom of more deep-seated weaknesses in the way in which policy is made in Britain. These weaknesses are traced to Britain's constitutional arrangements, and in some accounts, to the character of the British state itself.[14] But the conclusion is not that economic policy needs insulating from democratic pressures, rather that it ought to be decentralized to permit much greater participation both in the way it is formulated and, still more, in the way it is carried out.

This variant argues that the harmful effects of adversary politics should be sought not only in the discontinuity of economic policy but in its continuity as well. British government is centralized in too few hands and the internal organization of the political parties is one aspect of this. According to this view, the reasons why Britain at times appears ungovernable is not because government is too weak but because it is too strong. Overcentralization means there is not only considerable scope for arbitrary short-term shifts in policy, but also that there are few mechanisms for reassessing policies or challenging existing priorities. An adversary style of politics concentrates debate and party competition around a few issues, while policy in many other areas is relatively neglected.

In those areas that are heavily politicized the development of long-term policy becomes very difficult, whereas in those areas that are not, the long-term policies that are in force are never properly discussed in the political arena at all. On this view adversary politics reflects the degree to which decision-making has been centralized and its harmful effects are not limited to the disagreement and conflict it generates in some areas but include the consensus it upholds in others. This damage is compounded by the secrecy which still surrounds the operation of government in Britain. This view regards élite consensus and the development of corporatist bargaining structures as the most important realities of twentieth-century British politics, which have been accompanied by the decline of Parliament and the subordination of party organization to the party leaderships.

This third view of adversary politics also recommends constitutional changes, including PR, but not to generate a technocratic consensus or insulate economic policy-making from politics, but actually to make possible a more open debate about policy and the political requirements for successful modernization. This means exploding the consensus that has been sustained by adversary politics because this consensus has, in Tom Nairn's telling phrase, been 'erected against modernisation'.[15] Building a new consensus that can sustain a programme of modernization has to involve a considerable reform of the constitution and of civil society.

The Period of Manifesto Madness

What kind of prima-facie case exists for these three variants? This chapter concentrates on evidence for the first, since this is the most influential yet least discussed. Evidence for the second depends on evidence of a political business cycle, which has been extensively discussed in recent years.[16]

In order to assess the value of the first account the period 1960–81 is taken, during which four changes of government have taken place. Some attempt must be made to clarify the meaning of continuity and of economic policy. If continuity is not equivalent to inertia then the analyst is immediately confronted with the task of making not merely a quantitative but a qualitative assessment of changes. When are changes in policy to be regarded as evolutionary and not destructive of continuity, and when are they to be seen as fundamental reversals of policy?

There is also the problem that many observed changes in policy derive from changes in the context of policy-making rather than from the decisions of policy-makers themselves. Changes in the world economy are the most obvious source of such discontinuity in British economic policy, because of the degree of dependence of the British economy on the world economy. It may sometimes be hard to disentangle changes in policy that are primarily a response to changed circumstances from changes that are due to specific political influence. Similarly it may be very difficult to separate the influence of parties and politicians from the influence on institutions, groups, and interests. The problem of estimating, for example, the influence of the trade unions on policy is compounded because the influence of such external groups is itself discontinuous; it rises and wanes in accourance with specific circumstances and cannot be assumed as a static given in the policy-making process.

Continuity in policy can be considered in three ways. There is firstly continuity in policy goals and priorities, such as the pursuit of full employment or stable prices. Secondly there is continuity in the use of policy instruments, for example monetary and fiscal devices, or special government agencies like the Prices and Incomes Board (PIB), Industrial Reorganization Corporation (IRC), and National Economic Development Council (NEDC). Thirdly there is continuity in the consequences of policy. Whatever the intentions and whatever the instruments employed, is there any observable difference in the results? Attention will be concentrated on the first two. Richard Rose has analysed the third and has concluded that the trends of all the most important economic variables, including interest rates, the Public Sector Borrowing Requirement (PSBR), public expenditure, output, take-home pay, the distribution of income and wealth, inflation, and unemployment, are secular and resistant to party influence.[17] This conclusion is confirmed in Table 3 which shows how resistant broad economic trends appear to be to government changes.

In stark contrast to this the adversary politics thesis suggests that the first eighteen months of each new government is spent implementing partisan and ideological policies which have been adopted in opposition due to pressure from party activists. Such a partisan government will reverse the main policies of the previous government and repeal its major legislative enactments.

This proposition can be easily tested by asking two questions whenever a change-over in government has occurred. How many policies were reversed by the incoming government; and which policies and areas of policy were untouched? When this is done it can be seen that the main deficiency of this variant of the theory is that it is too selective. It generalizes from a few instances to the whole of economic policy. But of the three main areas of economic policy identified in Chapter 1, significant discontinuities in policy which can be attributed to the government changing hands are mostly to be found in the field of industrial policy, as Chapter 4 of this book illustrates in detail. They are generally absent from either foreign economic policy or stabilization policy. This is shown in Table 1. The principal adversary cycles are set out in Table 2.

This is most striking in the case of foreign economic policy. In the twenty-year period under consideration one of the most important initiatives in this area was the application to join the EEC leading to full membership in 1973. Although at different times this issue hovered on the edge of becoming subject to adversary politics it never did. The only instance when an incoming government reversed policy on the EEC was in 1974 when the Labour government attempted to renegotiate the

Table 1

Major new initiatives in economic policy
(following the changes of government in 1964, 1970, 1974, and 1979)

	Inherited policy	1964–6	1970–1	1974–6	1979–80
Foreign economic policy					
Treaties	NATO; GATT	–	EEC application	EEC renegotiation	EEC budget dispute
Sterling	Fixed exchange rates	–	Sterling floated	–	–
Capital	Exchange controls	–	–	–	Controls abolished
Trade	Multilateral trade	Import surcharge (abandoned 1965)	Acceptance of EEC Common External Tariff	–	–
Labour	Commonwealth Immigration Act (1962)	–	Immigration Act	–	British Nationality Act
Stabilization Policy					
Monetary	Discretionary regulation of credit	–	Competition and Credit Control	Announcement of monetary targets	Medium Term Financial Strategy

Fiscal (taxes)	Income (PAYE)	Marginal rates increased	Marginal rates reduced	Marginal rates increased	Marginal rates reduced
	Consumption (purchase tax etc.)	Selective Employment Tax (SET)	Abolition of SET, Purchase Tax. Replaced by VAT	–	
	Company (profits)	Corporation Tax	–	Petroleum Revenue Tax	
	Property (death duties)	Capital Gains Tax	–	Capital Transfer Tax	
Public expenditure:					
Control	Public Expenditure Survey Committee (1962)	–	Programme Analysis Review	Cash limits	Cash limits on local government spending
Programmes	Major expansion underway	–	Selective cuts	General cuts in expenditure plans	Planned cuts in absolute level
Prices and incomes	National Incomes Commission	National Board for Prices and Incomes (NBPI)	NBPI abolished	Pay Board abolished. Price Commission strengthened.	Price Commission abolished
Industrial policy					
Labour	Trade-union acts	–	Industrial Relations Act (IRA)	Repealed	
		–	National Industrial Relations Court	Abolished	
			Commission on Industrial Relations	Abolished	

continued

Table 1 *continued*

	Inherited policy	1964–6	1970–1	1974–6	1979–80
				Employment Protection Act Trade Union and Labour Relations Act	Amended by Employment Act
	Factory acts and general employment legislation	Redundance Payments Act	–	Health and Safety at Work Act	–
Public sector	Nationalization Acts	Renationalization of steel	Nationalization of Rolls-Royce. Limited privatization	Major new measures of nationalization: cars, aerospace, shipbuilding. Establishment of British National Oil Corporation	Major privatization programme launched
Private sector	Company Acts	–	–	–	–
	Competition policy	–	–	–	–
	Regional policy	Regional Employment Premium introduced (REP)	REP abolished		
	Planning (NEDC, NEDO)	Industrial Reorganization Corporation (IRC)	IRC abolished	National Enterprise Board (NEB)	NEB abolished
Land:					
Agriculture	Deficiency payments system	–	Common Agricultural policy	–	–
Planning	Town and Country Planning Acts	Land Commission established	Land Commission abolished		

Table 2

Adversary cycles 1959–83

	1959–64	1964–70	1970–4	1974–9	1979–83
Foreign economic policy					
None	–	–	–	–	–
Stabilization policy					
Marginal tax rates	Low	High	Low	High	Low
Incomes policy	Initiated	Extended	Rejected, reintroduced	Rejected, reintroduced	Rejected
Industrial policy					
Planning	Initiated	Extended	Abandoned, reintroduced	Extended	Abandoned
Nationalization	No change	Minor change	Minor change	Major extension	Major contraction
Regional policy	Active compensation	Extended	Major change	Small change	Major reduction
Trade Unions	No change	No change	Major change	Major change	Major change

Table 3

Major trends in the economy and government changes 1964–79

	1964	1970	1974	1979
Public expenditure (percentage of GDP)[a]	34.1	37.7	40.4	41.1
Inflation (annual percentage change, GDP deflator)[b]	3.1	7.8	16.9	13.4
Unemployment (000)[c]	372	555	542	1,344
Percentage of work-force	1.6	2.6	2.6	5.7
Industrial output (1975 = 100)[d]	86.2	99.9	105.7	112.8
Import penetration (percentage)[e]	n/a	17.1	23.3	25.7
UK share of world export of manufactures (percentage)[e]	14.4	10.8	8.8	9.7

Sources: a Leo Pliatzky, *Getting and Spending*, Oxford, Blackwell, 1982; Appendix 1, Table 2.
b M. H. Peston, *The British Economy*, London, Allen, 1982, Table 5.2
c *Economic Trends.*
d Peston, Table 9.2.
e C. J. F. Brown and T. D. Sheriff, *De-Industrialization in the UK* (Discussion Paper No. 23), London, NIESR, 1979.

terms of entry. But at most this was a partial reversal and little different in practical effect to the Thatcher government's attempts to reduce Britain's contribution to the EEC budget in 1980. All the other major issues of foreign economic policy have been marked by continuity – they have rarely entered the adversary debate at all. What look like changes often turn out on examination not to be related to parties at all. The import surcharge, for example, imposed by Labour in 1964 was one of several options prepared for the preceding government by the Treasury. Britain's continued membership of the Atlantic Alliance, including acceptance of the rules of GATT and the IMF, has never been seriously questioned; and immigration controls have been progressively tightened since 1960. The apparent discontinuities in policy on sterling and exchange controls are not the result of conflicting views on the issues. Both the 1967 devaluation and the floating of sterling in 1971 and 1972 were adjustments forced on the British authorities. Similarly, although exchange controls were lifted in 1979 the controls that had been operated had not hindered the expansion of overseas investment and production by British firms or the international business of the City. The continuity of policy in these areas and its generally non-controversial character is what is striking, even though it is the priorities of foreign economic policy which set the limits which shape the rest of economic policy.

Turning to stabilization policy, the evidence for continuity is rather more plain than the evidence for discontinuity. The major shift from Keynesianism to monetarism as a framework for managing the economy did not take place as a result of adversary politics. In the elections of 1964, 1970, and 1974 there was no difference in the principles of economic management espoused by either party and relatively little in the weighting which was attached to goals, instruments, and techniques of policy. In 1979 the Conservatives openly campaigned on monetarism and after the election introduced the Medium Term Financial Strategy. But the discontinuity is less than it appears because of the Labour government's conversion to monetarism in 1975–6. In the history of British stabilization policy the move to cash limits will probably be seen as a more important step than the introduction of the medium-term financial strategy.

In fiscal policy many new controversial taxes were introduced in this period, including Corporation Tax, VAT and Capital Transfer Tax. But few were ever abolished by the next government. Selective Employment Tax (SET) is the major exception but the introduction of VAT in the early 1970s made it superfluous in any case. Of much greater importance have been the constant changes in various tax reliefs and subsidies, particularly those covering investment and regional policy, and the constant variation of tax rates with important consequences for consumption and investment.[18] But although British economic management may sometimes have been inept it is difficult to identify these discontinuities as effects of an adversary style of politics.

The most pronounced effect of adversary politics on taxation has been the treatment of tax on high income earners. The last three governments have all reversed the treatment of such incomes and marginal tax rates have fluctuated enormously. But although policy on this issue is a potent symbol of what each party stands for, its wider effects either on the distribution of income or on economic performance are not paricularly great.

The one major exception in the field of stabilization policy, a policy area where adversary politics appears to have been important, is incomes policy. There was broad continuity between the Conservative and Labour governments in 1964. The National Incomes Commission

(NIC) was absorbed into the new National Board for Prices and Incomes (NBPI). But every succeeding change of government has been followed by the ending of the formal or informal incomes policy that was in force and the abolition of the agencies established to uphold it. The NBPI was abolished after 1970, the Pay Board in 1974, and the Price Commision in 1979. But alongside the turning of incomes policy into an issue in adversary politics, other factors were also important in explaining why a permanent incomes policy was not established, particularly the internal dynamics of those policies themselves.[19]

In stabilization policy a major change in policy did take place with the introduction of Competition and Credit Control in 1971. But this was not an issue between the parties, it was apparently not even discussed in Parliament, despite the fact that its effects were far-reaching. This important example shows how only a narrow range of issues actually enter the party political debate.

It is in the field of industrial policy that the adversary politics thesis comes into its own. It certainly does not fit every issue but there are at least four major issues where the parties have taken up adversary positions; industrial relations law, the size and operation of the public enterprise sector, planning, and land policy. The pattern, as will be seen, is certainly more complex than a crude version of the adversary politics thesis would indicate. Industrial Relations Law, for example, did not become a contentious issue between the parties until the Heath government's 1971 Industrial Relations Act, and that Act built upon Labour's aborted plans unveiled in *In Place of Strife*. The 1974 Labour government repealed the Industrial Relations Act but re-enacted certain of its clauses, while the Thatcher government has not repealed the Employment Protection Act or abolished ACAS (Advisory, Conciliation, and Arbitration Service), but has preceeded cautiously, introducing piecemeal modifications to the law. Nevertheless, the failure to introduce a permanent legal framework for industrial relations and a reform of trade union organization is widely regarded as one of the central failures of the modernization programme in the 1960s. The dependence of the Labour party on the trade unions was ultimately decisive here.

The boundaries between the public and private sectors and policy towards the public enterprise sector is another great issue of industrial policy which has been very contentious between the parties and has resulted in marked discontinuities in policy. But the discontinuities are often more modest than might be imagined from the rhetoric. A pure adversary model would predict 100 per cent nationalization by one government followed by 100 per cent denationalization by the next. Renationalization of steel was certainly contentious in 1964, but the Conservatives made no attempt to denationalize it in 1970. The Heath government's period of disengagement (1970–2) was marked by only a few minor privatization measures (sale of Thomas Cook and Carlisle Breweries, and some air routes hived off to private airlines). Many of the extensions of the public sector undertaken by the Labour government – British Leyland, the British National Oil Corporation, British Shipbuilders, and British Aerospace – were dictated only partly by the party's socialist goals, and most had to be accepted, reluctantly by the Thatcher government. Althouth the Thatcher government made privatization and the ending of subsidies such major priorities, and launched the first major programme of denationalization since the war, progress was slow. More serious perhaps than nationalization itself has been the constant party dogfight over not just the size but the legitimacy of the public enterprise sector, and one result has been the erratic handling of nationalized industries – their methods of accountability, their investment and pricing policies, and their relations with Government.

Conclusions

A few tentative conclusions can be advanced. In its two simplistic forms it is difficult to sustain the adversary politics thesis without substantial qualifications. The evidence that there have been significant discontinuities in economic policy-making caused by the adversary positions adopted by the parties seems to be limited to industrial policy, and in particular economic planning, although the consequent and persistent difficulties of sustaining modernization strategies may have been critical for Britain's post-war economic performance. Also the theory of an invariant cycle of policy-making is not convincing. The idea, for example, that every government performs a U-turn midway in its term of office appears largely to be a generalization based on the experience of the Heath government, and not well founded even here. The forced acceptance of devaluation in 1967 and the abandonment of the National Plan may be thought to qualify the first Wilson government for membership of this category, but failure was inbuilt in the Plan in so many of its aspects that caution is needed in generalizing from this instance. Similarly the dilution of Labour's industrial strategy after the election of 1974 owed more to the internal politics of the Labour party than to any belated recognition of external constraints by the leadership. The significance of the 1976 intervention by the IMF is overstated. The process of controlling public expenditure had already begun with the introduction of cash limits, and the decision to give containing inflation a higher priority than halting the rise in unemployment had already been taken.

There is also only limited evidence (not reviewed in this book) to suggest that governments have either attempted or succeeded in manipulating the economy to win electoral support. At first sight there seems to be a distinct correlation between the electoral cycle and the abondonment of incomes policies, but only in 1974 did incomes policies become a major issue in a general election. The abandonment of incomes policy in 1970 owed more to the perceived difficulties of its implementation than to electoral considerations.

The similar rejection in 1979 by an incoming Conservative administration was certainly influenced by monetarist doctrine, but the Labour government's incomes policy was already in ruins. There is some evidence that cuts in public expenditure consistently required by the demands of stabilization policy have, over the period in question, fallen disproportionately on public investment rather than on personal consumption, and this normally for political reasons. But, as against this, British governments since 1976 have been active, with a degree of success, in discouraging rather than promoting economic expectations.[20]

The thesis appears to work best when adversary politics is seen as an integral part of the organization of the British state and its political system, performing a range of functions. This means that at times such as in the 1950s adversary politics can be associated with stability and integration but at others with instability and polarization. It directs attention to the whole range of effects that an adversary system can have, not just to the erratic shifts in policy for which it is responsible, particularly in the fields of industrial relations law, the role of public enterprise, incomes policy, and planning, but also to the unchallenged consensus it helps support in so many other areas of policy, particularly in foreign economic policy and stabilization policy.

What the limited disintegration of the consensus in the 1970s has made plain is how consensus was achieved in the past by excluding certain major areas from political debate or active parliamentary scrutiny, encouraging a ritualized party conflict around a few issues. The major failures of British post-war economic policy are found in areas which have not been issues between the parties – such as the failure to enter the EEC in the 1950s, the narrowness of the tax base, the failure to generate long-term investment funds for industry or to subordinate foreign economic policy to the needs of the industrial sector – as well as the more publicized failures which have been the subject of acrimonious party debate, such as incomes policy and the reform of industrial relations.

The studies which follow show two different aspects of the party system and its effects on economic policy since 1945. Its apparent success in sustaining stabilization policy over a considerable period masked weaknesses in the political system, and in other agreed economic policies which it had sustained, weaknesses which became apparent as soon as attempts were made to transcend the limitations of demand management. The consequent failures have had profound effects on both major political parties and on the structure of the political system as a whole, the implications of which for Britain's political, economic, and constitutional future are as yet unclear.

3

STABILIZATION POLICY AND ADVERSARY POLITICS

A. M. GAMBLE

Introduction

The post-war history of stabilization policy does not at first glance appear to give much support to the adversary politics thesis. For a particular stabilization policy, which adopted full employment as a major objective and Keynesian techniques for managing demand, is generally seen as being at the heart of a consensus between the parties on policy priorities which existed in Britain until the late 1960s and early 1970s. The most important change in stabilization policy in the 1970s was the replacement of a broadly Keynesian by a broadly monetarist orthodoxy, but even this change was not accomplished through the mechanism of party competition, but as a result of policy responses to the economic problems of the 1970s, in particular the new world recession and the breakdown of the international monetary system. Only in the 1980s has this bipartisan approach to questions of stabilization policy finally broken down.

The maintenance of a bipartisan approach in this area over such a long period is puzzling. It even managed to survive the abandonment of Keynesian assumptions and techniques and the acceptance of monetarist ones in their place. For the options inherent in stabilization policy look peculiarly suited to being colonized by an adversary two-party system. Schattschneider once defined democracy as 'a competitive political system in which competing leaders and organisations define the alternatives of public policy in such a way that the public can participate in the decision-making process'.[1] Stabilization policy is framed around alternatives and trade-offs, particularly the priority to be given to goals such as full employment, stable prices, and rising living standards. It is also shaped by the extent and scope of public services and public provision, by considerations of public finance, taxation, and redistribution, and by wider political values such as equality, liberty, and efficiency.

All these are issues which are important in daily experience and which help shape popular attitudes towards economic policy and to those in charge of it. The link between the performance of the economy, both as nationally perceived and as individually experienced, and government popularity, has become significant. The awareness that governments have some influence over economic outcomes has generated expectations of what governments should achieve and therefore additional pressure on governments to act in particular ways and take particular measures. This new pattern suggested to many political scientists that there was now in existence a political business cycle. The economic business cycle of boom followed by slump followed by a new boom was superseded. Armed with their new powers to influence the level of demand and actively to set and then to try to achieve targets for employment, prices, and output, governments were expected to intervene in the economic business cylce to shorten and damp down the slump and prolong the boom. It was also thought that they would attempt to make the peaks of the new modified business cycle coincide with general elections.

If governments had really acquired the power to influence economic outcomes to this extent then the parties which competed to form the government would offer distinctive alternatives to the electorate based either on their ideological preferences or their psephological calculations. Electors would be able to vote for full employment or for stable prices, for greater equality of for greater liberty. Armed with the popular mandate the victorious party would translate popular preferences into government policy. Some observers thought this was happening in Britain in the 1950s. Given the convention allowing the British Prime Minister to choose the date of the general election and given the new techniques for estimating public opinion and for influencing it, there seemed for a time at the end of the 1950s, when the Conservatives had won three elections in a row, no reason why any government should ever lose office again.

After 1959 and until 1983 the pattern was very different. The political business cycle delivered results which worked against incumbent governments and the government changed hands every five years. No government was re-elected after serving a full term. The inability of governments to manage the economy was much more in evidence than their success, and each party while in government suffered on two occasions rejection by the electorate – the Conservatives in 1964 and 1974, Labour in 1970 and 1979. Yet despite these regular changes of the party in government the bipartisan approach to stabilization policy was barely ruffled. The adversary system did not function. The discontinuities in policy between different party administrations are relatively minor, even in 1979.

The detailed evidence for this assertion is presented later in this chapter. First it is interesting to speculate why this should be so. If few discontinuities in policy exist and if those that exist are unrelated to adversary stances taken up by the parties, what is the explanation? The most obvious is that stabilization policy was so successful in achieving its objectives and was so in tune with public preferences that no party saw any reason to alter it. This is not a common view. The overall record of stabilization policy in reaching its objectives has been poor. Moreover, it became less and less successful, and the economy became less and less stable. Unemployment has been rising since 1966, doubling between 1975 and 1977, doubling again between 1979 and 1981. Inflation accelerated in the 1960s, moving into double figures in the 1970s. Its annual average in the 1970s was 13 per cent. Output stagnated after 1973 and GDP fell in 1974–5 and 1979–81. The public finances as a result of these three failures were plunged into repeated and ever deeper crises over funding and control.

The failure of stabilization policy to achieve its central objectives in the 1960s and 1970s, in stark contrast to the 1940s and 1950s, did not go unnoticed. Since the early 1960s a torrent of advice, diagnosis, and criticism has been pouring out from academics and commentators. As Cairncross once remarked about the debate on growth:

> There has been no lack of discussion in Britain of economic growth . . . But it would seem . . . that the volume of discussion is inversely proportionate to the resulting improvement. In the countries where growth is rapid there is no similar public debate on how it might be accelerated.[2]

The criticisms of stabilization policy have differed. During the 1960s there was considerable technical criticism of the actual conduct of demand management, if not of the principle that lay behind demand management. Many of these criticisms fed into a more wide-ranging political criticism of stabilization policy – the thesis that Britain's domestic economic growth was being sacrificed by the priority being given to defending the sterling exchange rate and maintaining the balance of payments in surplus. This priority was in turn linked to the political decisions to maintain sterling as an international currency, to fund overseas military expenditure, and to permit investment overseas. In the 1970s with the series of shocks and failures in economic policy and the return of mass unemployment, the technical criticisms became broader and began to focus on the intellectual framework that the Treasury was using in formulating and carrying out its stabilization policy. The most influential criticism came from the monetarists, but also important was the Cambridge Economic Policy Group. These technical ideas again fed into and helped shape the broader political strategies that were emerging within the two main political parties – the social market strategy on the right and the alternative economic strategy on the Left.

What is striking about the criticisms made in the 1970s is that for the first time since the war the issues involved in stabilization policy were politicized and made the subject of an adversary debate between the parties. But the effects on policy remained muted. The impact of the Conservatives embrace of monetarism after 1975 was limited by the adoption of practical monetarism by the Labour government. The alternative economic strategy was first of all an alternative to the course which the Labour government was pursuing. Nevertheless, after the consolidation of monetarism under the Thatcher government the commitment of all the opposition parties as well as part of the Conservative party to varying degrees of reflation suggested that stabilization policy was to be sealed off from adversary politics no longer.

These changes follow on the end of full employment in the 1970s and the 1980s and the inability of governments to do anything about it. This has completed the undermining of the post-war consensus on economic policy, which inflation began, and has reopened to ideological debate many of the questions concerning the relationship of state to economy which had been ignored in the period of stability and mild reforms after 1945 and increasing prosperity after 1953. A substantial section of the Labour party and the dominant section of the Conservative party now wish to reorder the balance of private and public power, to reshape the mixed economy, and to change the balance of power between labour and capital. Stabilization policy is to be an instrument in this restructuring while the failures of past stabilization policies are cited as a major reason why such restructuring has become necessary.

There remain elements in both major parties committed to the post-war priorities of economic mangement. The Liberals, now joined by the SDP in the Alliance, have also reasserted their commitment to the mixed economy and to a Keynesian framework for the stabilization policy. The range of choice presented to the electorate has therefore substantially widened. Even though this does not mean that the discontinuities in policy will be as sharp as the rhetoric it nevertheless highlights the long period when stabilization policy was not contentious.

Why was there such continuity at least in the framework of stabilization policy, with the single major exception of the switch from Keynesianism to monetarism? Technical answers are clearly insufficient. There were always technical disagreements on what was the best policy and there were some major political disagreements, but except on a few minor questions these differences did not emerge as issues in the adversary contest between the parties.

One important reason is because, by accepting the overall framework of stabilization policy, parties competed by offering themselves as more competent managers of the economy. Each party claimed it could deliver higher employment, lower prices, and faster economic growth than the other. There was relatively little conflict over the objectives themselves. No party would openly campaign for a faster rate of inflation in order to raise the level of unemployment. Such trade-offs were clearly understood and much technical work was devoted to trying to clarify the relationships involved. But in their electoral campaigns both parties preferred to claim that all the major objectives of stabilization policy could be realized simultaneously.

This reflected the fundamental idea, still maintained by Keynesians, that any stabilization policy worth having must aim for satisfactory outcomes in a number of areas. To achieve only one objective at the expense of missing the others by a wide margin was considered short-sighted and self-defeating. The monetarists, at whom the criticism is aimed because of their single-minded concentration on the objective of stable prices, retort that by the middle of the 1970s it had become common for Keynesian fine tuning of demand to manage to miss all policy objectives simultaneously.

But there was a deeper reason involved. Politicians of all parties in the 1950s and 1960s came to believe that growth could be the solvent of all other problems. If stabilization policy could be pursued successfully and the economy kept expanding, then the problems of achieving greater equality, or a higher minimum of income and greater opportunities, and therefore social progress and political stability, would be greatly diminished. A set of levers and techniques that could guarantee a satisfactory economic performance proved a lure that few politicians could resist. It explains why many politicians from all parties came to see their role less as tribunes of the people and more as technocratic managers, administering the swollen public sector and intervening more extensively in the markets of the private sector.

The apparent removal of many issues from politics altogether in the 1950s was assisted by the world economic recovery and the unprecedented prosperity and rate of expansion of those years. But the temporary end of ideology, the narrowing of the scope of the alternatives for democracies to choose between and the consequent shrivelling of adversary party politics and parliaments had deeper roots. In Britain they can be traced most clearly to the compromises struck between the state and the major producer interests, a development which Keith Middlemas has traced back to the 1920s. What emerged was a new style of government in which the legitimacy conferred through party and Parliament was radically diminished. The crucial economic and political problems of a modern industrial and capitalist society, particularly all the aspects of the conflict between capital and labour, came to be resolved through bargains and compromises struck outside parliament between state and the major organized interests. The aim of all sides came to be the avoidance of major conflicts and the establishment of an economic order which could generate the fastest possible increase of national wealth.

The growth of corporate representation alongside parliamentary representation and the increasing willingness of governments to formulate and carry out economic policy in consultation with and often with the active assistance of the organized interests, diminished the importance of party and parliamentary contribution to economic policy-making. This was more marked in some fields than others. It was particularly evident in stabilization policy. The new framework of stabilization policy that emerged in the 1940s was the expression of the series of compromises and changes which became essential for the prosecution of the war, and whose permanence was confirmed by Labour's victory in 1945.

One major theme of this chapter is that the terms of the post-war settlement and the way in which it was arranged left only a minor role for party politics in stabilization policy. The new objectives of demand management and the new techniques to achieve them were made possible by the new agreement on how the economy should be managed, what the boundaries between public and private sectors should be, how public expenditure should be increased, how the tax base to fund it should be extended, and how the interests of the major producers groups should be protected and their status recognized. This was not initially a consensus between political parties. The parties came to acquiesce in it and ideological conflict over it gradually abated.

The ideologies however remained intact, to be resurrected at another time. In retrospect the shift in the balance of political forces that created the post-war consensus and post-war Keynesian stabilization policy was heavily dependent on their ability to deliver an adequate economic performance. The fact that for a while in the 1950s, the economy performed better than anyone in the 1930s or 1940s had imagined possible, disguised the weaknesses involved in the new stabilization policy.

Continuity is not necessarily desirable in itself – it can turn out to be restrictive and stultifying. One of the aspects of the adversary style of politics established in Britain since the war is that by concentrating party and parliamentary conflict on a narrow range of policy issues it underwrote a consensus on the other issues – often of far greater importance. Douglas Ashford has discussed the highly secretive and arbitrary nature of the policy-making process in Britain – faults he argues that are sustained by the willingness of parliamentary leaderships of both parties to collude in adversary rituals which often prevent the opening of key policy issues to public scrutiny and debate.[3] This is a point which will be developed further.

The nature of stabilization policy

The term stabilization policy immediately raises the question what is to be stabilized and how. The traditional aims and conception of stabilization policy were modest. What needed to be stabilized were the public finances and this meant achieving and holding a balance between revenue and expenditure. The idea of a balanced budget was the corner-stone of this kind of stabilization policy, both because it expressed the ideal of good housekeeping and because it was treated as the key to maintaining the confidence of the financial markets and the commercial markets.

The assumptions behind this kind of stabilization policy became formalized in the 'Treasury view' of the inter-war period, against which Keynes and others directed so much scorn and argument. But the persistence of the Treasury view and the rejection of all radical measures to tackle unemployment were not the result of faulty economic analysis but instead expressed a particular balance of interests and circumstances. A balanced budget was so prized because it was regarded as the key to maintaining a sound currency. With the exception of the period of the First World War, British prices showed remarkable stability between 1815 and 1940. Sound money and price stability were regarded as the most important elements in achieving the success of an economic system organized through free markets because of the bed-rock of certainty they provided for economic decisions on buying, selling, saving, and investing. They therefore provided the best possible basis for a prosperous and expanding economy. The more prosperous the economy, the greater the tax revenues accruing to government, hence the greater the scope for reducing the tax burden and providing those government services that were judged to be necessary, at the cheapest possible rate

A balanced budget was therefore linked with economy in government expenditure and a low tax burden in the interests of encouraging individual initiative, individual self-reliance, and a flourishing market economy. This implied a restricted conception of government responsibilities and fuctions. Only those necessary for markets to function were judged appropriate for governments to undertake. Market rules, but not market outcomes, were the province of government. The level of employment, the distribution of income and the rate of economic growth were not regarded as matters with which governments could or should concern themselves. The government had no responsibility to stabilize the level of employment or the balance of payments; in the nineteenth century unemployment was not regarded as an 'economic' problem which could be alleviated by government policies.[4]

This view of economic policy was reinforced by the equally strong commitment to free trade and an open economy. The consequence of such a foreign economic policy is to make the markets for money, for goods, and for labour, international rather than purely national. The greater the openness of the economy the more restricted will be the options open to the national government in its economic policy, because prices, productivity, profitability, and employment will all be determined through international competition. The commitment to sound money became reinforced by adherence to the gold standard, which fixed exchange rates between currencies and dictated domestic monetary policies in accordance with international flows of exports and imports. Since money supply was tied to gold reserves and outflow of gold necessary to pay for a trade deficit forced contraction of the money supply and a fall in prices and costs in the debtor country. In this way each national government helped to maintain the edifice of the world market, on which economic progress and prosperity were held to depend.

This traditional view of stabilization policy in Britain came under attack from two sides. Firstly the liberal world economic order, under strain from the 1880s onwards, fell apart in the 1930s. The collapse of the gold standard, the spread of protectionism, and the dislocation of world trade discredited the free-trade argument for persisting with traditional stabilization policy. At the same time the steady piecemeal expansion of public agencies and responsibilities had reached a point where the public finances in aggregate were a much larger component of national income than before, and this made a discretionary stabilization policy much more feasible.

The economic rationale for such a stabilization policy was formulated by Keynes. His ideas made a major impact on Treasury thinking during the war and helped shape the post-war 'Keynesian' view of stabilization policy. The crucial change that emerged was the change in the objective of stabilization policy. Instead of following the simple rules of balancing the budget and aiming for strict economy in expenditure governments now attempted the much more ambitious task of stabilizing the level of demand in the economy. The purpose was to moderate fluctuations of economic activity and to achieve a range of targets, most notably full employment, stable prices, economic growth, and a surplus on the balance of payments. Far from a balanced budget being a priority, the new Keynesian wisdom was that the budget should be unbalanced when necessary to achieve the wider goal of stabilizing demand in the economy. The government should so time its own expenditures and so vary its own taxes as to influence the expenditure of other sectors and to counter the emergence of either deficient or excess demand in the economy.

What Keynesianism meant in practice was that the traditional fiscal and monetary instruments of economic policy – such as direct and indirect taxes, interest rates, open market operations – should always be assessed in terms of their impact upon the balance between total demand and total output. If demand was excessive there would be an inflationary gap and strong pressure on prices; if it was deficient there would be underemployment of productive resources. The aim of Keynesian stabilization policy was so to manipulate public spending and the level and incidence of taxation that the harmful fluctuations in output and employment so characteristic of an unregulated market economy were largely avoided. In technical terms, Keynesian demand management was justified as a solution to market failure – the failure of the market economy to overcome the mass unemployment of the 1930s – but it was first used during the war to deal with a very different kind of market failure, the excess demand created by extra government spending in the war economy.

The abandonment of the gold standard in 1931 forced governments to develop a discretionary monetary policy, and created the opportunity for conceiving economic policy as the management of a national economy relatively insulated from world economic pressures. This was a major reason for the subsequent success of the 'Keynesian revolution'. Not just the war economy but the economy in the 1930s had become an object of political management. Keynesianism offered a specific rationale and identified a number of new instruments to give effect to government economic policy, such as national income accounting, which made it possible to calculate aggregates of consumption and investment. These were essential tools for an attempt by governments to influence the level of demand.

The new stabilization policy depended on the existence of a state budget that was large in relation to national income. Otherwise alterations in taxes and spending by government would only have a marginal effect on the level of total demand. Public demand for goods and services had to be a significant proportion of the total for stabilization policy to work at all. This made advocates of the new stabilization policy allies of high spending policies. The larger the public sector the greater the discretion and the influence governments could exert over the economy. Similarly there was a tendency for the advocates of a managed economy to favour redistributive measures through the tax system, because the higher marginal propensity to consume of those on low incomes would increase the overall level of effective demand, and because such transfer payments, although not so direct in their efforts as government purchase of goods and services, nevertheless gave governments another instrument with which to influence the level and the distribution of demand.

The existence of a large state budget, however, accounting for more that 40 per cent of national income, also brought with it a number of major constraints for the new stabilization policy. This was chiefly because the state budget was not expanded primarily to make the management of demand possible. It was determined by other things. It reflected both the identification by public agencies and the civil service of new areas where government intervention was necessary, as well as growing demands for collective provision and public subsidies channelled through and stimulated by the pressure groups and political parties of the new mass democracy.

This posed a major difficulty for the new stabilization policy. Public spending programmes and agencies once established acquired their own momentum and proved very hard to adjust to the requirements of the policy. Controlling public expenditure was difficult enough; varying it to offset movements of demand elsewhere in the economy proved even harder. Between 1955 and 1966, for example, the correlation between public expenditure and the margin of unused resources (an indicator of deficient demand) was actually negative, when on orthodox Keynesian arguments it ought to have been positive.

If all public expenditure were devoted to employing workers to dig holes and fill them in again it would be a more efficient instrument of stabilization policy. Actual government expenditure has a content – such as health or educational services – which makes it very resistant to short-term variations. Not only are there good reasons for a particular level of service (such as demographic trends) but particular programmes rapidly become institutionalized and protected by a bureaucracy anxious to preserve, and if possible improve, its position, as well as by the dynamics of a competitive two-party system. Parties attempt to outbid one another by promising higher levels of service and spending.

The greater the extent to which such practices are established the less easily will the objectives of stabilization policy be secured. The need to fund the public sector and its spending programmes becomes one of the most powerful constraints on government economic policy because it must be accomplished if possible in ways that do not conflict with the major objectives of stabilization policy – particularly economic growth and stable prices.

The second major set of constraints on Keynesian stabilization policy are the labour markets. By making full employment a policy objective the government apparently dispenses with the traditional means for curbing wage demands and restraining the share of wages in national income – periodic mass unemployment. If the target of full employment is achieved, then labour discipline may be eroded and groups of workers may make pay demands which companies can only afford to pay by raising prices. If governments allow such prices to become effective by allowing the money supply to accommodate the higher demand for money then full employment will be maintained by allowing prices to rise.

This is a fairly standard account of the dilemma involved in full employment policy as many Keynesians have seen it. It led some economists to argue that the new stabilization policy meant that prices were no longer determined by the gold standard, i.e. by international levels of productivity as reflected in the balance of trade, but by a labour standard, i.e. by the outcome of the wage bargaining process. This fixed a large part of costs which were then passed on in prices.

It is hardly surprising therefore, given this kind of analysis, that Keynesian economists from the outset saw the handling of pay as a major problem for stabilization policy. In order to achieve both full employment and stable prices it was essential that some way be found of restraining pay demands. Otherwise there could be accelerating inflation, or a forced deflation of the economy and a return to unemployment. The problem was complicated because the labour market was not a single unified market but a multitude of local and specialized markets, which were very difficult to co-ordinate with a centralized stabilization policy. One aspect of this, which exacerbated the problem of controlling public expenditure, was the different level of productivity in parts of the private sector compared to the public sector, coupled with the tendency for pay in the private sector to be fixed according to productivity and the demand for labour, and pay in the public sector to be fixed in relation to pay in the private.

If labour markets were perfectly competitive, composed of a multitude of individual workers making individual contracts with individual employers, the problem would still arise. At full employment there would be excess demand for some types of labour and the wages of those workers would accordingly be bid up, and prices, in a permissive monetary environment, would follow. But many labour markets in Britain are not perfectly competitive – the workers in them have been organized into trade unions and bargain collectively with employers who are likewise often organized collectively. In many industries, labour power was no longer a commodity whose price could be automatically lowered by creating an excess of supply over demand, i.e. by creating unemployment. This became one of the main starting-points for Keynesian analysis. If wages could not be pushed down because of the power of organized labour, then the creation of mass unemployment would work very slowly to reduce costs, restore profitability, and create the conditions for a new boom. The cost of prolonged stagnation and mass unemployment on social and political stability might prove explosive. From considerations like this came Keynes's conviction that it was better to raise profits by stimulating demand and raising prices (cutting real wages but not money wages) than attempt to reconstruct the profitability of the capitalist economy by directly reducing costs and confronting the power of organized labour. The losers in the long run from this policy would be *rentiers* and savers. It was Keynes who wrote:

Inflation is unjust and deflation is inexpedient. Of the two, perhaps, deflation is, if we rule out exaggerated inflations such as that of Germany, the worse; because it is worse, in an impoverished world, to provoke unemployment than to disappoint the rentier.[5]

The need to restrain spending in the public sector and the growth of earnings quickly emerged as major constraints on Keynesian stabilization policy. They led to experiments with various devices for controlling public expenditure, notably the Public Expenditure Survey Committe (PESC) launched in 1961, and different kinds of pay controls – the incomes policies of the 1960s and 1970s. But all these innovations took place within the general framework of Keynesian assumptions about stabilization policy. The overriding purpose of economic policy was to manage the level of effective demand so as to achieve a high level of employment, reasonable stability of prices, a favourable balance of payments, and a steady rate of economic growth.

Post-war stabilization policy became patterned by three annual sequences of events and decisions; firstly, the decisions on taxes, concentrated overwhelmingly in the annual budget announced in March or April; secondly, the decisions on public spending which determined how much revenue had to be raised; finally the annual wage-round – spread throughout the year, each group of workers having its own bargaining arrangements and its own date for annual settlements. The interaction of these three sequences established an annual policy cycle, the outcome of each process being determined by the balance which emerged between administrative neccessity, the influence of pressure groups, and political calculations.

Stabilization policy would have been difficult enough if it had been limited to striking a balance between the demands for higher expenditure and the political and administrative limits to higher taxation and to deciding on the rate of growth of earnings that would ensure the attainment to the wider objectives of economic management. But the constraints of the annual policy cycle, although frequently the most visible and most discussed aspects of economic policy, are not the only constraints. They are most visible because government has direct responsibility for fixing tax rates and determining levels of public expenditure, and the growth of the public sector has made the government a major employer with a major interest in and influence over the annual pay-round.

The success of post-war stabilization policy, however, was never solely a matter of how the government managed its own finances and the pay of its employees. The aspiration behind the policy was to stabilize demand for the whole economy and by indirectly influencing the decisions taken by private economic agents on consumption and investment promote the wider objectives of the policy. The main obstacle to achieving this was that it was much easier to influence consumption than to influence investment, because the latter depended on securing the confidence and co-operation of those who actually made the decisions on output, investment, employment, and prices in enterprises. This meant that governments had to conduct their management of the public finances and the pay-round so as to maintain the confidence of decision-makers in private-sector firms.

If governments failed to maintain industrial confidence by their policy the consequences could be dire – a slump in output, in investment, and in employment. Large though the increase in the public sector was, the success of any policy to stabilize demand depended on the active co-operation of the private sector. Even after the extension of public ownership in the 1940s over 80 per cent of economic assets remained privately owned. This characteristic of the organization of a market economy makes private business not just another pressure group but an interest which has a privileged status in partnership with government.[6] No government can succeed in its policies if it ignores the need to secure the co-operation and maintain the confidence of this sector. A fundamental requirement of successful government is that there should be prosperity, not just to promote social order but also to make possible the funding of public expenditure. Recession and slump if they are prolonged will always thrust the public finances into crisis.

But there is a further major constraint on stabilization policy. Its operation is crucially determined by the foreign economic policy which the Government maintains. For this concerns the relative openness of the national economy to the world economy and the extent to which national markets are fully integrated into international markets for goods, for labour, and for money. As was seen when discussing the gold standard, the greater the openness the less the scope for a national stabilization policy. Stabilization policies can be most effective when economies are closed.

The openness of the British economy has been a priority of Britain's foreign economic policy since the move to completely free trade during the first part of the nineteenth century. It was modified in the 1930s and 1940s as a result of events outside the British government's control. This was the period when ideas of managing the national economy as a single enterprise made considerable headway. In the post-war years, however, the commitment to an open economy re-emerged, although in a different form. The commitment was to participation in the new world economic order which the Americans established, and which encouraged steady progress towards the liberalization of trade and the convertibility of currencies. For a time this new liberal economic order permitted sterling to re-emerge as an international currency.

The result of the gradual increase in openness of the British economy after 1945 and its reintegration into a unified 'world' economy will be considered in more detail below. A few preliminary points should be noted here. Firstly it made national stabilization policy considerably more difficult because it introduced so many factors over which British governments had little or no control. The public sector in the UK might be a significant part of total UK demand but it was an insignificant part of total world demand. Successful stabilization policy in an economy where approximately 30 per cent of national output was traded abroad depends to a considerable extent on the policies pursued by other governments.

Secondly, it re-established the financial markets as an important arbiter of government policy, The markets in financial claims and foreign exchange became the most open of all in the post-war world economy and this has exerted powerful constraints on the financial and stabilization policies that governments have been able to pursue. The decentralized and competitive character of financial markets ensures that financial crises and sterling crises when they erupt do so with remarkable suddenness and generally force the government to modify its policies or introduce measures (particularly cuts in public expenditure) that can restore financial confidence.

Once stabilization policy is placed in its true international context the conditions for success and failure are no longer subject in important respects to government control or influence. Areas of discretion naturally remain since no national economy is ever completely integrated into the world economy. Even where there is perfect competition and all domestic and foreign goods are complete substitutes for one another, national governments can still influence the structure of relative prices by introducing tariffs or varying the exchange rate. More important is the fact that markets are never perfect. National labour markets have become most closed through restrictive immigration policies, and trade union organization and professional cartels. There is greater openness and competition in the markets for goods and services, but also great variations and many services are not supplied through markets at all.

A successful stabilization policy therefore becomes extremely hard to engineer, unless either policy or circumstances modify the constraints on its operation. The most important constraints identified here are firstly the organization of the public finances – the need always to balance the pressures for expenditure to increase with the political and administrative limits on taxation; secondly, the organization of the labour markets – the need to restrain the growth of earnings to prevent an escalation of costs in public and private sectors and win the co-operation of trade unions in the undertaking; thirdly, the organization of the private sector, the need to manage demand, taxes, interest rates, and pay, so as to maintain the confidence of industrialists; and finally the relative openness of the national economy to the world economy, which ensures not only that the level of demand, prices and employment are shaped to a significant extent by forces outside the national economy, but also that maintaining the confidence of the financial markets becomes essential for a successful stabilization policy.

With so many constraints and so many groups and agents to satisfy, it is hardly surprising if stabilization policy in the past has often appeared as a catalogue of errors, a lurch from one crisis to the next. This is even before the political dimension has been explicitly considered. It is to this that we turn next.

Demand management and the parties

There is another constraint on stabilization policy which so far has been considered only indirectly – the political constraint. The actual decisions which implement stabilization policy are taken by politicians at the head of government departments who must calculate the effect of them on their parties and on the wider electorate. Whatever the political regime one of the main results sought from a discretionary stabilization policy will be political and social stability. In a competitive multi-party system numerous channels are also established by which the preferences of party activists and voters can influence the priorities of stabilization policy.

The impact of party in a competitive adversary system on stabilization policy suggests a range of possible outcomes. The actual outcome will depend on the specific characteristics of the party system; the internal organization of the parties; and their relative responsiveness to (a) needs and problems defined by the public realm; (b) pressure groups, (c) their party activists; (d) the electorate.

A few examples will illustrate the different effects that could be expected, and which have been discussed in Chapter 2. If parties are mainly responsible to elite opinion and policy formulation then a durable elite consensus about stabilization policy might be forged, high on continuity, low on partisan input or interference. If parties, however, are more responsive to pressure groups, and if the main parties are more responsive to some pressure groups than others, then a more erratic stabilization policy would be likely, the choices reflecting the influence of particular pressure groups (of which civil servants would be only one) at different points on the policy cycle.

If on the other hand parties are more responsive to their activists and party organization, then the priorities for stabilization policy which each party in office seeks to maintain will reflect ideological preferences which may or may not be in line with elite opinion. Here again major oscillations in policy might be expected, as in the pure adversary politics model, particularly in the first two years of each new party administration. Finally, if the responsiveness of parties and those who direct them is greatest towards voters then parties will attempt to pursue a stabilization policy that maximizes votes. If voters' preferences are evenly distributed then competition between parties may force parties to seek the middle ground only slightly differentiating the choices they offer to the electorate. If voters' preferences do not bunch in the centre or if they cannot be ranked on a single preference scale at all then competition between the parties may produce much sharper policy alternatives for the electorate to choose between. In stabilization policy most of the issues likely to be presented to the electorate are 'valence' rather than 'position' issues. Everyone is likely, for example, to be in favour of full employment and of stable prices. There is unlikely to be sharp split in the electorate between those favouring high employment and those favouring high unemployment. Much more likely is a split in the relative importance attached to different policy goals. Not only may such valuations shift but they may be very unevenly distributed amongst the electorate.

These four approaches offer different ways in which the impact of party on stabilization policy can be assessed in relation to the actual record. What all presume, however, in the form in which they are stated above, is that party government does have the capacity and the means to pursue the stabilization policy of its choice and that a political business cycle in which key economic variables are manipulated and influenced by discretionary government intervention is not illusion but reality. Only if governments have this power is it reasonable to speculate about the relative influence of party competition on how they exercise it. What should be abundantly plain from the earlier discussion is just how constrained stabilization policy is.

Party attitudes to stabilization policy

Are there deep ideological divisions in the attitudes of the parties towards stabilization policy? Are these divisions reflected in the discontinuities in the conduct of stabilization policy? Or does the competitive adversary system have other effects which are less visible but still significant?

The two crucial periods for post-war stabilization policy are the 1940s and the 1970s. The first saw the commitment by all parties to the objective of full employment, the second saw the breakdown of the consensus on this objective amidst failure to prevent unemployment from rising. What was the nature of the commitment to full employment and where did the parties stand?

There is no doubt that a commitment to full employment became part of the rhetoric of all three main parties at the 1945 general election. Yet that commitment in itself was unsurprising. No party had ever declared itself the party of unemployment. What mattered was whether the parties expected full employment to arise naturally as an effect of their other policies or whether they proposed to take additional measures to ensure full employment was achieved. In the first sense traditional stabilization policy was a full-employment policy. It indicated the obstacles which hindered the working of the free market and which prevented jobs being available for all who wanted them. One problem in looking at the debate on full employment in the 1940s is deciding how much opinion (especially opinion in the Liberal and Conservative parties), really had shifted, and how far the politicians were merely adjusting their traditional rhetoric on economic policy to take account of the popular expectations about reconstruction which the war had created.

One unfailing source for party rhetoric is general election manifestos. The new tone in 1945 is unmistakable. The Conservatives, who had been in government almost continuously since 1916 and had presided over high levels of unemployment in the 1920s and 1930s, now took their stand on the reconstruction plans of the coalition government.

In the White Paper presented to Parliament by the late administration are sound plans for avoiding the disastrous slumps and booms from which we used to suffer, but which all are united in being determined to avoid in the future. The Government accepts as one of its primary aims and responsibilities the maintenance of a high and stable level of employment. Unless there is steady and ample work there will not be the happiness, the confidence or the material resources in the country on which we can all build together the kind of Britain that we want to see.[7]

The Conservatives were, however, not specific as to how this high and stable level of employment would be maintained. The Liberals were not much clearer. Although the party was later to claim that it was the architect of the full-employment policy because of its pre-war plans and the work of Keynes and Beveridge, the 1945 Liberal manifesto was a less radical document than in 1929. It was content to state 'Full employment can be maintained in a Free Society'. Since the 1920s the Liberals had come to support a policy of national development and economic growth although they had never abandoned their commitment to free trade. There remained a deep tension between the Liberal commitments to planning for social welfare and full employment and to the principle of individual economic freedom through free competitive markets. Keynes referred to it as the divide between real Liberals and true Liberals. At a later date the labels became radical reformers and radical individualists.

The party which had the clearest view on how full employment should be created and maintained was Labour. In a section entitled 'Jobs for All' the 1945 manifesto stated:

All parties pay lip service to the idea of jobs for all. All parties are ready to achieve that end by keeping up the national purchasing power and controlling changes in the national expenditure through Government action. Where agreement ceases is in the degree of control of private industry that is necessary to achieve the desired end.[8]

Labour's position in 1945 was firmly rooted in an analysis of the capitalist economy which identified a chronic tendency to under-consumption and deficient demand. Their proposals for stabilization policy emphasized, therefore, the need for central direction of the economy and the extension of public ownership:

In hard fact the success of a full employment programme will certainly turn upon the firmness and success with which the Government fits into that programme the investment and development policies of private as well as public industry.[9]

The difference between Labour's proposals on full employment and those of the Conservatives and Liberals were plain:

Our opponents would be ready to use state action to do the best they can to bolster up private industry whenever it plunges the nation into heavy unemployment. [They] are not ready to draw the conclusion that the sphere of public action must be extended.[10]

This injected a true adversary note into the debate. There was indeed all-party agreement that the government should do more to manipulate purchasing power in order to moderate booms and slumps in the economy. The war economy had demonstrated just how powerful a role governments could occupy. There was also agreement that there should be an extension of public ownership. Jo Grimond has recalled that there was little Liberal opposition in 1945 to the measures of nationalization that Labour was proposing. 'We were all to some extent socialist.'[11] The same was true for the Conservatives. But what both Liberals and Conservatives did strongly oppose was a progressive extension of public ownership in order to preserve the goals of the stabilization policy.

In 1945 Labour argued for a much more radical stabilization policy than it did subsequently. While it is true that Keynesian economic thinking was making increasing headway within the party, it did not displace older perspectives on unemployment but supplemented them. 'Keynesianism' in the sense of the commitment to manage aggregate demand, to counter fluctuations in economic activity, and to create conditions for, amongst other things, full employment became the common framework within which the parties discussed stabilization policy. But there remained important differences, most obviously over what should be done if demand management failed to achieve 'full employment'. Would such a failure constitute grounds for a further extension of government responsibility over the economy? How important was the commitment to full employment to be? Was the principle of 'work for all' to take priority over other long-standing principles such as economic liberty?

The implication of Labour's position was that the profitability of the private sector should not be allowed to become a constraint on the pursuit of the objectives of its stabilization policy. If the stabilization policy eroded company profits by maintaining a tight labour market and increasing taxes on companies to pay for welfare policies, then rather than acquiesce in unemployment and cuts in public spending in order to preserve investment, output, and jobs in the private sector, the government should take powers to ensure the level of production was maintained. This was one aspect of the process which Hayek described as the 'road to serfdom' – the progressive dismantling of the legal framework of the market order which ensured a clear distinction between the public and the private realms.

Labour valued its achievement rather differently. In 1950 its manifesto stated that a moral order had been created whose corner-stone was full employment, because 'jobs for all' was the foundation of economic security. Full employment was proclaimed 'the main but not the only achievement'. This theme was stated still more emphatically a year later in the 1951 manifesto:

> Full employment through six years of peace is the greatest of all Labour's achievements. It has never happened before. It has meant a revolution in the lives of our people. Under the Tories there never was full employment.[12]

On the other side the Conservatives' commitment to full employment had not slackened. They could not afford to be branded electorally as the party of unemployment. Both the 1950 and 1951 manifestos reaffirmed the party's commitment, 'We regard the maintenance of full employment as the first aim of a Conservative Government.' But the 1951 manifesto added an important qualification:

> The Conservative aim is to increase our national output. Here is the surest way to keep our people fully employed, to halt the rising cost of living, and to preserve our social services.[13]

By 1951 the Conservatives had swung decisively to opposing further extensions of public control over the economy. Labour remained committed to further measures of nationalization and the retention of significant central controls, notably over the financial markets. The 1950 manifesto promised:

Finance must be the servant and not the master of employment policy. Public ownership of the Bank of England has enabled the Government to control monetary policy. . . . We shall take whatever measures may be required to control financial forces, so as to maintain full employment and promote the welfare of the nation.[14]

The Conservatives, by contrast, although it did not appear as a manifesto pledge, wanted to restore freedom to the financial markets.

There was a significant difference in the attitudes of the parties to stabilization policy in the 1940s and it was linked to much wider conflict over the boundaries of public and private power. The post-war 'consensus' between the parties was only consolidated in the 1950s, by which time full employment was no longer such a central issue for economic policy. The Conservatives were able to claim in their turn that they were now the party of full employment. Their manifestos in 1955 and 1959 made full use of it:

Under Conservative administration a working population of record peace-time size has been kept fully employed, without Socialist controls and without continual inflation. Our record speaks for itself.[15]

In 1959 the claims were still greater:

We have cut taxes in 7 Budgets, whilst continuing to develop the social services. We have provided over two million new homes and almost two million new school places, a better health service and a modern pensions plan. We have now stabilised the cost of living while maintaining full employment. We have shown that Conservative freedom works. Life is better with the Conservatives.[16]

What made the election rhetoric of both Labour and the Conservatives rather hollow was that no post-war administration could properly claim credit for the existence of full employment. Governments had faced a problem not of too little but too much demand and the Keynesian techniques for overcoming unemployment were used to counter the problem of overfull employment, of an economy whose resources were periodically in danger of being overstretched so that inflation was a permanent threat. This theme grew in prominence in the manifestos. In 1950 Labour declared that:

Purchasing power and production must march together. Just as we have aimed at keeping purchasing power within limits in the last few years when there have been too few goods and too much money, so we will be prepared to expand purchasing power if the danger is too little money and too few goods.[7]

The latter danger did not materialize and in 1955 the Conservative manifesto was stating:

Any country pursuing a policy of economic expansion and full employment faces a constant danger of inflation. The risk is that home demand may take away from the export trade and swell the import bill.[18]

A new framework for stabilization policy designed to tackle the problem of slump and deficient demand was being used for the very different economic problems of the 1950s. The cycles of activity which governments attempted to stabilize were mild, and unemployment was extremely low. Most political and economic opinion in 1945 expected that once the post-war reconstruction boom was over there would be a return to mass unemployment. When this did not occur it rendered obsolete the adversary debate between the parties on how to achieve full employment. Full employment was a fact.

In retrospect we can see that this led to the degree of consensus on stabilization policy in 1945 being overstated. The groups which emerged to dominate their parties in the 1950s, were those which for a variety of reasons found Keynesian ideas a convenient source of justification for the new economic order now increasingly described as either the 'mixed economy' or the 'managed economy'.

In the Conservative party these ideas had become known as the New Conservatism and were strongly associated with R. A. Butler and Harold Macmillan. Butler was in charge of the Conservative Research Department after 1945 and was responsible for drawing up the statements on policy in the 1940s which signalled the acceptance by the Conservative leadership of many of the changes which the war economy and the Labour government had introduced. There was a minority in the party which bitterly attacked the accommodation to the new political realities which the leadership seemed intent on making. The Conservatives' acquiescence in the new level of public expenditure excited most alarm. Sir Waldron Smithers, MP for Orpington, speaking at the 1949 Conference in the debate on *The Right Road for Britain*, the party's new policy document, condemned it for promising a materialistic Utopia and making promises which would fail. The pledges in *The Right Road*, he declared, quoting an unnamed professor of economics, are 'irreconcilable with the reduction of public expenditure. We cannot hope for national recovery while public expenditure continues unabated. . . . It is futile to compete with the Socialists in promising a welfare state.[19]

There were many in the party like Smithers who were never reconciled to the 'New Conservatism' and who wanted the party committed to a stabilization policy which still put sound money, a balanced budget, and economy in public expenditure first. Concern in the party about inflation and high taxation was rife throughout the 1950s and early 1960s, but it never dislodged the central commitment of the party leaders to the new style and rhetoric of economic management, since they were determined that the party should lose the label as the party of unemployment. Butler's retort to his critics at the 1949 Conference was typical. The new policy document is, he declared:

as I see it a policy of humanity and commonsense – humanity because it associates the Conservative party with the spiritual, human and physical needs of our large population, and commonsense because it used the instrument of change where change is in the national interest, and accepts economic facts where these are unanswerable and ineluctable.[20]

Two years earlier he had defended the Industrial Charter. Waldron Smithers had urged the Conference to reject it in order to prevent the Conservative party being infected with the 'socialist bug'. Butler, however, declared that far from being 'milk and water socialism' the Charter represented the core of the Conservative tradition and an attempt 'to restate Conservatism in the light of modern economic theory'.[21] There was, he said, an urgent need to concentrate on the question of management not ownership of industry. In an introduction to a Conservative pamphlet, he wrote:

It is the task of the present generation of Conservatives to found our modern faith on the basis of two features of this age, namely the existence of universal adult suffrage and the acceptance by authority of the responsibility for ensuring a certain standard of living, of employment, and of security for all.[22]

These were themes which had been developed most strongly by Harold Macmillan, particularly in his inter-war writings such as *The Middle Way*,[23] which had been strongly influenced by Keynes. Macmillan wrote subsequently that he had wanted to devise:

Some coherent system, lying between unadulterated private enterprise and collectivism. It was a policy which I afterwards called 'The Middle Way'; an industrial structure with the broad strategic control in the hands of the state and the tactical operation in the hands of private management, with public and private ownership operating side by side.[24]

The political events of the 1940s placed the advocates of the New Conservatism in the ascendancy. They did not hesitate to scorn their critics. Butler, when Chancellor of the Exchequer, declared that those who talked about creating pools of unemployment should be thrown into them and made to swim.

The new Conservative rhetoric about full employment was not believed in the Labour party. Labour politicians argued at the elections of 1950 and 1951 that the return of the Conservatives would mean the return of mass unemployment. At the 1952 Labour Party Conference, Nye Bevan stated: 'It is a fact and even the Keynesians have to admit it that there is no means of preventing unemployment in capitalist society.' He was echoed by Bessie Braddock: 'Whatever we try to do, there will be mass unemployment while a Tory Government is in power, since that is part of the capitalist system that the Tory party stands for.' The traditional view of the Labour party was still that full employment could only be secured if the public sector was maintained and extended. Prosperity and socialization went together. It was the failure of the Tories to deliver unemployment in the 1950s that undercut many of the traditional Labour attitudes towards economic policy and allowed revisionists like Tony Crosland to argue that nationalization was not the priority it had appeared to be for so long.[25] It was merely one among many means to the central socialist goal, equality. Crosland and other revisionists took the success of world capitalism in the 1950s as a vindication of Keynesianism and argued that the new economics made obsolescent much of the ideological framework within which socialists had been accustomed to think about politics. The central issue was now how to achieve the fastest possible rate of growth so as to allow a continuing expansion of public services (not public enterprises) in order to eliminate social inequalities.

Crosland believed that the achievement of full employment by Keynesian fiscal and monetary policies constituted one of the structural changes that had permanently transformed capitalism and its politics. He thought that an economic system composed of a substantial private market sector and a Keynesian state prepared to use fiscal and monetary policy to achieve growth and maintain full employment had overcome many of the drawbacks of traditional capitalism and had rendered state socialism irrelevant.

In the 1950s full employment was maintained with ease, inflation was persistent but negligible, and growth was rapid. It was not, however, rapid enough when Britain's performance was judged against its main competitors. The question of Britain's relatively slow growth rate and the need to achieve a programme of modernization became the key issue of the 1960s for all parties. That it did so was a sign of how comprehensively the New Conservatives, the Labour revisionists, and the radical reformers in the Liberal party had won the ascendency.

The issue which the two opposition parties used to force the Conservatives back on the defensive was the stop–go cycle and the government's responsibility for it. The nature of this cycle will be examined in the next section. What both Labour and Liberal critics stressed was that the government was failing to achieve steady expansion of demand and output. This was already identified as a key issue in 1959. The task, declared the Labour manifesto is 'to combine an expanding economy with full employment and steady prices'. Labour still argued that the Conservatives could not be trusted to maintain full employment, but it was regional unemployment, not national employment, that was now identified as the problem. The issue, as the Labour party saw it, was whether even the moderate business cycle of the post-war years was necessary. The Conservatives were still suspected of a commitment to financial orthodoxy. The deflation of the economy instituted by Peter Thorneycroft as Chancellor in 1957 was often cited. The 1959 Labour manifesto argued:

After the Thorneycroft crisis of 1957 the Government deliberately created unemployment in an attempt to halt inflation. Unemployment is still heavy in some areas. The use of unemployment to halt rising prices is as obsolete as it is cruel.[26]

The preferred instruments for coping with inflation were a policy of expansion and a policy for incomes. By 1964, even though the Conservative government had launched its own modernization strategy and its own initiatives on planning and incomes policy, Labour claimed in its manifesto to be offering a real choice in stabilization policy:

Only a major change in economic and fiscal policy can break the defeatist stop–go cycle and prevent another bout of stagnant production, rising unemployment and declining national strength.[27]

Among the perceived consequences of stop–go in the 'thirteen wasted years' were slower growth, intermittent bouts of high unemployment, growing stagnation and unemployment in the regions, inflation and wage drift, and a climate of 'irresponsibility' and 'selfishness'.

All parties embraced modernization in the 1960s. The need for continuous expansion, for incomes policy, for greater co-ordination between government and industry, and for greater public spending in areas like roads, health, and education were all acknowledged. But there were significant differences of emphasis. Although the Conservatives initiated many of the modernization policies of the 1960s, the defence of sterling remained a very important constraint, and the younger Tories interpreted modernization to mean a more competitive free enterprise economy. These views were well expressed by Peter Walker proposing the motion on economic policy at the 1963 Party Conference. Full employment, he argued, depended on the success of the free enterprise economy, which should be extended so as to create a popular and positive capitalism:

Our educational services must be geared to the needs of modern industry and modern technology. . . . Free enterprise itself has a compulsive and exciting effect, demanding change, in contrast to the reactionary and Luddite effects of a system based on state domination. . . The Labour party is today the party of Luddites – Luddite towards modernization of our railways, Luddite towards the closing of exhausted collieries. . . . We have to be sure that we contrast with them as the party of change and modernization.[28]

Both the Labour and Liberal parties put greater emphasis on the possibilities of better state management. The Liberals were particularly influential in developing a powerful critique of post-war economic policy. They emphasized more clearly than any other party the need for a new foreign economic policy as an integral part of a radical modernization strategy. As Jo Grimond put it, growth must come before grandeur. Economic growth, the 1964 Liberal manifesto stated, 'must become a major aim through more skilful management of the nation', and this implied a major rethinking of the traditional priority accorded to the international role of sterling and other aspects of Britain's continuing world role, particularly the high level of overseas military spending.

Yet despite the fact that all parties agreed there was a need to escape the constraint of the balance of payments on domestic expansion, none in office proved able to surmount it. Every modernization programme in the 1960s was shipwrecked on sterling and the balance of payments. The failure to the new policies of state management in the 1960s had a profound effect on the parties' attitudes towards stabilization policy and led ultimately to the emergence of true adversary postures. It is a remarkable irony that only when unemployment began its inexorable rise after 1966 did the rhetoric and concern for full employment begin to diminish. Peter Bessell's impassioned declaration at the 1966 Liberal Party Conference that a single person unemployed was intolerable was already anachronistic. Inflation came to dominate party discussion of stabilization policies in the 1970s. The Conservative manifesto of 1970 stated bluntly; 'In implementing all our policies the need to curb inflation will come first.' Labour's compulsory wage control had been 'a failure and we will not repeat it'. In February 1974 the message was a little different but the theme was the same:

The gravest threat to our national well-being has been the menace of unrestrained inflation. . . . We shall press ahead with the pay and prices policy if necessary stiffening it in the light of the developing economic situation.[29]

In 1979 the party published its first monetarist manifesto. Full employment is not mentioned. The only reference to the high level of unemployment, 1.4 million in 1979, was that policies would be needed to create 'genuine new jobs'. But the first task that the party pledged itself to carry through was 'to restore the health of our economic and social life, by controlling inflation and striking a fair balance between the rights and duties of the trade union movement'. The new priorities for government economic policy were described as sound money, economy in government expenditure, and trade union reform. The problem of unemployment had once again become a secondary problem, the cure for which lay in sound money, improved incentives, and reform of the labour markets. It was no longer a problem which could be solved by measures to increase demand. The position of the Thatcher goverment was close to the Treasury view of the 1920s which Churchill so ably expounded when he was Chancellor of the Exchequer:

It is the orthodox Treasury dogma, steadfastly held, that whatever might be the political or social advantages, very little additional employment and no permanent additional employment can, in fact, and as a general rule, be created by State borrowing and State expenditure.[30]

Keynes's response to this was characteristic:

The Conservative belief that there is some law of nature which prevents men from being employed, that it is 'rash' to employ men, and that it is financially 'sound' to maintain a tenth of the population in idleness for an indefinite period, is crazily improbable – the sort of thing which no man could beleive who has not has his head fuddled with nonsense for years and years.[31]

The overthrow of orthodox ideas on stabilization policy by notions derived from Keynes has not lasted. With the disintegration of the Keynesian consensus on stabilization policy has come a much sharper adversary divide between the parties on the principles and priorities of stabilization policy. But this development appears to be an effect rather than a cause of the breakdown of consensus.

The record of stabilization policy

The evaluation of the adversary politics thesis requires an assessment of the changes that have occurred in stabilization policy. This is not an easy matter because there are several different patterns of discontinuity that can be observed, and the final judgement that will be formed on the adversary politics thesis depends upon the weight that is given to them. Five different criteria for identifying changes in economic policy are listed in Table 4. They give strikingly different periodizations for economic policy in the post-war period.

(i) *Party politics*

This is the criterion most obviously in tune with the adversary politics thesis. It allows the period since 1945 to be divided into six main periods; 1945–51, 1951–64, 1964–70, 1970–4, 1974–9, and 1979– . Change of the party holding government office marks the end of each period with the exception of the last. It is suggested that the economic policies pursued have varied according to the ideology and policies of the party in power. At its extreme this would suggest that the only period of consistent stabilization policy which Britain has experienced since the war is between 1951 and 1964. Otherwise the direction of stabilization policy has been changed every four to six years.

The plausibility of this view is enhanced because political parties need to differentiate their policies from their opponents and to present their programmes as marking a decisive change from what has gone before. The adversary conception of policy-making in Britain is further strengthened because of the convention that ministers have responsibility for formulating policy and civil servants for implementing it. The element of discontinuity rather than continuity in public policy-making is emphasized.

Using this criterion a familiar picture of post-war stabilization policy emerges. The period 1945–51 is dominated by reconstruction and planning. The Labour government used physical controls and high taxation to promote full employment, stable prices, and the recovery of

Table 4

Different criteria for analysing stabilization policy

1. Party Politics

	Chancellors of the Exchequer	Party in office	Keynotes
1945–51	Dalton 45–7	Labour	Reconstruction
			Full employment through planning
	Cripps 47–50		
	Gaitskell 50–1		
1951–64	Butler 51–5	Conservative	Set the People free
			Full employment through markets
	Macmillan 55–6		
	Thorneycroft 57–8		
	Amory 58–60		
	LLoyd 60–2		
	Maudling 62–4		
1964–70	Callaghan 64–7	Labour	The New Britain
			Modernization through planning
	Jenkins 67–70		
1970–74	Barber 70–4	Conservative	Britain in Europe
			Modernization through competition
1974–79	Healey 74–9	Labour	The social contract
			Managing the recession
1979–	Howe 79–83	Conservative	Sound Money
			Stable prices through financial discipline
	Lawson 83–		

continued

Table 4 *continued*

2. Actual priorities of stabilization policy			
1945–7	Full employment		
1947–60	External financial balance; full employment		
1960–75	External financial balance; faster growth		
1975–	Stable prices		
3. Instruments of policy			
1945–7	Manpower budget; physical resource planning		
1947–75	Financial budget; demand management. Fiscal measures / monetary measures / incomes policy / PESC		
1975–	Financial budget; monetary management. Monetary targets, cash limits		
4. Dominant intellectual frameworks			
1945–7	Physical planning; manpower budget		
1947–61	Demand management; national income analysis		
1961–75	Planned growth; fine tuning of demand, incomes policy		
1975–	Monetarism; monetary aggregates		
5. The external context of policy			
1945–53	Reconstruction:		
	Rejection of bilateralism, gradual progress to multilateralism, containment of inflation		
	Bretton Woods Agreement, 1944		
	Washington Loan Agreements, 1945		
	Marshall Aid, 1948		
	Sterling Crises:	1947	attempt at convertibility; abandoned
		1949	devaluation
		1951	

1953–73	The long boom:		
	Multilateral trade, reduction of tariffs, increase of capital and labour flows		
	Rapid growth, low unemployment. Low inflation		
	Full convertibility of major currencies achieved; exchange rates fixed (gold exchange standard)		
	Sterling crises:	1955	
		1956	
		1957	major deflation of domestic economy
		1961	major deflation
		1964–7	major deflation
		1972	pound floated
1973–	Recession:		
	Multilateral trade maintained, but protectionist strains		
	Exchange controls removed, immigration controls tightened		
	Floating exchange rates; removal of external financial discipline; rise of international monetarism		
	Acceleration of inflation, major increase in unemployment, growth sharply reduced		
	Sterling movements:	1974–6	major deflationary package; acceptance of international monetarist policies
		1979–80	sterling allowed to appreciate
		1982–3	sterling allowed to depreciate

output and exports, while at the same time funding major programmes of social expenditure and rearmament. There was a climate of austerity, many goods were still rationed, and there were continual appeals for national unity and social discipline.

The Conservatives campaigned during the 1951 election under the slogan 'Set the People Free'. They called for an end to controls and argued that the battle against inflation could be won by reducing public expenditure and taxation and by using monetary policy to ration credit and control the quantity of money. A quick return to free competition would increase output, and in the long run, tax revenue, and was the best means to achieve full employment. The 1951–64 period is accordingly associated with the 'freeing' of the economy, the ending of controls, the reopening of commercial exchanges, the liberalization of international trade and payments, the reduction of public spending and taxation (at least in the early period), and a much greater reliance on monetary policy.

The period also attracted negative labels – the thirteen wasted years, the years of stop–go. Economic expansion was constantly held back by sterling crises and balance of payments difficulties. The third period, 1964–70, is accordingly the period of the *New Britain*, of modernization and planning. Planning this time, however, was modelled not on the physical planning of the war economy but on the indicative planning techniques of the French. Priority was to be given to growth in stabilization policy which meant attempting on the one hand to improve the match between the growth of demand and the growth of productive potential, and on the other to raise the rate of growth of productive potential by new interventionist policies, while riding out any short-term difficulties on the balance of payments. There were important experiments with incomes policy and selective industrial intervention.

The new policies were not, however, accompanied by the expected rate of economic expansion and this encouraged a renewed assault by the Conservative Oppostion upon the level of public expenditure and taxation, and upon the degree of state intervention in industry. The theme of the 1970–4 period was still modernization and growth but this time it was to be achieved by the state disengaging itself from the economy and encouraging competition and private initiative. Inflation emerged at first as the leading priority of the government's stabilization policy, and its control was to be achieved not through government control over incomes and prices but through the creation of a more competitive and responsible climate and through monetary discipline.

The Heath government's programme for modernization was not shipwrecked as the Wilson government's had been upon the defence of sterling. The Heath government was able to float the pound when the system of fixed exchange rates broke down in 1971. But it was greatly damaged by the wave of industrial militancy certain of its policies provoked and by the failure of British industry to respond more quickly to the climate of opportunity that the government was trying to create by its policies on public expenditure, taxation, industrial relations, and the EEC. Several of the policies were modified, and growth emerged strongly as the leading priority of the stabilization policy in 1972. It was accompanied by a new statutory incomes policy and the creation of a legislative framework for selective intervention in industry.

The circumstances in which the Heath government lost office – the miner's strike, the three-day week, and the quadrupling of world oil prices – ensured that it allowed the incoming Labour government to offer in its place a social contract between government and the trade unions to end 'industrial confrontation', an exploration of the potential of new and existing tripartite arrangements, and institutions for contributing to a successful stabilization policy in the most adverse international circumstances since the early post-war years. Allied to this was a radical industrial strategy based upon selective nationalization designed to remedy the persistent industrial weakness which made stabilization policy so difficult. The radical industrial strategy was abandoned after sixteen months and the techniques of stabilization policy became predominantly monetarist, but the government clung to its formal co-operation with the unions.

The breakdown in the incomes policy in the winter of 1978/9 provided the perfect launching pad for the next 'party' episode in stabilization policy. Once more the Conservative theme was freeing the economy from state intervention and high public expenditure and high taxation. The control of inflation became the leading priority of government policy – full employment and economic growth were downgraded and were regarded as objectives about which governments could do very little. Stabilization policy became strongly influenced by 'monetarism' which was held to mark a break with the failed 'Keynesian' policies of the past. The government declined to intervene in the setting of wage levels in the private sector, it took various steps to privatize enterprises and services in the public sector, it abolished exchange controls, it raised interest rates and it welcomed the rise of sterling on the foreign exchanges in 1979–81. The serious impact of these policies upon British industry – the collapse of manufacturing output, investment, and employment – led the opposition parties to argue for alternative economic policies, in which the themes of reconstruction and full employment were again prominent.

This everlasting ping-pong between the advocates of planning and freedom is a real feature of the process of economic policy-making in Britain. But it does greatly overemphasize some aspects of economic policy to the exclusion of others. It suggests that the pattern of stabilization policy has been broadly as follows: 1945–51, full employment through controls; 1951–64, full employment through the free market; 1964–70, modernization through indicative planning; 1970–4, modernization through competition; 1974–9, stable prices through the social contract; and 1979–83, stable prices through monetary discipline. This contains an element of truth, but only an element. The international context of stabilization policy is generally ignored, and the role of parties and party ideology in policy-making is overstated. This is evident when the other criteria for assessing the history of post-war economic policy are used. For these make it clear that the major discontinuities in policy, the major turning-points, the major innovations, at least as far as stabilization policy is concerned, rarely coincide with the replacement of one party by another in government.

(ii) *Priorities of stabilization policy*

When the priorities of stabilization policy are examined the shifts are not what the adversary model would predict. The period of true full-employment policy lasted a very short time, 1945–7. In policy terms after 1947 the external balance and the threat of inflation associated with it became the central priorities of policy. Full employment was still important, especially in the rhetoric it continued to inspire, but as a policy objective it had become subordinate to other objectives and it receded in importance the more it became clear that the period of post-war reconstruction and high demand was not going to give way to a new slump. The period from 1947 through to the early 1960s is dominated, as far as stabilization policy is concerned, by the need to smooth the adjustment of the British economy to multilateral trading and free convertible currencies. The complexities of Britain's external position – the special role of sterling, the size of the sterling balances, and the peculiar structure of the British balance of payments – created the context in which governments struggled to implement disinflationary policies and ward off periodic sterling crises. The sterling crises in 1947,

1949, 1951, 1955, 1956, 1957, and 1961 were the major constraint on stabilization policy throughout this period and this constraint is traceable to the Chancellorship of Stafford Cripps, and even to the last budget of Hugh Dalton.

There was a change in the 1960s in the priorities of stabilization policy but it does not come in 1964. It took shape before the major disinflationary package of 1961, prompted by the sterling crisis. The new priority was expansion because of the increasing awareness that the performance of the British economy had suffered as a result of repeated balance of payments difficulties and inflationary pressure during every boom. Balance of payments deficits had weakened financial confidence, creating fears about possible devaluation, which frequently triggered a run on the pound. To protect the rate the government would announce cuts in spending, increases in taxes, and restrictions on credit. Investment was usually hardest hit.

The policy was a success because it maintained external balance and prevented a devaluation of the pound after 1949. while at the same time keeping inflation to very low levels, 2–3 per cent per annum, without sacrificing full employment. What was sacrificed, or at least not achieved, was a rate of growth equal to other industrial economies in Europe.

The new priority given to growth in stabilization policy was accepted by all parties in the 1960s. As so often with stabilization policy the dispute was not over the objective itself but about which party was best equipped to achieve it. Labour's rhetoric attempted for a while to capture growth for the party's image but the two most determined attempts to put growth first were undertaken by Conservative Chancellors, Reginald Maudling in 1963–4 and Anthony Barber in 1972–3. Labour's attempt to pursue an expansionist policy collapsed because of the repeated sterling crises between 1964 and 1967. The government gave a higher priority in practice to achieving external balance than to encouraging expansion, without, however, altering many of the policies which had assumed a much faster rate of economic growth. The external balance the government had achieved by 1970 was, like its predecessors in the earlier period, real enough, only this time inflation was higher, unemployment was rising, and output and productivity were still far behind European competitors.

Stabilization policy in the 1961–73 period is therefore ambiguous. There is no mistaking the new emphasis upon growth and the battery of different measures to achieve it, but in practical terms the commitment to external balance, the defence of sterling, and the control of inflation remained supreme. Between 1947 and 1972 when the pound was inflated the only serious attempt to alter decisively the external constraints on domestic stabilization policy occurred in 1952 with the 'Robot' plan. This would have made the pound freely convertible and free floating while freezing sterling balances and retaining import controls. Although supported by Butler and Lyttleton and a number of Treasury officials it was opposed by the Bank of England and eventually defeated in Cabinet.[32]

Floating exchange rates, a commodity price boom, and the first major world recession since the war created a very different environment for stabilization policy after 1973. The control of inflation quickly became the dominant priority and all other objectives were subordinated to this end. There is not great gulf between the Labour government of 1974–9 and the Conservative government of 1979–83 as regards their priorities in this area. The conquest of inflation was taken to be the essential first step before there could be a return to employment or growth and, as will be shown below, the means that were adopted did not differ to the extent that might be imagined from party rhetoric.

(iii) *The instruments of policy*

If the main shifts in the priorities that the government has followed in practice in its stabilization policy do not coincide with changes of the party in government, is the same true of the techniques of stabilization policy? Some writers on the political business cycle, for example, have argued that governments of the Left show a marked bias in favour of fiscal policy, while governments of the Right favour monetary policy. If there was a constant alternation between techniques of stabilization policy whenever the government changed hands, then even if the objectives and priorities remained the same, there could be considerable uncertainty and instability created.

Two of the major changes in techniques (listed in Table 4), the re-introduction of monetary policy after 1951 and the history of incomes policy, appear to conform to an adversary model. The other major changes do not. Many commentators have argued that the Labour government between 1945 and 1951 ignored monetary policy and relied mainly on fiscal policy to contain inflationary pressure. The revival of monetary policy under the Conservatives, the readiness to use interest rates and hire-purchase restrictions to ration credit and reduce excess demand, was certainly a distinctive new feature of economic management in the 1950s. Large fluctuations of investment were one result. As one economist commented at the time, the Conservative government had abandoned physical controls and retreated from the use of fiscal policy to restrain consumption: 'The main method of ensuring adequate full employment without excessive demand has become one of encouraging or discouraging investment. . . . Trying to control the economy by controlling investment is like controlling a dog by its tail, when you are not even sure how much and how soon you can make the tail move.'[33]

Comparing stabilization policy under Labour 1945–51 and under the Conservatives in the 1950s, there appears a clear difference in the readiness of the two parties to use tax changes to manage demand. The Conservatives were pledged to reduce taxes and on several occasions when an increase in taxation appeared justified (especially in 1955 and 1960) the government preferred to rely on monetary policy to restrain demand. This was criticized because while the effects of fiscal changes on the economy were reasonably certain and predictable, the effects of monetary policy were very hard to predict, the timing even more so.

It would be wrong to imply, however, that there was a very dramatic shift from fiscal to monetary policy after 1951 which corresponded to Labour's faith in central planning and the Conservatives' faith in the free market and minimal government intervention. In the first place the downgrading of monetary policy under Labour was inherited from the wartime economy when monetary policy had played a very minor role. The cheap money policy which kept interest rates down to 2–3 per cent despite the pressure of demand was not challenged by the Conservatives. It was a bipartisan policy which followed on from the low interest rates of the 1930s and the wide recognition that funds should be made available for reconstruction at the lowest possible cost.

There was also a major internal shift within the Labour government's own approach to stabilization policy. The wartime physical controls on every aspect of economic activity were retained for a while into the period of reconstruction. Between 1945 and 1947 stabilization policy was framed around the manpower budget – the attempt was still being made as during the war to plan economic activity according to the manpower available in each sector, allocating raw materials and fixing production targets accordingly. This gradually gave way to the financial budget as controls were used to influence production and costs indirectly by influencing the level of demand through fiscal policies.

The conception of stabilization policy as the management of aggregate demand in order to achieve full employment, stable prices, and economic growth became firmly established after 1947 and was inherited and developed by the Conservatives. Labour's indifference to monetary policy was not absolute. The government had been forced to accept the strong case for devaluation in 1949. This was part of the price of moving towards a free, multilateral trading system. The government could not hope to cope with the problem of external balance without the use of controls on trade and capital movements. Precisely this option, however, had been closed, and the adjustment of the exchange rate was one of the few instruments the government could employ.

The reintroduction of an active domestic monetary policy by the Conservatives is best seen as part of the general trend of British policy towards removing controls and preparing for full participation in the new world economic order. It did not signify the abandonment of fiscal policy, which given the size of public expenditure continued to be of major importance. A mixture of monetary and fiscal techniques was now used to maintain a stable growth of demand.

Subsequent changes of government did not lead to any such marked shift in the relative importance of fiscal and monetary policy. All later governments used a mixture of both techniques. This was because the real alternatives were either a return to controls or a return to the Treasury doctrines and sound money policies of the past, where the objective was not to balance aggregate demand but merely the budget itself.

The critical assessment of stabilization policy in the 1950s led to a number of new developments in the 1960s. Many interventions by governments in the 1950s were criticised for being either 'too little too late' or 'too much too late'. Many economists argued that the time lags between the recognition of a new trend, the government policy response, and the eventual effect on the economy were not sufficiently understood by economic policy-makers and that a much more flexible response to economic trends was necessary as well as a move away from annual budgets.

This led to the experiments with 'fine-tuning' demand in the 1960s, but this change of technique had little to do with party politics. Similarly the overhaul of the planning of public expenditure following the report of the Plowden Committee brought the setting up in 1961 of the PESC system for monitoring public spending. This system of planning spending five years ahead and trying to establish the impact of programmes on resources in physical not purely financial terms, was refined and modified by subsequent governments, but survived until the imposition of cash limits in 1975. The acknowledgement under the PESC system that public expenditure programmes had to be planned over the medium term and could not be turned on and off like a tap helped to educate politicians in the complexities of the modern budget, emphasizing the small room for manœuvre that generally existed for large reductions in expenditure.

The attempts to institute an incomes policy were an integral part of the modernization strategy of the 1960s and an essential adjunct to stabilization policy. The need for a permanent incomes policy had long been advocated by many economists. As G. D. N. Worswick argued in response to the first Brookings study of the British economy:

> It is as though we have been playing a game of musical chairs among our policy objectives of full employment, growth, stable prices and so on; stop the music in any year you like from 1952 to 1967 and you will find one and perhaps two of the objectives without a chair. The mistake of the authorities was that instead of fetching more chairs, they simply started the music again, selecting a different tune.[34]

The extra chairs Worswick believed were needed were firstly a permanent incomes policy, 'which will enable us to get at the level of money incomes and prices and their movement by means additional to the influence which can be exerted by fiscal and monetary policy of the traditional kind'; and secondly control of capital movements and imports. The second never entered the adversary debate while the first was perhaps the major casualty of the alternation of the parties in government after 1959.

The other major change in techniques which should briefly be discussed here, and is considered from a different angle below, is the adoption of 'monetarist' techniques such as cash limits on the greater part of voted expenditure, and monetary targets for the growth of money supply. Monetarism certainly introduced some novel techniques into stabilization policy and also helped to transform the framework within which stabilization was discussed. But it is very difficult to treat the adoption of monetarist techniques as an effect of adversary party competition. The Conservatives were always most shrill in their denunciation of the evils of inflation, and inflation was a major issue at the elections in 1950, 1951, 1970, and 1979. But the actual adoption of new techniques for controlling inflation have in practice been the work of Labour Chancellors. The disinflationary strategy adopted by Stafford Cripps from 1947 onwards, the targets for Domestic Credit Expansion imposed by Roy Jenkins after 1967, the introduction of cash limits in 1975 by Denis Healey and Joel Barnett, and the imposition of targets for the growth of money supply by Denis Healey after 1976 – none of these changes were the result of party competition. One of the minor ironies of British politics has been that in contrast to the images they cultivate, Labour has more often been the party of financial probity and the Conservatives of financial profligacy.

The Conservative government of 1979 was not therefore responsible for introducing a monetarist counter-revolution in stabilization policy. It continued the policies of its predecessor. The main innovation was the promulgation of a medium-term financial strategy in the 1980 budget, which set precise target bands for the growth of money supply (using the £M_3 definition) and gave projections for the expected path of the Public Sector Borrowing Requirement. The intention was to bind the government to a steady reduction in the growth of money supply, in order to create expectations throughout the economy that inflation would fall. This strategy of gradually easing inflation out of the economy by altering expectations and behaviour was intended to be accompanied by only a small rise in unemployment and reduction of output. As so often in the history of stabilization policy the strategy was overwhelmed by events. The new downturn in the world economy and doubling of oil prices caused a major new recession in Britain. Unemployment doubled and manufacturing output fell by 18 per cent between 1979 and 1981. The severity of the recession in Britain was partly caused by the rigidity of the financial strategy which the government had adopted. That rigidity was to some extent an effect of adversary politics, because of the way in which monetarism as a technique of stabilization policy had been employed as an anti-socialist ideology within the Conservative party between 1975 and 1979. But the actual move towards 'sound money' policy comes long before the election of the Thatcher government and is not merely a British but an international response to the new phase in world economic development in the 1970s.

(iv) *Adversary economics*

A fourth criterion of change in economic policy in Britain in this period is the intellectual framework which guided policy. It is not necessary to endorse Keynes' famous aphorism[35] about the power of ideas to recognize that ideas play an important role in shaping how issues and problems are constructed and solutions proposed to them. A conventional wisdom about economic policy does tend to crystallize and be recognizable as belonging to a certain period. In Britain three phases are commonly indentified – the pre-Keynesian phase when neo-classical orthodoxy was dominant; the Keynesian era inaugurated by Kingsley Wood's 1941 budget; and the monetarist era, which began as an intellectual revolt against some of the key assumptions of 'Keynesianism' in the 1960s, and came to dominate policy-making by the end of the 1970s.

If less emphasis is placed upon the intellectual debates among economists and more on the practical contexts which have shaped policy-making, then four main shifts have taken place since the war. The first phase was dominated by physical planning and the manpower budget; the second by demand management, the financial budget, and the development of the technique of national income analysis; the third phase from the 1960s onwards saw attempts to supplement Keynesian demand policies with additional policies, particularly attempts to control wages and prices directly and to influence decisions on investment and industrial location; these 'Keynesian plus' policies, which gave such high priority to growth, then gave way in the 1970s to monetarist policies which placed chief importance on controlling inflation and creating a stable financial environment by announcing and adhering to target rates of growth for money supply.

It has been argued above that considering the record of stabilization policy from the standpoint of either the major priorities of policy or the techniques of policy, the major changes do not often coincide with government changes. In this field adversary politics appears to play a minor role. Yet the shift from 'Keynesianism' to 'monetarism' is often portrayed as highly political – not a matter of economic techniques but economic ideologies involving quite contrasting assessments of how the economy works and how it should be organized. If there was once an 'economic consensus' this is now much less evident. One sign of the fragmentation of opinion is that there is no agreement on what the history of stabilization policy since the war actually shows. There are rival Keynesian and monetarist histories, and these will be summarized here for the different light they throw upon the events and episodes of stabilization policy. They can be usefully contrasted with the 'party political' accounts outlined above. What is common to all of them is the indifference they display to the influence of party politics upon the development of stabilization policy.

The Keynesian interpretation for a long time was the standard and possibly still remains the most widely accepted account among British economists. It describes the growing influence of Keynesian ideas on official thinking, before the Second World War, the decisive breakthrough during the war itself with the acceptance by both the Bank of England and the Treasury of Keynes's ideas on war finance. The Kingsley Wood budget of 1941 for the first time identified the need to balance aggregate demand in the economy, and this was followed in 1944 by the publication of the White Paper on full-employment policy, the Magna Charta for the dawning Keynesian era. The progress of the new thinking was hindered by the continuation of physical controls and manpower planning into the post-war years, but from 1947 onwards controls began to be removed and the financial budget emerged as the centre-piece of the government's stabilization policy. The financial budget in turn depended upon the steady refinement of national income analysis and the associated development of short-term forecasting of how different elements of national income interacted and could be expected to behave.

Keynesians have not been slow to claim credit for the results of their revolution. In the 1950s there was an orgy of celebration. The main objectives of stabilization policy were generally achieved in the 1950s and the trade-offs between objectives were mild. It was not surprising that Keynesianism should have been hailed as a major advance in knowledge, a wonder drug which banished unemployment and moderated business cycles as surely as antibiotics banished infections.

For Keynesian histories the major problem of stabilization policy in the 1950s was reconciling internal with external balance. The openness of the economy imposed restrictions on domestic expansion. The solutions pursued in the 1960s were the attempts to reduce the priority given to protecting the balance of payments and defending sterling, and to developing a permanent incomes policy. These attempts were not very successful but most mainstream Keynesians still argue that the record of both national and international Keynesianism between 1945 and 1973 was excellent. Very high rates of employment and economic growth, very low rates of inflation, combined increasing trade liberalization and economic interdependence.

What destroyed the successful post-war stabilization policy according to the Keynesians was the series of internal and external shocks that the British and the world economy suffered in the early 1970s – the commodity price boom, particularly the quadrupling of oil prices in 1973, and the wages offensive. The world recession of the mid-1970s is on this account a sign of the still immense fragility of the liberal world economic order so laboriously reconstructed after 1945. The inability of governments to pursue the common policies which could refloat the world economy is seen as the major obstacle to an early return to full employment and growth. But Keynesians continue to insist that the Keynesian analysis remains valid. Blaming Keynesianism for the breakdown of prosperity is entirely rejected. A return to Keynesian principles remains an essential element in any possible recovery. Ian Gilmour expresses the essential Keynesian position very well:

> Two things . . . are clear. We have an old-fashioned slump and we need to climb out of it. There is severe and chronic deficiency of aggregate demand: millions of people cannot get jobs at any wage, and firms in general cannot expand their sales because people cannot buy whatever they have to sell.[36]

The mainstream monetarist approach differs fundamentally from this analysis. Like Keynesianism, monetarism is composed of several different strands, but what is common to all monetarist writing is a denial of the validity of Keynesian assumptions about how the economy works and the effectiveness of Keynesian policies. Monetarist concede that governments since the war have maintained full employment, but it is argued they have only done so by a stablilization policy that has sacrificed price stability. For monetarists the main characteristic of Keynesian stabilization policy was that governments tried to spend their way to desired levels of employment and rates of economic growth regardless of the effect this might have on the money supply. The consequence was an accelerating inflation because the doses of higher demand that were required to achieve the targets for employment and growth became ever greater with each cycle. The pattern of demand in the economy became distorted, expectations of rising inflation became entrenched, and were reflected in the behaviour of economic agents, until the point was reached where governments had to choose between maintaining employment in the short run and lurching towards hyper-inflation, or abandoning targets for employment and growth, bringing the money supply under control and so precipitating a slump.

Where this view agrees with the standard Keynesian history is in ascribing to post-war stabilization policy a high degree of continuity. There is a Keynesian phase which lasts up until the mid-1970s followed by the introduction of monetarism, rather grudgingly at first, more enthusiastically after 1979.

This adversary economic model, however, has been challenged. The problem with both monetarist and Keynesian standard accounts of stabilization policy is that they credit policy with such a decisive influence on events. But it has been convincingly argued that full employment was maintained in the 1950s and the 1960s not because of Keynesian policies but because of the bouyancy of the world economy. R. O. C. Matthews, for example, argued in 1968 that the decline in unemployment in the post-war years when compared to the period before 1914 was to a considerable extent not a Keynesian phenomenon at all. He pointed out that throughout the post-war period the government far from injecting demand into the economy had been running a substantial current account surplus. He concluded that fiscal policy appeared to have been quite strongly deflationary in the post-war period.[37]

His explanation of why full employment had been maintained emphasized the investment boom in the post-war years which, far from petering out after the reconstruction phase, continued into the 1960s. He argued that the long-term trends of economic development displayed an increasingly full absorption of the labour force and increasing security of labour relative to capital. In the inter-war years these trends were overlaid by an acute lack of demand which required, but in Britain did not receive, Keynesian remedies.

From this standpoint the renewed slump in the 1970s has been caused by a new acute lack of demand and by the failure to maintain the investment boom. It is therefore a great irony that in the period when the influence of Keynesian ideas was at their height Keynesian remedies were not needed, while in the periods before and since Keynesian remedies were available but were not applied – in the latter case because they had been discredited by monetarism and blamed for inflation.

The monetarist sceptics put the point rather differently but the conclusion is strikingly similar. The maintenance of full employment is here ascribed to the investment boom and partly to the maintenance of monetary discipline through fixed exchange rates. Governments wanted to pursue expansionary policies that pumped demand into the economy but were prevented from doing so by the need to safegaurd the parity of the currency. Sterling crises held domestic demand management in check and ensured reasonable price stability. On this view Keynesianism only became a serious menace when the post-war international monetary system broke down in the early 1970s. Floating exchange rates removed external restraints on domestic monetary expansion and swiftly produced the 1972–3 boom and the subsequent crash. Monetarism became essential as a means of establishing internal financial discipline in a world of floating exchange rates. Monetary targets replaced employment targets, and annual cash limits replaced spending plans which assumed a particular rate of growth of national output.

(v) *The external context of policy*

The arguments of the sceptics as to how the stabilization policy has developed are reinforced by considering the fifth criterion. If the focus of attention is shifted from the national economy and domestic stabilization policy to the development of the world economy, the result is greatly to reduce in importance the autonomous impact of domestic policy and therefore of the forces that shape domestic policy such as party competition. The post-war period can be divided into three main episodes – Reconstruction, 1945–53, the period of the establishment of a new liberal world economy under American leadership, based on fixed exchange rates, the supremacy of the dollar, commitments by member states to full convertibility of their currencies and free multilateral trade in return for substantial American aid and military protection; the long Boom, 1953–73, the period of rapid and for many countries uninterrupted economic growth, during which currencies became freely convertible and barriers to trade and capital movements were substantially reduced, and high levels of employment and low rates of inflation were achieved; and Recession, 1973– , the period of renewed generalized recession in the capitalist world economy, signalled by a decline in profitability and investment opportunities, and the weakening of American power, which led, amongst other things, to a collapse of the system of fixed exchange rates and the former dominance of the dollar. This in turn reflected a narrowing of the gap between the United States and some other economies, notable Japan and West Germany, and the commodity price boom of the 1970s, which turned the terms of trade decisively against the industrialized economies. This period has not been associated with the very steep falls in employment and output characteristic of the Depression of the 1930s, but the rate of growth of output has declined markedly, while in the weaker economies it has fallen absolutely. Recoveries have been weak, inflation and interest rates have been high, and levels of employment have deteriorated substantially.

The British economy, being so dependent on world trade and also being one of the weaker economies throughout the post-war period, has had very little scope for an autonomous stabilization policy. The crucial post-war debate was over whether Britain should be incorporated into the emerging American world economy and on what terms. The debates in the reconstruction period of the merits of bilateralism and multilateralism, on the convertibility and post-war role of sterling, and on rearmament were resolved by Britain's full participation in the Atlantic alliance and the new institutions of the American world economy.[38] The Atlantic orientation of British policy ensured that from 1947 onwards (the period of 'Keynesianism') Britain no longer had an independent full-employment policy. The level of employment now became increasingly an effect of the level of activity in the world economy.

In the period of the long boom the requirements of convertibility, fixed exchange rates, and free multilateral trade, when combined with the unique role of sterling and the overseas commitments and investment of British government and British business, ensured that domestic stabilization was dominated by the problem of external balance. As argued above, the most potent factor that has structured post-war stabilization policy is the succession of sterling crises. Floating exchange rates finally eased this constraint for British policy-makers, but Britain has experienced more sharply than many other countries the effects of the world recession because of the uncompetitiveness and low productivity of such a large part of its industry. The policies necessary to restrain inflation in Britain have imposed a more severe slump on Britain than experienced elsewhere, with few signs of any lasting improvement in the condition and prospects of British industry. This has been the background against which the consensus on the priorities of stabilization policy has finally ruptured, and party politics has once again become important in defining different alternatives. But in stabilization policy at least, the adversary policy-making appears more as an effect than a cause of the failure of policy.

Stabilization policy and budget strategy

What even this brief survey of the different ways of analysing stabilization policy indicates is that stabilization policy in Britain is surrounded by myths. When Jim Callaghan as Prime Minister declared at the 1976 Labour Party Conference:

> We used to think that you could just spend your way out of a recession and increase employment by cutting taxes and boosting government spending. I tell you in all candour that that option no longer exists, and that insofar as it ever did exist, it worked by injecting inflation into the economy. And each time that happened the average level of unemployment has risen. Higher inflation followed by higher unemployment. That is the history of the last twenty years,

he cannot have consulted his own or Roy Jenkins's record as Chancellor. For if he did once think like that, he never acted upon it. Between 1964 and 1970 there was not a single expansionary budget. Similarly, many monetarist myths about British economic policy do not stand up to examination. British stabilization policy in the 1950s and 1960s has been criticized as being on balance destabilizing because of the timing of the interventions, but the fluctuations were mild. Economic conditions were highly stable throughout this period and policy had relatively little to do.

This suggests that few of the important developments in post-war stabilization policy took place as a result of changes of the party in government. The parties did not take up adversary positions on stabilization policy because, whether managing demand or controlling the money supply, the content of stabilization policy was determined by the priorities of foreign economic policy. Both these crucial areas of economic policy generally stayed outside adversary political debate, until events in the 1970s began to thrust them into the political arena.

The nature of the consensus on stabilization policy can be illustrated by surveying the budget strategies as revealed by successive Chancellors in their budget speeches. Full employment was usually taken for granted and was given little attention on these occasions. It was rarely cited as a reason for taking action. Most surprising of all, concern about unemployment appeared to move in the opposite direction to the unemployment statistics.

Several Chancellors in the early post-war period made statements of Keynesian intent on employment – particularly Cripps, Butler, and Macmillan. Cripps treated his budgets as part of the wider national economic plan. The budget, he argued, gave direction to the whole economy and was to one of the main instruments in achieving the government's objectives, one of which was full employment. In his first budget speech in 1952, Butler referred to the high and stable level of employment as one of those priciples guiding the construction of the budget. (In January 1954, registered unemployment stood at 373,000 – with 270,000 vacancies.) When Butler was forced to introduce a deflationary budget after the 1955 election, he argued that it was important to avoid a major cut-back which might create unemployment. This theme was emphasized by Macmillan in 1956 in the midst of the first deliberate deflation. Macmillan defined the problem as one of overemployment – the economy was 'overheating' with serious consequences for prices and the balance of payments. But Macmillan rejected the idea of cutting demand to take pressure off the economy. This would be deflationary and would risk a return to the unemployment of the 1930s. The correct policy was not to restrict demand but to raise output. This was to become the rationale for the growth policy of the 1960s, though Macmillan did little to bring it about in his year as Chancellor.

What is most striking about the budget speeches considered as a whole is the way in which the external balance is cited again and again as the most pressing problem facing the economy and as the major constraint upon stabilization policy. This recognition is what unites the budgets from Stafford Cripps through to Roy Jenkins. Not full employment but a surplus on the balance of payments and the defence of sterling appear as the major priority for stabilization policy. This was stated very clearly by Butler in his 1953 Budget speech:

Our economy, like our island climate, is always exposed to changes in the world economic weather, which are to a large extent outside our control . . . Only by increasing our national wealth can we continue in our proud position of leader and banker of the sterling area. Only thus can we regain our economic independence.

The emphasis on increasing production to solve the balance of payments problem and reduce inflationary pressure continued a major theme of Stafford Cripps's budgets. But subsequent Chancellors, starting with Butler himself, showed themselves ready to sacrifice growth if it conflicted with the defence of sterling and sterling's international role. Thorneycroft made this explicit in the 1957 speech. He stated his first objective as:

the earning of a surplus on overseas account substantially larger than that of recent years in order to build up the reserves, to repay borrowing, to finance overseas investment, and to provide for further drawings by the holders of sterling balances. We need this not only for our own security as a trading nation, but also to honour our commitments as a world banker.

He praised the successful dampening of economic growth in the previous twelve months, arguing that 'the process of growth cannot be absolutely regular. There will be years of growth and years of consolidation. Our long-term growth will be all the sounder for the consolidation we undertook in 1956.'

Throughout the years of the long boom, when the relative decline of the British economy gathered pace, Chancellors continued to stress that the basis for faster growth and full employment remained a strong pound, and that this in turn required strict control of prices. Amory defined the first two objectives of his 1958 Budget as maintaining the value of the pound and building up reserves. He referred to a major problem of inflation brought about by wages rising too fast, 'our Achilles' heel'. This seems to have become the standard view of British economic policy, at least in government circles. Macmillan commented in 1961:

At present we dare not inflate, because our system is open at both ends – wages and imports. Increased wages mean (without increased productivity) more imports and less exports.[39]

This was the background to the new policies of the 1960s designed to raise productivity and control wages. The new policies were introduced, however, during another sterling crisis and another deflation. Selwyn Lloyd, like his predecessors, reiterated that maintaining confidence in sterling was the supreme objective of policy.

The Labour budgets of 1964–70 began with declarations of the need for a major change of direction of policy and a rejection of past deflationary remedies to balance of payments problems. Callaghan argued in November 1964 that the imposition of the import surcharge was preferable to using the methods of Selwyn Lloyd, a credit squeeze, a pay pause, low growth, and unemployment. In his 1965 budget speech he again castigated the stop–go policy of the Conservatives and promised: '1964 was a year of reckoning for a decade of mistaken policies and false pride.'

The note was already different in 1966 (before the July measures). Callaghan apologized for appearing so preoccupied with the balance of payments, but argued that it was necessary to get the balance of payments right before attention could be switched to other things. He pleaded that the government should not be judged month by month; it would be more realistic to see where the country stood in five years time. In 1967, following the July measures and the abandonment of the National Plan, the emphasis was still more heavily on the balance of payments. A balance of payments surplus had become the government's main objective. But despite all its efforts the pound had to be devalued at the end of that year. Once again a sterling crisis and the attempts to avoid it had dominated stabilization policy; Roy Jenkins's period as Chancellor was concerned with making sure that the devaluation of sterling resulted in a large balance of payments surplus.

Only twice during the long boom were budget strategies based on the need to promote expansion – 1963–4 and 1972–3. Maudling declared in his 1963 budget speech: 'The theme of this Budget is expansion, expansion without inflation, expansion that can be sustained.' In 1972 Barber declared, after announcing that he was planning for 5 per cent growth and had given a large temporary boost to public expenditure: 'We now have a rare opportunity to secure a sustained and a faster rate of economic expansion over a considerable period of time.'

These phases were short-lived. Budget strategy in the period 1947–73 is dominated by the balance of payments, and this constrained all other options. The reason for this dominance lay in the need to defend sterling. It was a constraint imposed by a fixed exchange rate system. This meant that the defence of sterling and the containment of inflation went hand in hand. The disintegration of the fixed exchange rate system in the late 1960s and early 1970s meant that inflation itself became the number one priority of stabilization policy and the economists' debate shifted from the rival merits of cost-push and demand-pull explanations of inflation to the rival merits of Keynesianism and monetarism in providing techniques for stabilizing the economy in the face of the slump.

Conclusions

In the field of stabilization policy the first model of adversary politics discussed in Chapter 2 has little application. Apart from incomes policy there are no major adversary cycles. The second model which predicts that politicians manipulate the economy to secure re-election has little support from empirical studies or from the attempts of successive governments after 1959 and before 1983 to get re-elected, but not succeeding. The third model is more relevant since it suggests that the adversary system created both conflict and consensus; a ritual conflict around political symbols and an actual consensus on most of the fundamentals of policy. This narrows political debate and limits the evaluation of existing policies and alternatives to them. Stabilization policy is a good example. Despite some adversary rhetoric at election times, the priorities of stabilization policy have in practice remained unchallenged and unassessed, and have been heavily influenced by the commitments of post-war foreign economic policy, Monetarism is not a great ideological reversal of thirty years of Keynesianism and social democracy. It is a logical development of the stabilization policy required by the manner of Britain's integration into the world economy. The surprising thing about adversary politics is not that it destroys continuity of policy in some areas, but that it protects a narrow and unreflecting consensus on some of the most important determinants shaping economic policy.

4

ECONOMIC PLANNING AND DYSFUNCTIONAL POLITICS IN BRITAIN 1945-1983

S. A. WALKLAND

The limited nature of this chapter should be made clear at the outset. It is not intended to be a comprehensive analysis of the many factors, from the technical to the social, which have influenced economic policy-making and determined its outcome over the last thirty-five years. It is a selective attempt to separate out the impact of the party political system in Britain on the supply side of the economy. But immediately the artificiality of such an analysis has to be admitted – like a fish which loses its irridescence when taken out of water, the operation of party politics in this field cannot be appreciated in isolation from the historical and cultural environments which essentially condition it, some discussion of which appeared in Chapter 1 of this volume, and which will be developed in the context of particular situations in the course of this narrative.

The focus of this chapter is on the measures which attempt to operate directly on the national economy, by deliberate improvements in investment and production. It largely ignores government's role in the indirect management of the economy, which was dealt with in the previous chapter, and is concerned with a different time-scale than that involved in the short-run control of aggregate demand. Whilst the political system has been reasonably geared, with some major reservations, to the demands of stabilization policy, it is the main thesis of this chapter that it has been dysfunctional for the development and implementation of positive industrial strategies over the time-scale necessary to produce substantial results. The period under review has been marked by a considerable degree of economic analysis and prescription, but also by a lack of sustained initiatives which would have provided a consistent approach to self-evident problems of the economy. This lack of effective links between analysis, prescription, and action is all the more marked in terms of international comparison, especially with France, West Germany, and Japan.

The activities of government in this context have been numerous; direct investment aid, direct or indirect subsidization; location incentives and directives; industrial rationalization, often by selective public ownership for economic rather than ideological reasons; other measures aimed at higher productivity and import substitution, including aid for new technology, industrial training, changes in the corporate tax system with a view to increasing competitiveness, export promotion, regulation of monopoly and at the far end of the spectrum prices and incomes policies, both statutory and voluntary, and measures aimed at changing the conduct of industrial relations. The list is seemingly endless. Many of the policies reflect civil service influence as much as political initiatives – the modest achievements of experienced administrators. Without the measures, and *pace* the arguments of the extreme neo-liberals, the performance of the economy would have been much the poorer, although their net impact has only been to retard, by how much it is impossible to quantify, its relative decline. Many of the above supply-side measures have been uncontroversial, and represent a long history of bipartisanship; the more important policies, which depend for their long-term impact on a measure of agreement between the political parties and their respective clienteles, have a history which, as this chapter tries to show, has been extremely mixed.

Some of the policies noted above are more susceptible to explanation in terms of an adversary politics thesis than others, and have been fundamentally affected by the operation of the political system to the point where their impact has been drastically reduced. Areas other than that of comprehensive industrial planning would perhaps demonstrate the party system at its most destructive, in particular the fields of incomes policies and industrial relations, the post-1945 histories of which, from the perspective adopted in this volume, have yet to be written. Wage bargaining, for example, when stripped of its confrontational overtones, points to a recurrent chronic institutional disorder in British political and industrial life. Lack of authority in the political system – no post-war government has represented a majority of the electorate – and since the early 1960s a rapid alternation of governments, have produced a customary disorder. Policies have usually been disowned by incoming administrations with the result that there is a clear correlation between the breakdown of incomes policies and the electoral cycle. It should also be now apparent that the two-party system is incapable of producing a clear and sustainable framework for the conduct of industrial relations; the familiar negativism and hostility of the unions during periods of Conservative rule all too often give way to the indulgencies of Labour administrations, which, whatever private reservations Labour politicians may have, usually act as the pliable arm of the TUC.

If a typology of planning is attempted, then the definition assumed by Professor C. T. Sandford is useful as a starting-point: 'Planning, or more fully national economic planning, is taken to mean all attempts by the government to exercise conscious direction over the economy as a whole . . . which distinguishes planning from individual policy measures.' Within this broad definition he distinguishes overall financial planning, which consists primarily of monetary and fiscal policies to influence demand and prices; administrative planning, an attempt to manage the economy by an apparatus of controls backed by statutory compulsion, as in the immediate post-war period; and indicative planning, long-term voluntary programmes for the development of the public and private sectors of the economy, which depend largely on a consensus view of likely movements over a period. All governments since 1945 have engaged in financial planning; administrative planning since about 1948 has been restricted to the brief periods of statutory prices and incomes policies, and industrial location and a few other specific initiatives. Voluntarism has been the major form of comprehensive industrial strategies, although their formulation and adoption have been fraught with political difficulties. The situation regarding this particular form of planning has been much more complex than Sandford's typology would suggest. It has never been the case that a comprehensive industrial strategy could be arrived at simply on its technical/economic merits. In Britain, unlike France, for example, the notion of state intervention in the economy produces complex ideological resonances, largely flowing from the corpus of theory which each governing party assimilated in its formative period. Comprehensive supply-side policies and their institutions have suffered intensely from the major ideological differences between the parties, their characteristic modes of analysis of economic problems which derive from these, and from the mechanics of the operation of the two-party system which they embody.

Given the prevalence of voluntarism in Britain, it is not surprising that in the sphere of planning the usual mode has been tripartitism between industry, unions, and government, a structural form that has characterized most of the institutions of economic intervention created since the war, from the early and short-lived Development Councils of the late 1940s, to the NEDC and its attendant EDCs, the Industrial Reorganization Corporation, the National Enterprise Board, the Manpower Services Commission, and others. It is a form of organization which has attracted scathing criticism from observers more accustomed to different West European modes of economic management, but few of them have managed to suggest alternatives which would not run counter to the deep-seated cultural imperatives which inform the character of British government and determine the style of its operations. It is in any case a subsidiary thesis of this chapter that the potential of the British tradition of voluntarism has never been fully realized, and that it has operated in the face of considerable and often crippling difficulties. Those institutions which have been created to observe this form of participatory government have been denied their full potential, partly because successive governments have been unable to ensure the advantageous overall economic climate within which they could function to capacity, but also as a result of severe political fluctuations, leading to the overt politicization of the institutions themselves. All too often the policies and the institutions associated with them have been subject to reversal, drastic change, or abandonment. Some explanation has to be found for the piled wreckage of economic initiatives and their associated agencies which litters the landscape of post-war Britain, and which, as far as the author can detect, has no counterpart in any other Western state. It is intended to show that a systemic explanation can be found for this phenomenon, predicated on the operation of a two-party political system, fortified by the remarkably durable ethos and culture of the parties themselves, which have regularly and consistently conditioned their responses to the problems arising in the economy. It is worth while to examine briefly the intellectual status of planning as it has emerged in post-war British politics, and to attempt to identify the responses which it has evoked in both Labour and Conservative parties.

The political economists

It may be useful first to make a brief analysis of the main publications in the field of political economy of the last thirty years or so which have dealt with these themes, to identify any common ground of analysis or prescription, and the extent, if any, to which the main lines of this section have been foreshadowed. Studies of the deficiencies of the political system in relation to economic policy have largely been a product of the 1970s, an offshoot of a broader critique of the system as as whole, with renewed interest in electoral and constitutional reform. To a large extent the critique concerning economic policy has in the process of popularization been magnified and distorted, until it has come to be widely accepted that a two-party adversary system of national politics is bound to manufacture severe discontinuity which applies across the board of national policies. In this critique, changes of policy due to changes in administration have been held to be only slightly more important than mid-term changes forced on successive governments as a product of electoral overbidding and a more realistic perception over time of the economic and political restraints with which they are faced. There are areas of economic policy where this crude analysis holds brutally true – the most obvious, as has been noted, is that of incomes policy. But except perhaps for the decade of the 1970s there are difficulties in applying this simplistic analysis to the formulation and sustainment of a comprehensive industrial strategy, largely because these intitiatives have hardly got off the ground. Other characteristics of the British political system are equally important in this sphere, in particular the role which the peculiar character, ethos, and doctrines of the parties have played in shaping that delicate balance of confidence which is a prerequisite of planning in the British style. No strict division is possible here; there is no doubt that the mechanics of the two-party system have played a role, but the system develops from the character of the parties, whilst the character in part emerges from the ineluctable dictates of the system.

If the literature of the 1970s which concentrates on the theme of adversary politics and the effects on economic policy of a two-party system is examined, there has been little attention paid to economic planning even broadly conceived. In the most direct and systematic critique of the present political system – the collection of essays published in 1976 under the editorship of Professor S. E. Finer, entitled *Adversary Politics and Electoral Reform*[1] – the bulk of the work deals with the political rather than the economic dimension. Comment by economists is restricted to two essays, by Professor Tom Wilson and Professor D. K. Stout, and in the short space allotted neither is able to develop a systematic analysis. Wilson pays brief attention to three areas – to policies for economic stabilzation through the management of aggregate demand, i.e. policies relating to domestic investment and the balance of external payments; to regional policy; and to pensions policy. On stabilization policy his thesis is less than convincing; he is dealing with a policy area where until recently there was a marked consensus between the parties, and where the discontinuities in the application of the policy – the notorious stop-go effect of the 1950s and early 1960s particularly, which was so powerful a factor in initiating movements for more stability and predictability via planning – owed more to fluctuations outside the control of governments than to changes induced by the operation of the party system. The adversary system perhaps inhibited in this area consideration of basic objectives and of appropriate techniques, and marginal votes in elections often proved an overriding consideration for governmemts; but the prime cause of stop-go, the intermittent triggering of deflationary measures on domestic demand, was the fluctuating but general adverse balance of external payments, which can in large part be attributed, as Stephen Blank has pointed out, to a policy of high overseas expenditure on defence, not basically an issue between the parties in the 1950s.[2] Professor Stout tackles briefly but penetratingly the area of inflation and incomes policy, and here the contribution to instability made by an adversary system of parties competing on this front for marginal electoral advantage cannot be denied.

What is noticeable about these contributions to the debate is the separate discovery by the authors of characteristics of the political process in Britain which seem functional to the system, and owe as much to the automatic mechanisms of political response in a finely balanced electoral situation as to any doctrinal differences between the parties, although these do support and facilitate the phenomena. Wilson, when discussing the strong bias in favour of rapid changes of policy which he believes in inherent in the party system observes: 'each party as it assumes power, will wish to ensure that its policies are visible different from those of its predecessor, and change is thought to be necessary in order to establish distinctiveness', an inherent feature of the two-party system which even the civil service, with its instincts for stability and continuity, will find ultimately defeating. Similarly Professor Stout has this to say on the same theme (in relation particularly to incomes policy, but the proposition holds true generally): 'Electoral advantage has lain in persuading voters that a policy which has failed is the property of the other side, and must be abandoned, rather than revised and strengthened . . . In its turn the new government is driven to intervene and control . . . however the new intervention is dangerously delayed by the commitments made in opposition and by its wish to differentiate its product from (its) rival.' This automatic tendency towards the mutual exclusivity of policies between the parties has been marked in domestic policies (and may now be extending to foreign and defence policy) and the mechanics of its operation will be explored more closely in relation to economic planning later in this paper.

Wilson also makes a passing reference to an associated phenomenon of the two-party struggle – the ambitious nature of the programmes put forward, particularly by the Labour party, a characteristic which again owes as much to the zero-sum mentality engendered by the political system as to a doctrinal urge to alter fundamentally the economic and social structure (an urge which, in the 1970s, has not been confined to the Labour party). A system which puts complete political control for a term of office in the hands of a party gaining a mechanical majority in the House of Commons encourages unrealistic ambition in government. The concept of the 'fresh start', of the remaking of society and economy in a different image over the period of a single Parliament is engrained in the psychology of the major parties. Success as well as stability is the more difficult to achieve as a result, and this particular syndrome is also important in any discussion of economic planning movements. It is largely responsible for the mid-term shifts in policy which have become a characteristic of British government of either party.

This theme is taken up and made the central focus of a study of British economic policy since 1964 by Michael Stewart, in his book *The Jekyll and Hyde Years.*[3] In contrast with *Adversary Politics and Electoral Reform* it is disappointing. A highly readable and detailed account of economic policy-making since the advent of the Wilson governments of the 1960s, it lacks both theory and depth of analysis. Dedicated to the proposition that the most disturbing instability in the development and administration of a coherent economic and industrial policy has been the marked tendency for governments to shift ground mid-term, there is little analysis of some of the innate characteristics of the two-party system, such as those touched on by Wilson and Stout, nor any analysis of the policy-making process within the parties, particularly in opposition, which is a neglected area of political study and one which is critical for Stewart's general thesis. His account of the national planning movement of the 1960s, with which he was closely connected, is conventional, and the book was published too early to take fully into account the misfortunes of the National Enterprise Board in the 1970s. Whereas the essays edited by S. E. Finer explore the possible consequences on policy of electoral reform and political realignment, Stewart, probably because of his former attachment to the Labour party, contents himself with an unrealistic plea for more co-operation between the parties, a plea which ignores the mechanics of the operation of a two-party system, which makes co-operation seemingly impossible except in times of national crisis.

If the recent literature dealing directly with the influence of the political system on economic policy-making and its implementation is still fairly skimpy, it is worth while briefly investigating the contributions of political economists who have not addressed themselves primarily to the specific themes of this chapter, if only to examine the extent, if at all, to which they take into account the cultural and political dimensions to economic planning. I am not here concerned with the protagonists in what Trevor Smith has called 'The Great Debate' – the argument which raged throughout the 1930s and 1940s between the advocates of social and economic planning on the one hand and an open market economy on the other, political and economic argument on the grand scale which, in the writings of Mannheim, Hayek, Popper, and Schumpeter *et al.*, drew out some of the great and still unresolved themes of political and economic philosophy. Rather the review concentrates on the more mundane issues of planning and national politics, and on the predominantly British writers of the 1950s and 1960s who were concerned with this issue. It is, generally speaking, surprising how little attention was given to the political dimension, reflecting perhaps that marked disassociation between economic and political enquiry which has been a feature of British social science. A further reason for this omission, as Trevor Smith has pointed out in his odd but important book *The Politics of the Corporate Economy,*[4] is that as the case for planning became more widely accepted, the arguments tended to pass out of the hands of those who, whether advocates of planning or not, were primarily concerned with the values of Western liberal democracy as secured through the political process, into the hands of the economists and technicians, who in the 1950s and 1960s were largely motivated by considerations of economic growth, technique, rationalization, and efficiency. In general, political considerations took second place to technocratic criteria. At the same time it has to be admitted that the British political system until about the mid-1960s seemed more unassailable and immune from criticism than in the late 1960s and the decade of the 1970s, and had not attracted the reservations which later experience produced. In so far as political discussion occurred, it sprang from an appreciation that planning required both consensus and continuity, but the devices that were canvassed to this end tended to be highly artificial and unlikely. A typical reaction was that of Barbara Wootton, an earlier proponent of planning, who, in addition to her passionate concern for the preservation of democratic values, was also aware of the discontinuities which would inevitably arise as between the political order and the planning order. Her solution was highly implausible. Believing that when she wrote *Freedom under Planning*[5] in 1945 party political differences were in any case diminishing, she canvassed the possibility of an inter-party agreement on common planning goals, and the creation of independent extra-parliamentary planning agencies insulated from party politics and incapable of being dissolved except by a qualified vote of Parliament, with general elections fought on residual issues outside the central field of planning. These proposals, and the rest of her reforms reflect a typical faith in an ability easily to change ingrained political attitudes, which seems to attach to a particular breed of reformer, and which stems from an ineradicable tendency to see individuals and institutions as material for technocratic manipulation.

More realistic analyses of the same problems of political stability can be found in the early publications of Michael Shanks, one of the more durable members of the technocratic school of planning and now a member of the SDP. His early polemic, *The Stagnant Society*, published in 1961, is a wide-ranging account of what he considers to be the defects of British society and its institutions, which captures the spirit of impatience which beset the vaguely left-wing technocratic establishment of the early 1960s and which was a moving force behind the election of Labour in 1964. A period piece now (although the book was republished in 1971), it is worth rereading for its political analysis. A fervent advocate of central planning and a prices and incomes policy, Shanks is sceptical of the ability of the party system to deliver this. His Chapter 7 foreshadows almost exactly the arguments now current concerning the state of British politics – he forecast an early split in the Labour party after the Gaitskell revisionist debate, a realignment of moderate Labour with the Liberals to provide the major vehicle for his policies, with a corresponding split in the TUC, etc., etc. His belief was that the ambivalent structure of the Labour party, with left and right wings, together with its reliance on union support, was an electoral handicap, and that the party as a result would grow progressively weaker. That this diagnosis was correct has been demonstrated in the 1970s, but Shanks's analysis severely underestimated the durability of the system that he criticized, and the power of the forces, in particular the electoral system, which sustain it. His most acute observation was that Labour, because of its doctrinal ambivalence, conveyed a 'blurred image', a factor of considerable importance in any discussion of its ability to induce confidence in the private sector in any voluntaristic style of economic planning.

Omissions of analysis of another sort, so far as the section on Britain is concerned, attend the most important account of European national economies of the 1960s, a trail-blazer in political economy – Andrew Shonfield's *Modern Capitalism*, first published in 1965.[6] By any standard, *Modern Capitalism* is a *tour de force*, covering the economic experience of Western nations since 1945. Shonfield accepts that capitalism's basic nature has changed, a proposition which has been strengthened in the fifteen years since he wrote, and which in Britain is only denied by the doctrinaire left. The change, he believes, has been brought about as much by the imperatives of technology and the need for state management as from the divorce between ownership and control. He is perhaps the best analyst of the Victorian liberal culture which is twentieth-century Britain's intellectual inheritance, and the extent to which this has determined the style and content of British government, especially in relation to the economy. As he remarks, 'British post-war experience provides . . . illustrations of the way in which a living tentacle of past history loops itself round, and holds fast to a solid block of the present. The striking thing in the British case is the extraordinary tenacity of older attitudes towards the role of public power.' (*Modern Capitalism*, p. 88.) He is at pains to stress the cultural and administrative differences between Britain and European states such as France and Italy – his comparison of the ensuing differences between British and French economic planning is the best there is, surpassing in this regard even the later analyses of Professor Hayward.[7] He does not, however, discuss in detail the administrative and institutional changes which would be required in Britain if British planning were to accommodate itself to this model, nor from whence the political will to make these changes would come. Whilst he believes that British government should follow the best practices of Europe – Sweden's industrial relations, French planning and its civil service, Italy's organization of state-owned industry – there is little discussion except by implication of methods by which the vastly different political and cultural traditions of Britain could be reshaped for this task, and little appreciation of the highly conservative character of British political and administrative processes, the former particularly. As Trevor Smith points out,[8] Shonfield's instinctive approach is much more managerial and technocratic than political. He believed in the need for a political consensus on planning, without in any way analysing the changes required to produce this, and in a new relationship between parliamentary politics and the experts – in Smith's words ' a new breed of planner-politician', in which the 1960s abounded, engaged in sympathetic negotiation with the processes of Parliamentary politics. Shonfield's last chapter in *Modern Capitalism*, which should nave been devoted to analysing the political preconditions for the changes he wanted, is taken up with a discussion of the parliamentary reforms needed to make planning accountable – fairly standard stuff in which he echoed other writers of the period on Parliament, in particular Bernard Crick.

It is difficult not to see Shonfield (and Michael Shanks and a host of others) as a product of a particular moment in history, when disillusionment with Conservative rule and relative economic decline produced a powerful move for the overhaul of much of the industrial, social, and governmental structure of Britain. The political mood which they took advantage of, some consciously but for the main part unconsciously, was Butskellism, the depoliticization of Britain which briefly occurred in the decade between 1955 and 1965. This mood was summarized by Professor W. A. Robson as follows:

> There is now, at long last, unmistakeable evidence of profound changes in public opinion. People are disturbed; they are more realistic; and they want change. They have acquired postive attitudes to education, to science, and to planning. They are dissatisfied with Britain's position in the world and want to make it better. From these discontents a new dynamic could arise. It must be guided and harnessed by government, but this can be done only of the Government itself is more dynamic.[9]

The man to match this moment appeared in the shape of Harold Wilson – a better managerialist than a principled politician, and embodying in his personality the essential superficiality of the events that were to come. For a time it seemed as though nothing was to escape the reforming urge – the planning of public expenditure, the institutions of economic management, of science and technology,

Parliament, the civil service, the universities, and ultimately, the structure of local government and of some institutions of the welfare state. all were brought into the reformers' net. It is depressing in retrospect to see how little was in fact achieved by this vast and expensive movement. Either the political conditions for its success were not analysed or given sufficient weight, as in economic planning and in the case of Parliamentary reform or the cultural dimension was ignored, as in the case of the Fulton investigation of the civil service.[10]

Little else has been published since Shonfield's work with a direct bearing on the theme of this chapter. The most remarkable publication of the 1970s, in an excellent translation by Martin Harrison, is Jacques Leruez's *Economic Planning and Politics in Britain,*[11] which in extraordinary detail analyses the many aspects of economic policy adopted by post-war British governments up to 1975, and relentessly exposes the failures of most. Yet despite the title of his work, and his sophisticated knowledge of the British political scene, Leruez does not develop a systematic approach to the politics of his subject, nor produce any notable insight into the philosophies which sustain the main British political parties and condition their attitudes towards the economy. Much the same can be said of Professor J. E. S. Hayward's numerous writings on French and British economic policy, which include the Preface to the Leruez volume. Scathing in his criticism of the half-hearted and largely unsuccessful industrial strategies followed by British governments, he, like Leruez and Shonfield, advances no solution to the problem of how British governments can recover the will and capacity to steer economic development successfully. Hayward is aware of the difficulty in Britain of depoliticizing the economic planning process, as successfully happened in France for twenty years, if we discount a weak and uninfluential Communist party; he is also aware that planning in Britain has always carried ideological overtones and has been 'charged with ideological polemics'. Yet he fights shy of analysing the political changes needed if a similar sustained will to that which has prevailed elsewhere is to be developed in Britain. This is an omission which this chapter sets out to correct, without doing violence to some of the valued and rewarding characteristics of British public life.

Economic planning and the political parties

The history of thought on economic planning in the doctrines of both major parties derives largely from their nineteenth-century origin and the broad philosophies that each fundamentally assimilated in that period. It is essentially a history of ambivalence, predicated on uncertain conceptions of the role of the state and beset at each stage by ideological differences based on a nineteenth-century conceptual division between public and private powers, perhaps the least fruitful of the intellectual inheritances of the Victorian period. If one examines the movements towards economic planning in the pre-1939 gestation period, whilst there is considerable discussion leading to a measure of agreement on the ends and means involved in planning, an essential ambiguity stems from the fundamental disagreements between individualists and socialists over how far the economy should be socialized in the process, and over the question of ownership and control of the means of production. The ambiguity has continued to bedevil discussion of planning even when, in the post-1945 period, the right wing of the Labour party has, until recently, been in the ascendant, and when Clause Four of Labour's 1918 constitution has been largely ignored, though never formally dropped. As this chapter hopes to show, this ambiguity has been the main factor militating against the development of a broad continuous political consensus on a comprehensive industrial strategy; in retrospect, it appears to have guaranteed the failure of the main post-war initiatives in this sphere.

The intellectual problems posed by planning have proved somewhat less difficult for the Conservative party than for the Labour party, paradoxically enough, since the Conservative advocates of planning assumed naturally the continuance of a private enterprise economy, and even when talking of a mixed economy envisaged no fundamental change in the economic system. The capitalist firm would remain the basic unit in the economic community. Whilst Conservative thinkers such as Harold Macmillan showed a keen awareness in the 1930s that capitalism had been unable to solve the problems of poverty and insecurity, Macmillan could still say 'I want to argue for the deliberate preservation of private enterprise in a field lying outside the range of minimum human needs. I support it for the purely economic reason that it ensures initiative, the adoption of new methods, the exploration of the market possibilities of new products, and speculative experimentation with new scientific discoveries.'[12] In this basic commitment the Conservative advocates of a planned economy were provided with an unquestioned foundation which avoided fundamental disagreements about the basic structure of society and the economy. No such certainties have attached to the Labour Party's attitudes, either to the economic system in general or to the aims of planning in particular. In the 1930s, when much of Labour's theory was developed, so far as the socialist theoreticians were concerned the 'anarchism' of capitalism could not be eliminated by planning without abolishing capitalism itself, without socializing the means of production, distribution, and exchange. This essential precondition of planning was epitomized by G. D. H. Cole: 'Capitalism, by reason of its very nature, cannot plan, whereas Socialism can and must.' Such an axiom was so much a part of pre-war socialism as not to warrant discussion, although the programmatic means of achieving socialism remained hazy and largely unexplored. Yet by the 1920s British socialists had largely rejected the concept of the transformation of society by violent revolution. Most socialists, and certainly the British Labour party, had come to accept the principles of attaining power by parliamentary means, the logical consequence of which in economic and other matters was the abandonment of the idea of a radical and fundamental transformation of society and an acceptance of the Webbs' 'inevitability of gradualism'. Yet the underlying principles of the Labour party, particularly as they concern public ownership, have shown considerable durability, and the paradoxes inherent in the attainment of socialism by electoral means have never been clearly faced. If they had been the party would have had to surrender its unifying faith.

In his perceptive but essentially ambiguous book *Doctrine and Ethos in the Labour Party,*[13] Henry Drucker makes this particular point – that whatever happens to specific Labour doctrines, the ethos of the party remains: 'The point about socialism is not efficiency, nor the equality of income which might result from its realisation, but the fact that it represents the replacement of one order by another, the rule of the capitalists by that of the workers' (p. 41), and, as a Labour supporter, he welcomes the persistence of the ethos even in the face of declining class consciousness, whether the result of affluence or nationalism, and the rise of other parties. The continuing socialist project, as Drucker rightly says, is contained in the slim Clause Four of the 1918 constitution, which has resisted all attempts at revision. Whether one welcomes, as Drucker does, this persistence in basic and fundamental dogma or not, its influence in economic and industrial matters in the post-war period has been manifest. It has not mattered whether the socialist intention has been there – often the rhetoric has been enough. As Brian Magee has observed in discussing socialist rhetoric, 'it is only the Right of the (Labour) party that is guilty. The entire party, throughout most of its history, has said one thing and done another . . . this means that there is usually an element of hypocrisy involved in public discussion amongst Socialists.' Whilst this hypocrisy is an essential element if the survival of the party, its failure to inspire confidence in economic matters has generally been fatal. To explain the point in more brutal terms than the sentimentalism of a Drucker allows, and to emphasize the main reason why Labour governments have failed to develop confidence in the planning process, one can quote Aneurin Bevan, once a darling of the Left of the Labour party, and no Croslandite. In his personal testament *In Place of Fear*, he wrote (p. 118):

It is clear to the serious student of modern politics that a mixed economy is what most people of the West would prefer . . . I have no patience with those socialists, so-called, who in practice would socialise nothing, whilst in theory they threaten the whole of private property. They are purists, and therefore barren. It is neither prudent, not does it accord with our conception of the future, that all forms of private property should live under perpetual threat.

But his line of thinking leads to revisionism, and to the collapse of the intellectual structure of Labour. As Drucker says, although the problems which moved Gaitskell and Crosland in the 1950s to doubt the wisdom of further nationalization are now revealed to be much more deeply seated, criticisms of public ownership are beside the point. Nationalization plays an essential role in solidifying the ethos of the party, and to doubt it would leave an unbridgeable intellectual gap. Similarly the concept of planning plays its own role in the edifice of Labour thought – it is to be used to fill the vacuum left when the capitalist order has been destroyed. In practice, as will be demonstrated later, this intellectual apparatus has had a crippling effect on Labour's industrial policy.

It its nineteenth- and early twentieth-century intellectual origins have prevented, and continue to prevent, a pragmatic adaptation of the Labour party to the problems of running a modern industrial economy, the Conservative party in the same period has shown equal fundamental resistance, being moved to innovation and the expansion of state authority largely as a result of economic crises, and not through deep-seated conviction. Attachment to a comprehensive industrial strategy, to a guided rather than a market economy, has seldom been more than skin-deep, and has been associated with a remarkably small if influential number of personalities. That there has been a symbiotic relationship between the two parties on planning cannot be denied – Conservative opposition has been shaped and strengthened in reaction to both the doctrine and ethos of the Labour party, without which its attitudes towards the state and the economy might well have been different. What techniques for government management of the economy it accepted in the post-war period were Liberal rather than socialist in origin, and their flirtation in the 1960s with an industrial strategy derived more from European example than from socialist precept. If the Labour party managed to erect a complex, necessary, but highly artificial structure of thought on planning and the role of the state in the economy, the history of Conservatism, particularly in the immediate post-war years, is littered with hotly contested initiatives, most of them failures, designed to bring the party to intellectual terms with the need for a measure of planning, and to slough off its pre-war reputation. Although the party managed to adapt to the welfare state and a degree of nationalization, in retrospect we can see that a fundamental conversion to an industrial strategy and a creative use of state authority in the economy, never happened.

The difficulty Labour governments find in operationalizing an intellectual conviction on state ownership has been matched by the opposing Conservative difficulty of intellectualizing pragmatic and necessary responses to changed economic and social situations. And working powerfully on an essentially reactive Conservative party have been the mechanics of the two-party system, with their tendency towards the mutual exclusivity of policies, which will be analysed later in this chapter. To try to develop from this intellectual ambiguity, and the operational imperatives of a particularly rigid political system, the consensus needed for planning in the British style, would seem a recipe for certain failure. And so it has proved. It is possibly the case that no political rearrangements could create a more advantageous environment for planning, given the tenacity of the liberal tradition in Britain – an inherent cultural disadvantage which commentators such as Professor Hayward and Alan Budd have consistently emphasized. What seems certain is that innovation on a purely institutional level, whether in planning mechanisms or in other specific areas, is likely to fail as a result of disregarding the political and cultural context in which it has to operate. It is worth while exploring these dimensions in some instances of post-war planning in order to demonstrate this fact. Such an analysis may not lead to any prescriptive conclusions, but may clear the ground for some discussion of possible future developments.

Labour and Conservative governments: 1947–1953

Despite the intense theorizing over planning which had characterized the pre-war Labour party, the first majority Labour government after 1945 was never able to develop a coherent medium-term economic strategy, although the vocabulary and general discourse of the period were dominated by planning metaphors. The economic achievements of 1945–51 were relatively good, but were largely due to favourable world conditions and a high level of demand for consumer and capital goods. In the immediate reconstruction period, short-term planning was undoubtedly effective in smoothing the path from war to peace – but at the expense of a long-term philosophy – depending as it did on the physical controls which were a legacy of the war. These constituted a cumbersome structure, which from 1948 onwards was fairly rapidly abandoned. It was no new technique of economic planning, as the French were then developing, but an inheritance from the emergencies of the war. The abolition of controls, however, in response to considerable demand for more consumer choice via market mechanisms, was not replaced by a more systematic medium-term plan less dependent on the rationing of resources. There was in this area a marked lack of imagination at the level of a comprehensive economic policy on the part of Labour, and this was matched by a similar lack of interest in the Conservative party. Much time and energy were in any case devoted in this period to social welfare provision, which tended in the minds of many members of the Labour party to take priority over the economy.

Whilst retaining a declining structure of physical controls, the administration engaged in extensive but largely uncoordinated consultation to work out, in terms of OECD requirements, new patterns of co-operation in order to renovate the economy. But long-term programmes developed by the government's Central Planning Staff were little more than a statement of economic strategy in broad terms. Some instrumental policies were adopted, but adequate instruments of detailed planning were not created. From the point of view of this chapter, perhaps the most instructive initiative in the search for a new industrial strategy was the Development Councils, which had a brief life between 1947 and 1953. The device was not new – it had its origin in the thinking of Macmillan in the 1930s. But Labour's Development Councils, set up by Sir Stafford Cripps under powers given by the 1947 Industrial Organization and Development Act, have the dubious honour of being the first in the relentless procession of failed economic institutions which has characterized post-war Britain. They were the vehicles of an industrial strategy developed by Cripps after his appointment as President of the Board of Trade in 1945. Reorganization and expansion of industry were the Board's primary concern, after a decade and a half of slump and war in which investment-led development had suffered. The Councils were set up under the 1947 Act, following reports by a series of industry-wide working parties, seventeen in all, which by 1947 and 1948 had all revealed scope for improving productivity, quality of product, investment, the share of production for export, and so on. The Councils which ensued followed the parallel French development of *commissions de modernisation*, which had the same broad development functions and were the original building-blocks of French post-war economic planning. The French commissions prospered and were developed; the British Councils, an experiment of great potential significance, never really got off the ground.

The history of the genesis and subsequent difficulties of the Development Councils has been well charted, and only a broad outline needs to be given here.[14] Eleven Councils were proposed under the 1947 Act; only three (or four if one includes the pre-existing Cotton Board) ever saw the light of day. As conceived by Stafford Cripps, Labour's industrial policy rested on co-operation between state and producers, for the most part from private industry. The refusal of private industry to co-operate spelled the first failure of post-war planning. There were other reasons for failure than non-co-operation in what at the time was a complex situation, and each commentator on this period has tended to concentrate on that facet to which his general analysis attributes the greatest importance. Shonfield, for example, in *Modern Capitalism*, with his disregard for the interplay of party politics, is concerned to point out the contrast between the Councils and the French modernization commissions, and to emphasize the weaknesses of their structure and underlying philosophy. The Councils were an early venture into the field of tripartite consensus. The establishment of a particular Council depended on the agreement of an industry; there was little active role allotted to government; and attitudes were formed not by the industrial front-runners, as in France, but by the average backward firm, and the resultant machinery was little improvement of existing industrial associations. In sum, the experiment revealed the characteristic difficulties attaching to the traditional liberal view of the relationships between public and private power, which is Shonfield's central thesis and which has subsequently been developed in more detail by other commentators such as Professor Hayward. This emphasis by Shonfield and others, accurate but limited, tends to discount the political context – not entirely, since Shonfield admits that 'the political atmosphere of this time . . . was not propitious to the venture', but his conclusion, which appears in retrospect quite mistaken, was that it was doubtful whether the change of government from Labour to Conservative in 1951 made any real difference to the outcome, since failure was inbuilt in the structure and philosophy of the Councils.

Jacques Leruez rightly traces much more influence to the political context, and the characteristics of post-1945 party politics, in order to explain the failure of this early attempt to use the apparatus of government to foster the development of a large section of British industry. The experiment took place when the Labour government's relationship with industry had deteriorated sharply, despite the government's attempts to conciliate the private sector. The major factor in increasing industry's suspicion of the Labour government's intentions, and which ruled out co-operation, was the continuing and growing fear of nationalization. It is perhaps difficult in retrospect to recover the atmosphere of the first majority Labour administration, and the extent to which the issue of nationalization dominated it. In particular, the last three years of the Labour party's hold on government was dominated by the battle over steel nationalization, which, unlike the nationalization of the other industries that Labour had taken over, was thought to introduce a radical change in the nature of public ownership. Fuel, power, and transport nationalization measures had attracted little opposition, since the need for radical reorganization with increased investment in these areas was demonstrated beyond question. Iron and steel were different – the industry under the Iron and Steel Board had succeeded in reconciling private ownership with state direction and had made a major contribution to the economic recovery of 1948–9. The government's decision to press ahead with steel nationalization was seen as evidence of doctrinaire socialism, and was bitterly fought from within and without the industry, provoking also a controversial constitutional amendment to the powers of the House of Lords in the 1949 Parliament Act.

In this atmosphere, the government's assertions that the Development Councils should not be seen as trojan horses for public ownership of the industries concerned were ineffectual, although there is plenty of evidence that the Labour administration understood the fear and went some way to allay it, although without success. It is probably the case that the government deliberately chose industries for development by the Councils that it had no intention of nationalizing in the foreseeable future. Stafford Cripps went so far as to deny publicly (*HC Debates*, 13 February 1947, col. 552) that the Industrial Organization and Development Act portended further nationalization, but his speech did not rule out a later programme of state ownership, and in January 1950 a list of proposals for the nationalization of another six industries was published. This sparked off considerable opposition from the industries concerned, who began a campaign against nationalization and the Labour party which was to set the tone of the 1951 general election campaign. The campaign became something of a crusade by industry against the concept of a socialist state, particularly when the election of 1950 produced a much reduced majority for Labour which threw doubt on the government's capacity to last a full term. *Pace* Andrew Shonfield, the attitude of the Conservative party was of considerable importance at this stage. It is difficult to account for the deterioration of government/industry relationships in anything other than strictly political terms – the prospect that the Conservatives would return to power sooner than expected. When the Tories took over in 1951 they were wholly unenthusiastic about both the Development Council project and the philosophy behind it, and were already launched on their support for the free market which was to last for the next eight years. The remaining Councils were disbanded by the Conservative government in 1953, although the 1947 Industrial and Organization Act was not repealed and was used by the Conservatives in minor ways ten years later, when opinion in the party towards state intervention in industry had marginally changed.

In retrospect, it is easy to conclude that the attitude of private industry towards the 1947 Act was misplaced and its reaction to the Development Councils excessive. But the reaction was not surprising given the exaggerated atmosphere of the period, and the extent to which doctrinal disagreement was over-emphasized by the political parties. In particular the Labour party was at fault – less confident than its 1945 majority might indicate, it developed a mood of strident self-justification, especially after 1948 when confidence in the government was waning. It felt constrained to publicize its record and intentions by inflated claims, couched in customary hyperbole and in a fashion which considerably misrepresented and exaggerated its achievements. In particular it felt compelled to establish its socialist credentials. As Clement Attlee himself said, 'Our policy was not a reformed capitalism but progress towards democratic socialism, and this we largely achieved'. But most observers in retrospect would agree that there was no serious social change during the period 1945–51. Although the goverment might have set out to build a socialist society, or at least to lay its foundations, its achievements in this direction were modest in the extreme. And the Labour government and party did not accept any modifications to its central ethos derived from its constant experience of the constraints placed upon the freedom of action of a government by the structure of a pluralist society, or attempt in its thinking to resolve the paradoxes, demonstrated to a majority Labour government for the first time, which are inherent in the pursuit of both socialism and democracy. Perhaps more important for the purposes of this analysis is that this period showed all too clearly the weaknesses engendered by a too close association of the more powerful economic groups with the political parties, and by the lack of an independent voice in economic policy-making. The experiment with the Development Councils demonstrated, for the first but not the last time in the post-war era, the facility with which the two-party system can block innovation. Non-co-operation, in anticipation of a change in party government, has since become a standard feature of the relationships of economic groups with British government, until it is now an ingrained characteristic of British two-party politics, although each administration seems to come to it afresh, and with surprise.

Conservative and Labour governments: 1959–1969

The narrative of planning in the 1960s, which was firstly and hesitantly undertaken by a Conservative government, then by Labour after 1964, is well known. It is not intended to repeat the account in this chapter; only to offer some general observations in line with the thesis which underpins this chapter. The most detailed and knowledgeable version of the events of the period is given by Jacques Leruez. But whilst Leruez is acutely aware of the political background of this episode he does not generate a comprehensive political critique, contenting himself with commenting shrewdly on the outstanding political events of the period, such as the devaluation crisis between 1964 and 1967. We are primarily concerned in this chapter with a different focus, the initial development of a political consensus on voluntary indicative planning between the various participants, and then with its inexorable destruction by the operation of the party political system. There is also an attempt to explain other characteristics of the period by reference to the same factor, and assess the gains and losses which can be recorded by 1969.

The beginning of the movement towards planning in the 1960s grew from the perceived inadequacies of demand management in the late 1950s, and its inability to provide for economic growth of the order which a number of West European countries were enjoying. By 1960 most comparative economic indices were unfavourable to Britain (see, for example, G. Worswick and P. Ady (eds.), *The British Economy in the 1950s*). A typical analysis of what needed to be done was made by J. C. Dow, a former civil servant in both the Cabinet Office and the Treasury, who in *The Management of the British Economy 1945–1960* gave a practitioner's view of the problem.[15] The main theme of Dow's work was that whilst stabilization policy had been successful in reducing unemployment and maintaining business confidence, defects in its management had contributed to rather than militated against slow economic growth. The conclusion was that even successful demand management needed to be supplemented by action on the supply side of the economy, by an industrial strategy and incomes policy, and by a shift of emphasis from macroeconomics to microeconomics. Such analyses received wide support, and perhaps only put in the form of detailed prescription what was by the early 1960s a generalized conviction.

The development of a consensus on planning, and on other major reforms in this period, responded to many impulses. The time seemed right – a deep sense of dissatisfaction with the general social, political, and economic state of Britain was manifesting itself, although this reflected no particular political ideology. The outcome of the 1939–45 war had not produced a social revolution of any magnitude. Rather it had confirmed and strengthened most social and political traditions in Britain. The post-war British social revolution, such as it was, was to take place in the 1960s, guided by, to quote the 1964 Labour party manifesto, the 'New Thinking', whatever this may have been. But by 1960 the conditions for a massive pragmatic and technological initiative were building up, although the failure in the late 1950s of the Gaitskell attempts to alter fundamentally the nature of the Labour party meant that essentially the political structure remained unchanged. But a few years of Butskellism had ushered in the 'end of ideology' debate, foreshadowed by Anthony Crosland's 1956 revisionist tract *The Future of Socialism*. Convergence theory had taken hold in international relations, and superficial prosperity had worn away the edges of sharp economic inequalities. As Trevor Smith notes, a generational change in politics and society was making itself felt; angry young men were questioning some fundamentals but in a curious non-political and unideological fashion. A great movement of critical opinion was discernible, which the economy and economic management in general were not to escape. Certainly a technocratic consensus on planning was rapidly built up in these years, encompassing economists, some business men, civil servants, and academics, and research institutes such as PEP (Political and Economic Planning) and NIESR (National Institute for Economic and Social Research), not perhaps sufficient itself to engineer a change but powerful enough to act as a political bell-wether.

In the Conservative governments of the late 1950s and early 1960s opinion in favour of more positive intervention in the economy was led by a few key personalities, in particular, Harold Macmillan, whose sole budget in 1956 had adumbrated new techniques of economic management. A much advocated instrument, new to the 1950s, was incomes policy, which Peter Thorneycroft as Chancellor first, if unsuccessfully, introduced in 1957, signalling a departure from the reliance on reductions in the overall level of demand as the sole means of controlling inflation. The move to economic planning – responding to a feeling that economic policy needed to be considered over a longer time-scale than the two-year period which was imposed by the limitations of demand forecasting, and which was successfully achieved in relation to public expenditure by the 1961 Plowden Report – followed rapidly, a main causal factor being the favourable attitude adopted by the Federation of British Industry after its 1961 Brighton Conference. While it is quite possible that the majority of the FBI membership were either opposed to or apathetic towards planning, the FBI Report was seen as a significant step in the building of a consensus. Continental example played its part, indicating to many Conservatives that planning on the French model could be divorced from socialist ideological concern with public ownership of industry and imposed physical controls – prominently associated with planning at that time as a result of the experience of the post-war Labour governments.

The writer has been unable to trace any detailed records of the informal meetings with French planners which in 1961 culminated in a London conference which discussed economic planning in France, but the proceedings are summarized by Leruez (pp. 87–8). As Leruez says, 'at this time there was a steady stream of visits by businessmen and civil servants between the rue de Rivoli and the rue de Martignac, the headquarters of the Ministry of Finance and the Commissariat du Plan, and the Treasury and FBI headquarters, preceding the London conference early in 1961'. The conference was high-powered, addressed by Pierre Massé, the Commissioner-General of the French Plan, and other high-ranking planning officials and heads of the relevant sections of the Ministry of Finance. Also present was a strong contingent of French business men from the sectoral modernization committees. Massé was at pains to emphasize the non-ideological nature of French planning, and minimized the risk to free enterprise. He laid great stress on the smallness of the Commissariat's operative staff – less than 100 (as opposed to the lavish staffing of 900 of the Department of Economic Affairs (DEA) when this eventually emerged) – to allay the fears of an extensive bureaucracy. The cultural and administrative differences between the French and British situations were played down, although Massé did suggest a system of financial incentives, if the British were to adopt a similar system. Probably out of deference to his audience Massé stressed the need for a wide consensus on planning, giving the impression that with this basic element the plan would be self-executing. Probably this explains the lack of emphasis on implementation which was so marked a feature of the British National Plan when it came to be developed some four years later.

It is useful at this stage to trace the development of the political consensus on planning in the early 1960s. In this assessment the records of the party conferences of the period are invaluable. The Conservative conferences are perhaps the more interesting, revealing the way in which the idea of planning was originally evolved, nurtured, claimed as Conservative policy, then swiftly disowned in the face of the arrogation of the idea by Labour. The 1960 Conservative Conference was, in its economic debates, largely only concerned with criticisms of the use of the regulators, as being violent and crude and militating against economic stability. The following year the debate in Conference on planning really sprang to life, with attempts by Peter Walker and Harold Macmillan, in his address as leader of the party, to move Conference towards more positive intervention in the economy, speeches which adumbrated the creation of the NEDC. The 1962 and 1963 Conferences, with the NEDC plan in operation, were notable for the growing enthusiasm in the Tory party for planning, with, amongst others, MacLeod, Maudling, and David Howell united in willing planning on the party. Many Conservative speeches at this time could have been made by Harold Wilson or George Brown. Cross-party similarities, especially amongst the leaderships, were striking. In the run-up to the 1964 election the Conservative manifesto included a section on 'The NEDC and Planning' which said, *inter alia*, 'the NEDC gives reality to the democratic concept of planning by partnership. In contemporary politics the argument is not for or against planning. All human activity involves planning. The question is: how is the planning to be done? By consent or by compulsion?' It would appear that planning had been accepted, in a document designed for public consumption, as a new Conservative philosophy.

The conviction was not, however, to prove lasting. It is fascinating to trace, in conference reports and party manifestos, the working of the process of mutual alienation which seems part and parcel of a party system such as Britain's, exploiting any weaknesses of conviction there may be, instead of sustaining and developing beliefs. The period 1964–6 saw the total destruction of any agreement which might have peeped shyly over the parapets in the early 1960s. The start of the process can be discerned at the Labour Party Conference of 1961, when Harold Wilson, introducing the pamphlet *Signpost for the 60s*, stated that planning was the most important of the five themes included in the text since it was so central to the socialist strategy. On the socialist belief in planning, Wilson said:

> There is nothing new in this. We have proclaimed this, year after year. What is new is that suddenly last summer planning ceased to be a dirty word in Tory circles . . . it is said that they have stolen our clothes. They have not. They have stolen the label sewn into the back of our trousers, but it is only a label, and will be a mighty poor cover for their nakedness.

This is the real beginning of the 'Tory planning is not real planning' argument, to be put with increasing emphasis by Labour as the 1964 general election grew close. Wilson in 1961 makes this point repeatedly, comparing at one stage the Tories to an alcoholic who signs the pledge whilst still drunk. He went on to explain that Labour planning was more than the co-ordination of basic industries. It had purpose and direction towards a socialist (not communist – he was careful to make the distinction) state. Conference's interest in more and extensive nationalization pointed up this leitmotiv. A national plan, in Richard Crossman's words as chairman of Conference, was intended 'to curb ostentatious waste and privilege and extend public ownership without any violation of personal freedom'.

At the Labour Conferences of 1962, 1963, 1964 (truncated because of the election), and 1965, these themes were developed, but public ownership was de-emphasized and an attempt was made to instil a more sober assessment of what planning entailed. But the inter-party struggle and the constant denigration of the Conservatives continued, to the point where it was argued in 1962 that the main virtue of planning was that the Conservatives really didn't believe in it. A realization on the part of the unions that planning could lead to some structural unemployment was evident, but perhaps the only worthwhile and cautionary contributions which came to puncture the general euphoria were made in 1962 by the newly elected William Rodgers and in 1963 by Anthony Crosland, both very much on the Right of the party. Rodgers in 1962 talked about the limitations of planning, and stressed the necessary long-term nature of any such exercise, in which he was echoed by James Callaghan, summing up on behalf of the National Executive Council – a similar stress on the growth aspect of planning and the need for at least a twelve-year perspective. In 1963 the pattern of the future election manifesto takes on more clarity, with the technological revolution introduced in debate and more details on the structure of planning. But Anthony Crosland's short contribution was particularly perceptive in view of what was to come – not exactly sceptical, but aware of the long-term nature of the task of industrial regeneration, and the need for a broad consensus, to break down opposition in industry, the trade unions, the co-operative movement – an attack on conservative and traditional attitudes right through society. Planning also needed a long-term research and educational dimension, according to Crosland, and could not be done overnight. In a prophetic passage he asked for restraint and responsibility, instead of trying to do everything in the first few years, a jarring note amid speeches which were considerably more euphoric.

If the Labour debate on planning became more integrated in the years 1962–4, it hit the heights of rhetoric at the 1965 Conference, with the party jubilant after the election win, and with the National Plan published. There was much blowing of trumpets sounding in the New Era. The Conservatives came in for criticism on a variety of grounds, and any previous reservations were totally unheard. It was at this time that a rapid and ultimately complete disenchantment with planning set in in the Conservative party. Whatever tensions existed inside the party over planning before 1964 disappeared when it lost office. The non-planners, and those who had only a moderate commitment, were very much to the fore, and found unity in attacking the ambitious and seemingly theoretical nature of the National Plan. What enthusiasm remained by 1965 was geared to a more limited and pragmatic exercise than that currently in full swing. But the current was ebbing, and significantly Mr Heath's speech to the 1965 Conference contained no reference to planning. The Conservative election manifesto of 1966 was very different from that of 1964. The word planning does not appear, and no attempt is made to justify government intervention on any scale.

There were many reasons why the National Plan would in any case have failed, if not necessarily as soon as it did. But by 1966 one thing was crystal clear – it would not have survived a change of government. The rest of the 1960s saw a steady and continued retreat from intervention on the part of Conservatives, with free-market enthusiasts such as Nicholas Ridley making the intellectual running, Notable was the resurfacing of ideology in the party, which ultimately in 1970 was to submerge those agencies of intervention which had survived the debacle of 1966.

The abrupt abandonment of the Plan as a result of the run on sterling and the consequent deflationary measures raise a number of questions which go to the root of the British political system of the 1960s. An immediate reaction in Labour circles was that it had been wrecked by the civil service – that the Treasury had taken its revenge on an initiative which was largely predicated on opposition to Treasury influence in the 1950s. It served to increase left-wing paranoia regarding the civil service, which has tended to surface in all financial crises – earlier in 1931 and later in 1976. But the theory that it was civil service and notably Treasury influence which prevented the devaluation of sterling in 1964 which might conceivably have avoided the 1966 crisis – promoted most explicitly by Rodger Opie, himself involved from the beginning with the DEA – whilst containing some truth, does not persuade. The Treasury had prepared an option paper to deal with the 1964 balance of payments crisis, one option being devaluation, another an import surcharge. It is likely that for a number of reasons concerned with the role of sterling at that time as a reserve currency the Treasury and a few other departments – 'the sterling-first lobby', as Opie dubs it – defended the 1949 parity of the pound for as long as was possible. But any such opposition would have crumbled in the face of a clear political lead on devaluation. But this had been ruled out by Harold Wilson himself on attaining office in 1964, the main reason being not only consideration of the resulting pressure on the US dollar at a time when the Labour government was basing its foreign policy on continued Anglo-American co-operation, but also on the political penalty which would have been incurred as being seen as three times the party of devaluation. Labour had a special complex concerning this sphere. It was also likely that Wilson's faith in the ability of Labour's planning policies to deliver quickly (and there was a need for this, given the parliamentary situation), encouraged him to believe that devaluation would not be needed. But the events of 1964–6 on the external payments front saw the beginnings of a financial policy in which the government eventually lost all freedom of action. What should have been a technical decision was inevitably politicized, and the first casualty was the National Plan.

It is with hindsight incredible that oppostition to Treasury influence should have led to an institutional split in economic responsibility in 1964, and have resulted in a lack of articulation of the Plan with other factors in the economy. No element of the Plan recommended a change in the parity of the pound. This factor, institutionalized in opposition to the Treasury – the equivalent of killing the messenger who bears bad news – and the consequent inflexibilty of the Plan, were the main reasons for its failure. But as Trevor Smith points out, failure was inbuilt in other ways. The time was not propitious, as opposed to the situation in the late 1940s when French planning got under way. Subsequent tariff liberalization had made most Western economies more sensitive to international economic movements, whilst sterling was still a major reserve currency and Britain was still spending heavily on overseas defence, all factors which made for sensitivity in the balance of payments. But inherently the Plan was far too inflexible and ambitious for both national and international circumstances. Apart from its lack of essential articulation with the sterling balance, it was inflexible in the sense of being a huge deductive exercise, from one major rigid premise – an annual growth rate for the economy as a whole of just under 4 per cent for an indefinite period. As Alan Lord of the Treasury commented in 1979, looking back on the post-war political economy of Britain, 'The difficulty about the (National) Plan was essentially that it was imposed from the top; a growth target was selected and this was translated into separate rates of growth for individual industries. There was some consultation with the two sides of industry about what the appropriate growth rate for them would be, but the sectoral growth targets did not flow from those consultations and consequently the Plan did not carry with it the commitment of management and unions in the private sector . . . the Plan was effectively discarded because it operated from the top downwards rather than from the bottom up . . . It did not have the flexibility to adapt itself to changes in the external environment. Because it was essentially the detailed exfoliation of a central growth rate which was seen to be incompatible with the measures needed to maintain the parity of the pound the Plan was in some curious sense thought to have failed and it was abandoned instead of being revised, as it might have been.'[16]

But perhaps more important in assessing the possible viability of the Plan was its ambition. A huge and theoretically coherent set of economic prescriptions and corresponding institutional arrangements was devised and set up, fully articulated except at the level of the individual firm and embracing the results of a massive econometric exercise. Modesty had no place – the reaction of Labour from the years of Conservative rule was to be complete and overwhelming. Whilst a more low-keyed, flexible, and pragmatic exercise, articulated with other economic factors, might have got off the gound, the sudden imposition of a comprehensive theoretical framework on the complex structure of British industry stood little chance of sucess. Trevor Smith makes the point that the French suffered from the same syndrome at the same time – the fourth French Plan, intended to run from 1962 to 1965, was the most extensive of the French exercises, and was of necessity radically slimmed to an emphasis on industrial restructuring as the 1960s wore on. It still, however, had more modest goals and organization than the National Plan of British Labour, a point which George Brown was to underscore at the Labour Party Conference of 1965, where it was put over as a point in favour of the British Plan, quite ignoring pleas for modest beginnings and long-term consistency which had been made in earlier Conferences. It is an illustration of the ambition generated by a zero-sum system of politics, in which a temporary monopoly of political power produces the familiar syndrome of an assumed ability to make society and the economy over completely in the space of a Parliament. There is some doubt about whether George Brown's commitment to planning was genuine and wholesale, or largely an expression of an ebullient and enthusiastic personality, and probably his performance at the 1965 Labour Conference, with Labour installed in office and the National Plan published, was somewhat of an exercise in personal trumpet-blowing. But his claims to Conference should have been enough to set the alarm bells going concerning the whole exercise:

We are not claiming I think too much when we claim that no comparable exercise to this has ever been conducted in any major democratic industrial society in the world. We often hear the French Plan lauded to the skies. Anybody who compares the French indicative plan with this must be struck by the enormous differences between the scope and comprehensiveness of what we have done compared with the French plan, for all the praise lavished on it. The sheer effort of collecting, checking and evaluating the information on which to base it has itself been a most monumental exercise.

And this when the Plan was scarcely one-year old, and when the difficulties of implementation had yet to be faced. Statements such as these signalized a singular reversal of received national cultural attitudes – a British reliance on comprehensive deductive theory as against the patient and flexible French pragmatism – an uncharacteristic British reaction which can only be explained in terms of a comprehensive ideological response designed to flatten opposition.

As a result of this and other characteristics there is in retrospect something insubstantial about the whole episode – and episode it proved to be – of the National Plan. It is not only the hurried nature of the preliminary exercise – the DEA thought up in the back of a taxi by Wilson and George Brown, according to legend, or the claims made for the accompanying 'technological revolution' – Wedgwood Benn's promise of 'cathedrals of technology' in every city on his appointment to the new Ministry of Technology, for example. There was a consistent tendency to mistake form for substance, as in George Brown's claim to the 1965 Labour Conference after the Plan had been published for only eleven months, that 'in less than a year the whole job had been done'. Richard Crossman's diary entry is pertinent at this point. In July 1965 Crossman wrote about a recent Cabinet meeting: 'This is the first time we have discussed the National Plan. And it is clear that, so far, no effort has been made to do more than a kind of book-keeping job of accounting; that has been the substitute for adequate economic planning . . . George Brown at the DEA just isn't a planner by nature.' Writing much later in 1979, Ralph Dahrendorf, the German director of the London School of Economics, reflecting on his failure to get political support for a new policy studies institute – a British Brookings – whose concerns would have been primarily long-term economic analysis, commented on 'the extent to which the political, and to some extent the business communities, of Britain are in fact enamoured with the excitement of the immediate . . . (where) one can bathe in the illusion of changing the world by doing things, changing interest rates 22 times in two years, pension schemes with every other government . . . it remains true that excitement is as characteristic of decision making in Britain as continuity, and as a result, confidence is precarious.' The period of the 1960s illustrates this observation precisely. There is much truth in the cynical comment by Professor Hayward that the main purpose of the plan and the brouhaha which surrounded it appeared to be to enable Labour to win the 1966 election with an increased majority.

But the main effect of these years was the inexorable and inevitable destruction of political consensus, which after 1966 worked to destroy whatever attachment there had been of industrial and trade union elements to the planning exercise. Initially much more reluctant than the FBI to commit itself to planning, largely because of an inbred reaction to the incomes policy which this entailed, the TUC remained committed to planning for much longer than industrialists. It showed concern at both its 1965 and 1966 Conferences over the effect of the deflationary measures. By 1967, when it was obvious that the Plan had been abandoned and that the government was prepared to forgo growth to protect the balance of payments, the TUC was unhappy, feeling let down and abused. Criticism centered on the institutionalized division of responsibility between the Treasury and the DEA, but such recriminations were too late. Although one current of TUC opinion favoured soldiering on with some form of planning, this opinion was set back as a result of devaluation and the obvious lack of interest of government in proceeding further with medium-term planning. The consequent isolation of the NEDC was much regretted – union attachment to the NEDC had always been greater than to the DEA, which tended to take decision internally and without union consultation. By 1969 it was evident that the dialogue with government had finally ended, largely due to government indifference and its single-minded concentration on the external balance. Had a Conservative government been in office the breach would have occurred earlier. In such fashion was the unions' initial enthusiasm for planning, which had seemed to give them much-needed political involvement and a chance of departing from their usual sense of impotence, dissipated.

The loss of confidence in planning of the FBI was more swift and marked and even antedated the abandonment of the Plan. As early as its 1965 Conference the Federation's Economic Policy Committee's views on planning were emphatically less ambitious than at the Brighton

Conference, which had marked the beginning of the planning honeymoon. In 1965, taking realistic stock of the deteriorating balance of payments, the CBI seemed resigned to the continuance of demand management, with its necessary deflationary consequences, and was sceptical about the growth targets of the National Plan. This attitude was confirmed at the end of 1966, after the Plan had been abandoned, and a new emphasis appeared on the solution of structural problems via the NEDC.

The collapse of the Plan led ultimately to the winding-up of the DEA in 1969 after it had produced a more modest and flexible strategy, which, however, by that time neither political party was interested in. With it went many of its sectoral and regional agencies, and those which survived were left without a *locus*. In the case of the Industrial Reorganization Corporation this proved to be no bad thing – it was free to operate pragmatically and commercially under industrialists such as Sir Frank Kearton, and followed a commercial philosophy of mergers and rationalizations of small-firm industries which it was hoped would allow more effective competition against overseas manufacturers both in the domestic market and in the export field. Its impact on British industry was quite widespread, in sectors such as nuclear construction, motor vehicles, ball-bearings, electrical engineering, and others. The creation of International Computers in 1968, and the building of two aluminium smelters, although due to the 1968 Industrial Expansion Act and not to the IRC, were moves in the same direction. But intervention such as this, more interested in method than in political dogma, was not to survive a change of government in 1970. The creation of the IRC had been opposed on dogmatic grounds in 1966 by the Conservative Opposition, which raised again the bogy of possible back-door nationalization, and ultimately it was doctrinaire considerations plus pressures from small companies which ensured its demise under Mr Heath. It joined the dismal wreckage of institutions and initiatives associated with the 1960s.

The fate of the Ministry of Technology was different – formed to modernize British industry on a basis of new methods of production and of applied research, it survived the 1970 Heath government at the cost of its merger into the Department of Trade and Industry, and became a strand in the considerable continuity in the basic machinery of economic government of the 1970s. The NEDC survived changes of government, and took on a number of functions whose potential were considerably more than the achievements, as a result of the limited backing it enjoyed through most of the decade. In the late 1960s it became the primary forum for intense arguments between the TUC and the Labour government over the rate of economic expansion and unemployment. Its later work on overseas trade policy, overseas investment, productivity, and prices and incomes agreements, and as a forum for consideration of the sectoral reports of the little Neddies had been valuable, if low-keyed, but has inevitably suffered from the intermittent lack of essential political support. The failure of the National Plan tended to emphasize the work of the NEDC's development committees; whilst difficult to quantify the results of this effort, the Council nevertheless retained the support of the TUC and industry which other, more ambitious, agencies had forfeited in one way or another, and proved to be a forum for the minimum achievement of keeping the concepts of tripartitism and concertation alive.

If we come to strike a balance for the 1960s, it is possible to begin with the positive achievements, which were numerous if not particularly startling. George Brown had some considerable justice on his side when he outlined to the 1965 Labour Party Conference the deficiencies of the government machinery for economic policy which Labour inherited in 1964. Machinery for industrial stimulus hardly existed, nor any for correcting regional imbalances. Training facilities were sparse, and industrial and economic statistics out of date and inadequate. The modernization of the machinery of government, and the beginnings of civil service reform, were considerable achievements, if not as thoroughgoing as might have been wished. A further legacy was that management of the supply side of the economy, virtually non-existent in the 1950s, was established in a number of ways by the experience of the 1960s. Perhaps the most important, in the light of the deepening inflation of the late 1960s and 1970s. were the attempts of successive governments to effect prices and incomes policies. although these were profoundly affected by political fluctuations. Similarly, a considerable degree of selective intervention, supported by regular and concerted consultation with both sides of industry, carried on from the impetus provided under the name of planning into the 1970s, by such means as direct or indirect subsidization, selective public ownership in sectors such as British Leyand, the British National Oil Corporation, British Shipbuilders, and British Aerospace, and the pursuit of microeconomic objectives such as continued rationalization, labour mobility, higher productivity, and import substitution. Although subject to political fluctuations, these initiatives provided for a certain continuity of policy which probably made the economic performance of that decade better than it otherwise would have been. This type of intervention has also survived, in the structures of the NEDC and the Department of Industry, the advent of the 1979 Conservative government, and its policies of disengagement.

On the debit side, however, the costs were great. The concerted efforts of the 1960s to make economic growth a priority ended in failure. It was in this decade that Britain was decisively overtaken by other European countries in both the growth of GDP and capital formation, as Tables 5, 6, and 7 show. Admittedly so far no British government has been able to maintain a fixed set of objectives, such as growth, without compromising with other conflicting demands or without surrendering to economic contingencies requiring emergency measures, as in 1947 and 1966. But the defeat of the economic strategy of the 1960s was much more massive and complete than the circumstances required, largely as a result of the operation of the political rather than the economic system. As Leruez remarks, 'the July 1966 deflationary measures meant not abandoning a particular plan, whose passing few would mourn, but the torpedoing of the entire policy of planning set up in 1962. For in the wake of this failure neither the public nor the civil service would be ready to give much weight to the planners for a long while to come.' If the lessons of the decade had only been to produce some appreciation by all parties of the difficulties of maintaining unequivocal choices in a diverse economy and some scepticism about the technical possibility of prediction and dependence on fixed targets, this would have been healthy, whilst not ruling out more limited and flexible modernization and growth strategies, aimed directly at the structural problems of industry. This would have required an emphasis on and the development of the work and philosophies of the NEDC and the IRC in particular, which with some careful handling might have recaptured the co-operation of the FBI.

But the concerted political will for this was effectively destroyed by the end of the decade. The political results of the failure of the 1960s were long term, and profoundly affected the future of British politics. They signalled a decisive and long-term reversal in the Conservative party of its early-1960s attitude to planned intervention in the economy, and to the oblivion, amongst some of the leadership at least, of strong sentiment in favour of a purposive industrial strategy. Mr Heath's genuine U-turn of 1972, by an administration converted to the need for positive economic intervention, only served, after the electoral failure of 1974, to strengthen the convictions of the neo-liberals within the party, who gained much ground as a result of the events of these years, to the point where they captured the leadership of the party after Mr Heath's dismissal. The reverses of the 1970s for Labour, plus doctrinal discontent, also had considerable effect on that party. The move for constitutional changes by the Left followed almost immediately the defeat of 1970, whilst the disillusionment of the trade unions, who felt, with some justification, that they had been made to bear the brunt of economic failure, contributed to the move to the Left in the union leadership which occurred in the next few years. Simultaneously the perception of the electorate of the dysfunctionality of the political system, always more acute than that of the politicians, accelerated the decline in support for the two major parties which became a marked feature of the next decade. If the 1970s proved to be a period of confrontation and political uncertainty, it grew from the massive alienations of the 1960s.

No simple theory of adversary politics fits the events covered in this section. Total reversals of previous policy did not attend the change of government in 1970. The only Labour initiatives to disappear were those connected with the IRC and an incomes policy, the latter soon to

Table 5

Comparative statistics of gross national product and gross fixed capital formation in UK, France, and EEC (billion of dollars – 1963 prices)

	UK		France		EEC	
Date	GNP	GFCF	GNP	GFCF	GNP	GFCF
1960	78.9	12.4	70.1	14.0	221.6	49.2
1961	81.7	13.6	73.9	15.7	234.4	54.5
1962	82.7	13.5	78.9	17.1	247.1	58.6
1963	86.1	13.8	83.4	18.6	258.5	61.5
1964	90.8	16.0	89.0	21.1	274.2	67.3
1965	93.1	16.7	93.1	22.6	287.4	69.4
1966	95.1	17.1	98.3	24.6	299.8	72.6
1967	97.1	18.3	103.2	26.1	309.9	73.3
1968	100.0	19.2	108.0	27.6	328.4	78.6
1969	102.0	19.0	116.3	30.6	352.3	86.3
1970	104.1	19.3	123.3	32.9	372.0	93.6
1960–70 Yearly average rate of increase (percentage)	+2.9	+4.9	+5.7	+8.7	+5.2	+6.0

Table 6

Evolution of the growth rate (percentage of GNP – 1963 prices)

Date	UK	France	EEC
1960	4.8	7.1	7.5
1961	3.5	5.4	5.8
1962	1.3	6.8	5.4
1963	4.1	5.8	4.6
1964	5.4	6.6	6.0
1965	2.6	4.7	4.8
1966	2.1	5.6	4.3
1967	2.1	5.0	3.4
1968	3.0	4.6	6.0
1969	2.0	7.7	7.3
1970	2.0	6.0	5.6

Table 7

Gross fixed-capital formation (percentage of GNP)

Date	UK	France	EEC
1960	15.7	20.0	22.2
1961	16.6	21.2	23.3
1962	16.3	21.7	23.7
1963	16.0	22.3	23.8
1964	17.6	23.7	24.5
1965	17.9	24.7	24.1
1966	18.0	25.0	24.2
1967	18.8	25.3	23.7
1968	19.2	25.6	23.9
1969	18.6	26.3	24.5
1970	18.5	26.7	25.2

Source: Revue economique de la Banque Nationale de Paris, Oct. 1972.

be resurrected. Otherwise what remained from the débâcle of the National Plan and its associated institutions was picked up and fashioned into some sort of basic machinery of economic government, which provided for some minimum degree of continuity in the management of the supply side of the economy in to the 1970s. But on a deeper level, the adversarial thesis is amply justified. The 1960s illustrated the destructive potential of the political system; its capacity to manufacture conflict on a wide front; its subordination of policy-making to the urgent requirements of electoral victory in a finely balanced two-party situation; the unrealistic and technically dubious ambition generated by a zero-sum perception of politics, massively supported by the doctrinally conditioned reactions of Labour to the solution of economic problems. In trying to perceive and evaluate weaknesses of approach within the deadly symbiosis which is the overriding characteristic of the system in this period, it is perhaps this latter consideration which provides a clue. In the conclusion to his short book *The Politics of Economic Planning,*[17] Alan Budd, in discussing why attempts at comprehensive planning in the West, even when apparently desirable, are likely to fail, quotes C. E. Lindblom on the sociology of planning.[18] Lindblom distinguishes broadly between what he calls the intellectually guided society and the preference guided society, the former dependent on the application of reason to determine how society should be organized, the latter dependent on social interaction and decentralized decision-making. The intellectually guided society finds its apotheosis in an ideal form of totalitarianism; the preference guided society in a system which stresses the importance of choice, markets, and politics, and finds its closest affinity with a pluralistic liberal democracy. Lindblom points out that the style of planning adopted in some liberal democracies, including Britain, has had many of the features of and has been based on ideas close to the concept of the intellectually guided society. British Labour has always found an affinity with this methodology, with its emphasis on the central direction of both society and economy. The alternative is what Lindblom calls strategic planning. As Budd defines it, the task 'should be to consider how objectives could be met within a system which emphasises the recognition of and response to individual demands, rather than the efficient administration of centrally-determined plans'. (p. 153.) It is not a system which rules out intervention in the economy, as extreme economic liberals do, but one which urges the weakness of a generalized approach dependent on comprehensive economic models, stresses the need for a realistic analysis of markets, and provides for intervention which is largely demand-led.

That this broad analysis can be applied to the differences between the two political parties and used to illustrate a basic incompatibility of approach seems obvious. It was evidenced by many of the developments of the 1960s, in particular in the characteristics of the National Plan as devised by Labour, and in the different philosphies of the Conservative-created NEDC and Labour's DEA. Also in their respective personnel – industrialists and trade unionists in the NEDC, 'arrogant elitists', to use Alan Budd's phrase, in the DEA. The approach associated with the DEA is bound to be mistrusted by industrialists operating in competitive market conditions. who recognize instinctively that their control over their particular environment is limited, and rubs a Conservative party which is instinctively cautious of change, pragmatic, and sceptical (until recently at least) of comprehensive solutions, very much the wrong way. This essential difference of approach is probably more destructive of mutual trust between the parties and between Labour and industry than the threat of public ownership, itself an illustration of Labour's centralizing syndrome, but hardly present in the 1960s. But when central direction and public ownership become combined elements in a Labour strategy, as they were to do in the 1970s, then the result was bound to be fatal to the intentions.

Labour and Conservative governments: 1970–1981

The period of Labour rule from 1964 to 1970 probably saw more effort and resources, in terms of legislation, institutions, and cash, put into the problem of industrial modernization than any other similar period. Before the 1970 election *The Economist* produced figures estimating that the government would spend in 1970 £2,000m on industrial aid, and commented 'it has taken an inordinately heavy priming of the pump in the four years since the last general election to produce a modest growth of 10 per cent in Britain's industrial production, equivalent to an annual 2½ per cent, well below the other industrial economies of the West'. The article went on, 'The inescapable conclusion is that much of the aid has been ill-directed', and concluded that what was called for was an overhaul of the machinery of government, of planning techniques in particular, and recommended a merger of the two departments most closely concerned with industry – the Board of Trade and the Ministry of Technology. Again institutional reform was on the agenda, although the problem could not be solved purely in this fashion; without a favourable economic climate, impossible with a continuing payments deficit and constant deflation, efforts at modernization were bound to produce disappointing results. Nevertheless the Labour government undertook a considerable reorganization in 1969, the main plank of which was the abolition of the DEA and the transfer of its medium- and long-term forecasting division to the Treasury, an admission that, as was by then commonly realized, it would have been better if the functions had not been separated initially.

A further overhaul of the machinery of economic direction was undertaken by the new Heath government immediately on taking office.

It reflected a widespread feeling that the numerous institutional creations of Labour had led to overlapping and competing responsibilities, had considerably increased the civil service, and had tended to overwhelm those few institutions which were worth retaining. It was this consideration, plus an acute attack of dogma, which guided the Conservative reorganization of the early 1970s. Its main departmental result was the merger of the Board of Trade and the Ministry of Technology to form the Department of Trade and Industry (DTI), which together with the Department of the Environment ushered in the brief age of the super-department, which lasted until Labour split the DTI in 1974 into four smaller ministries.

Despite this reorganization, there was some element of continuity between 1969 and 1974, each administration's developments foreshadowing the next, as in Mr Heath's creation of a Ministry of Energy from the DTI just before the 1974 election. To some extent these measures of continuity reflected civil service influence, particularly that of Sir William Armstrong, but the continuity should not be allowed to mask an essential difference of political philosophy between Labour and Conservative governments. It was not just that the creation of the DTI was in part designed to co-ordinate an approach to negotiations to join the EEC, to which Labour was opposed; Labour in 1969 was concerned with a rationalization which would produce stronger control of the economy; the aim of the Conservatives was to reduce the burden of intervention. The overt manifestations of a new philosophy were to be seen in the government's reaction to other interventionist agencies inherited from the 1960s, notably the IRC and the NEDC. The Conservative attitude had been set out, significantly enough, by the then Mr Keith Joseph, immediately before the 1970 election, in his capacity as Shadow Minister for Industry and Technology. He envisaged abolition of the little Neddies, and of the Prices and Incomes Board. Whilst the fate of the IRC was not made clear, it was to be 'stripped of its power to impose its will on the market', a degradation of the original concept that in any case would have emasculated it.

Action followed quickly. In October 1970 the IRC was abolished, an act designated by the Opposition as 'ritual slaughter'. This was followed by the demise of the Prices and Incomes Board in November. Although there was no serious threat to the NEDC, supported as it was by both the TUC and the CBI, a reduction of five in the numbers of its EDCs was obtained in December 1970; but the appointment in 1971 of Sir Frank Figgures as Director-General of the National Economic Development Office (NEDO) underlined a basic commitment to its continued existence. Nevertheless, efforts to expand its functions, to promote expansion, to initiate a cautious new planning exercise, got little in the way of government support in the early 1970s and its functions remained minimal. The sort of industrial self-government which is epitomized by the NEDC approach requires for its context a positive and comprehensive commitment on the part of government to industrial development. It has been rapid fluctuations in this commitment which has denied the NEDC its full potential, and which provoked Sir Ronald McIntosh, a later Director-General, to remark in 1978, in a speech which earned him a Prime Ministerial rebuke from Mr Callaghan, that 'the success of the NEDC depends on a reasonably stable policy environment . . . the proviso is important. Political uncertainty inevitably leads people to question the durability of an exercise of this kind.'

The Heath government's brief two-year neo-liberal phase, with its emphasis on reducing the role of government and cutting the level of public expenditure, on greater freedom for industry and a wider resort to market mechanisms had not been consistently intellectualized at that time within the party. But an early sign that a new orthodoxy was in the process of being born came in November 1972, when Mr Heath had already made a genuine U-turn and was negotiating a new interventionist strategy with the TUC and CBI, including a policy for incomes restraint. It was the latter in particular which led the 'Economic Radicals', a group of monetarist economists headed by a Conservative back-bencher, to publish a pamphlet setting out the classic monetarist case, including cuts in the money supply, a reduction in the budget deficit whether by higher taxes or reduced borrowing, a lower growth rate, and a stress on the fact that an incomes policy could by definition play no part in bringing down inflation. It is worth noting that at roughly the same time the left wing of the Labour party was making considerable advances, largely through the Campaign for Labour Party Democracy, towards constitutional change in the party. Orthodoxies were coming under attack from both sides; from monetarism on the Right; from protectionism on the Left, with opposition to membership of the EEC as its rallying point. It is perhaps too cosy a picture to dub the era which ended in the 1970s as one of consensus politics; the co-existence of the two major parties had seldom been more than uneasy. But what can be discerned at this time are the beginnings of the breakdown of the basic post-1945 political and economic settlement. Its achievements had been many and various, but its full potential had never been realized. As a result of intellectual movements in the two major parties its abandonment has been secured, although the Labour Left had for some years to contend with a right-wing parliamentary leadership. After 1974, however, the new orthodoxy of monetarism moved very quickly to make an intellectural conquest of the new leaders of the Conservative party.

The circumstances which brought about the conversion of the Heath government to intervention in 1972 were numerous. In particular it was the rise in unemployment, which reached a national average of 3.7 per cent in November 1971, resisting the reflations of the previous two years and demonstrating, in circumstances of both rising inflation and unemployment, the inapplicability of the economic reasoning behind the Phillips curve. The influence of the new Central Policy Review Staff (CPRS) played some part, as did fears of social unrest if key state industries were allowed to founder. Apart from on the prices and incomes front, the interventionist period to 1974 entailed no new methods or institutions, but in industrial and regional policy worked with machinery which had been largely inherited. It focused on the DTI and in particular its uprated regional offices. The new role of the department was signalized by the replacement of Mr John Davies by Mr Peter Walker, whose interventionist credentials were believed to strengthen politically the new policies, and by the appointment of Mr Christopher Chataway as Minister for Industrial Development, with responsibility for implementing the Industry Act of 1972, which revised the system of investment incentives for the assisted areas and reorganized the administration of development aid. If one adds to the regional aid the policy schemes for vocational training, and the Fair Trading Act of 1972, which continued a tradition of bipartisanship in the area of restrictive practices, restraint of monopolies, and consumer protection, the government after 1972 can fairly be said to have been the most pragmatically interventionist Conservative administration since the war.

If one uses the typology of planning set out in the introduction to this chapter, then the Conservative government followed a strategy of modest administrative planning in its aid to industry and financial planning in the fields of monetary and budgetary policy. It was unlikely that an incoming Labour government would be satisfied with a piecemeal and pragmatic approach to the problem of modernization, prefering, as is inevitable with Labour, something more comprehensive and more ideologically conditioned. As originally devised by Labour's NEC the strategy of the 1974 Labour government falls squarely into the category of administrative planning, resting on a general basis of legal compulsion and statutory control and direction. As diluted through the internal policy processes of an increasingly divided party, it emerged yet again as largely an indicative planning policy, dependent on a voluntary response from industry, and yet again demonstrating how fragile such voluntarism can be, given the ideological undertones which condition the character of even the most right wing of Labour's initiatives. From the point of view of an adversary politics thesis, the events of 1974–81 cannot in general be bettered; they illustrate the growing dependence of party policy on dogma; the inability of the political system to produce a continuous industrial strategy without interruptions caused by ideological lurches; the resulting tendency for such a strategy to represent the lowest common denominator rather than the highest common factor of the political system; the role of the civil service in maintaining a minimum strategy when the political system had failed to elicit the needed broad agreement; and finally the inevitable politicization and short life-span of yet one more valuable interventionist agency, the National Enterprise Board.

The process which produced the industrial strategy of the 1974 Labour governments is frightening in its implications. It illustrates how the fortunes of what is still a great industrial nation can be affected by a handful of ideologues, seemingly unaware or dismissive of the complexity of the situations which governments face and with neither regard nor enthusiasm for continuity of policy, for the further development of the patiently devised instruments of economic government which had painfully emerged from the bruising experiences of previous administrations. The original Labour proposals as contained in the Opposition Green Paper of 1973 display such an ignorance or calculated indifference to the processes of change and development in a liberal society, governed by periodic elections and free political choice, as to be unbelievable. They are an example of a zero-sum perception of politics at its most developed; an exercise carried out in the face of the electoral reality of declining public support, as manifested by a Labour government in 1974 which depended on the votes of only 28 per cent of the electorate. Only zealots could assume, if any thought was given to this factor at all, that an overwhelming mandate, renewed continuously at subsequent elections, was likely to emerge to produce the conditions for the massive corporate transformation of the basic structure of British industry which was envisaged.

It is the intellectual who is the vehicle of ideology; he seeks to criticize and to change. At the back of his mind there is always an ideal to which he is emotionally attached and which he would like to see generally adopted. The incongruence of his vision with reality arises partly from emotional commitment and partly from the imperfections of his information. The left wing of the Labour party has never been short of such individuals. It is a manifestation of a general psychological tendency —as E. H. Carr has observed, the radical is necessarily a Utopian, and the Conservative a realist; this antithesis of Utopia and reality, of theory and practice, reproduces itself in the antithesis of Left and Right. It is a sad commentary on the recent degradation of the British Conservative party that realism can no longer characterize its leadership. But if for the present we stay with the Left of the Labour party, then the characteristic mode of analysis that one might expect is that of the syllogism, a logical deductive process from given premises. For all its attendent paraphernalia of economic terminology, the analysis fits precisely the method adopted by Stuart Holland, the left-wing economist and later Labour MP for Vauxhall, whose book *The Socialist Challenge* became the blueprint for Labour's strategy in the period before 1974.

The development of a new and comprehensive left-wing initiative seems to have been born in Labour party circles out of the failure of the National Plan, and in particular the July 1966 measures. The Left took the view that the Plan had failed because it was not a radical departure from state capitalism. As early as 1969 the Labour party conference was passing resolutions calling for the public ownership of specific firms rather than whole industries; for the direction of investment to areas of high unemployment and for new companies to have workers' control. In 1968 Holland started on his book, which was to be published in 1973. In the Introduction he admits the very close ties he has had with the Labour party, his ideas often being expressed to the left-wing members of Labour's NEC. He is 'especially indebted to Judith Hart, Tony Benn, Ian Mikardo, Eric Heffer', and others, 'without whom there might well have been less coincidence between this book and Labour Party policy in the mid-1970s'. Most of the names he acknowledges reappeared as the authors of the 1973 Opposition Green Paper on the concept of a National Enterprise Board.

American political sociologists have noted in political life what they call 'the issue-attention cycle', to which the British Labour party, and especially its left wing, seems particularly prone. In such a cycle an issue or problem, perhaps as a result of a number of incidents which attract publicity, achieves overwhelming importance, only to fade and die as other problems supervene, or a longer perspective emerges, or the costs of dealing with the problem appear too great, or, as is usual, some combination of these factors. To the Labour Left in the late 1960s and early 1970s the issue was the multinational corporation – the air was full of ITT and Lonrho. It is the development of an ingrained hostility towards multinationals operating in Britain from which derive the primary and many of the secondary premises of Holland's book, and his macro-economic argument, microeconomic analysis, and institutional recommendations. But he also declares war on Keynes (Keynesian economics consists of little more than keeping the wheels of the capitalist machine well oiled) and also on the Labour revisionists, particularly Crosland. As Alan Budd remarks, this latter attack was somewhat odd: 'If the intention (was) to convert the revisionists, the tone is far too hostile; it appears instead to be written for the Left, who already believe in public ownership.' (*The Politics of Economic Planning*, p. 125.)

The leitmotiv of Holland's attack on British capitalism was its presumed inefficiency, in particular the inability of national industry to compete with the massively advantaged multinationals. It is difficult in a short space to summarize the complex and highly theoretical analysis of *The Socialist Challenge*, but the main premise is that the increasing dominance of the economy by multinational corporations renders Keynesian theory obsolete. They can operate whilst disregarding the multiple pressures exerted both by the market and by government policy. Their development means that a stabilization-policy approach which aims to control the main economic factors by regulating total demand, leaving the market to operate within the framework so fixed, is stultified. The national market as a focus for regulation has become outdated because of the multinationals and their capacity for transfer pricing, which in Holland's analysis is largely responsible for the continuing strain on the UK balance of payments. Through their monopoly power and consequent freedom to set prices the multinationals feed inflation, and by investing profits abroad they frustrate policies for growth and full employment.

But what failures of Keynsianism there have been rest largely on other factors – the mistiming of intervention, the speed of response of industry, and constant attempts to run the economy at too high a level of demand. Holland's obsession with the multinationals blurs and confuses analysis and hampers prescription – as Alan Budd has remarked: 'There must be grave doubts about his analysis, since it is based on a long list of things that multinationals could do rather than on a list of things they are likely to want to do or have been doing. Further, it does not satisfactorily explain why the UK's economic performance is relatively so poor, since multinationals operate in all non-communist economies.' (Budd, p. 128.) Despite, or rather because of its intricate economic argument, *The Socialist Challenge* smells powerfully of the lamp, an example of that tendency to seek all-encompassing explanations, to conflate the subject-matter of its obsessions, and to see the world as a vast and often conspiratorial jigsaw puzzle in which all the interlocking issues can eventually be made to fit, which is characteristic of the Left of the Labour party. Holland's work, in the final analysis, weaves just this sort of tightly meshed ideological web out of the problems of the British economy. It is a sad reflection on the processes of policy-making in Opposition that the book should have had such influence. Its prescriptions were the take-over at minimum cost of the leading twenty-five firms (why twenty-five?) from the top hundred ('the state investing in success rather than failure') to act as market leaders and 'feared competitors' of the multinationals, with vigorous state-funded investment policies; the control of the remaining private sector through statutory planning agreements, in order to produce a 'successful planning strategy' which would place 'all our dealings with the major companies onto a systematic and coherent basis', according to Labour's *Programme 1973*, and which, supported by powers given under a new Industry Act, would provide for the ministerial direction of the major commercial decisions of the remaining leading companies.

This seems to have been a recipe for a full-blown corporate state which would not have disgraced pre-war Italy. How Holland's concepts and vision would have squared with the imperatives of liberal democracy is not a question to which either he or his left-wing colleagues on the NEC seem to have addressed themsleves, probably for reasons which require no elaboration. But this doubt seems to have been present in the mind of *The New Statesman*'s reviewer of *The Socialist Challenge*, who wrote to the effect that it was all very well for Holland to propound grandiose schemes, but essential continuity of policy must be taken into account:

he (Holland) might consider whether we ought not to be looking for an industrial policy which would be continued rather than dismantled by a future Conservative government . . . There is widespread agreement that governments need a tighter grip on the activities of the multinationals, and that their planning perspective needs to extend beyond the life of one Parliament. But all that suggests precisely the bi-partisan approach which Mr. Holland denounces as social democratic treachery to socialism.

Given the nature of Holland's analysis and prescriptions, it is by no means surprising that it was to Italy, with its corporatist traditions, that the Labour Party turned for its institutions for the 1970s. Italy, and a miscellany of other national agencies, were to be the exemplars, much as France had been in the 1960s. The idea of some form of state holding-company seems to have developed out of the failure of the National Plan, and Holland's book fleshes it out. His pattern is the Italian Industrial Reconstruction Institute, developed considerably in the mid-1960s as an agency of both public ownership and commercial direction of a large Italian state sector, although nowhere near so large as that which Holland envisaged for Britain. Its success, as would now be recognized, has been limited, but Holland felt that a left-wing British socialist government could make better and considerably wider use of this instrument. Nothing if not thorough, he talks also of two further state holding-companies, the British Insurance Corporation and the British Bank, which would result from taking both these industries into public ownership.

The development of the concept in Labour circles can be traced from Conference and NEC reports. It is first mentioned in the NEC statement for the 1969 Conference; reappears again in an NEC document in 1971; appears as a National Enterprise Board at the 1973 Conference, and as a concept is fully developed in the policy discussion document which the NEC was asked to prepare for Labour's 1973 Programme. The rationale for the NEB, and the international examples on which it rests appear in considerable detail in the 1973 Opposition Green Paper, the authors of which are nearly all mentioned in the preface to *The Socialist Challenge*, and include Stuart Holland himself. Whilst the Italian IRI was seen as the pattern for the NEB, the paper also referred to examples of state holding-companies in Sweden, West Germany, Israel, Belgium, Canada, and Australia, without mentioning the small-scale operations of these institutions and their largely non-ideological character.

At the same time as the concept of a holding company was being firmed up, some preliminary dilution of the NEC's total strategy was progressing. Yet as late as October 1973 the Labour Party Conference was reaffirming its belief in wide public ownership in the Programme prepared for the occasion, largely based on the NEC document. If any industrialist or elector was to be in doubt about the continuous commitment of the party this section should have disabused them:

There are many strands of socialist thought and belief which throughout the history of our movement have made the theme of public ownership of our national industrial resources central to the achievement of a socialist society. At a time when the advance of technology has raised the stakes, and when the ownership carried with it has become more concentrated in fewer hands, they have never been more relevant.

Although manifestly wrong in fact, this section, in view of what ultimately happened to Labour's strategy, turned out to be pure rhetoric in another sense; but as has already been pointed out, rhetoric has its role in the conditioning of attitudes, and in determining the responses of the sections of the economic community whose support is solicited for the implementation of policy. But the reasoning persisted in the subsequent manifestos for the two elections of 1974, again putting public ownership and economic planning at the centre of the party's programme, on the basis of an analysis which was still recognizably Holland's. The emphasis on public ownership was probably the main reason, again, why only one voluntary planning agreement was signed by private industry during Labour's term, and this by Chrysler, who had its own urgent reasons for soliciting government support.

The dilution of the party programme at the hands of the Labour government between 1974 and 1976 was rapid and thorough, although at the expense of consistency and coherence, and ultimately of results. Once in office, and facing an equivocal parliamentary situation which the second election of 1974 did little to improve, the government became more acutely aware of the need to minimize opposition both in industry and the country, and to retain the support of the international financial community. Also as time wore on the government became increasingly preoccupied with the problem of inflation, and managing the oil price rises (the price after quadrupling in 1973–4 tripled again in the late 1970s), and the deficits which the rises entailed. By 1976, when the tardy development of a more pragmatic industrial strategy was just under way, the government faced a financial crisis far larger in its implications than that of ten years earlier, not helped by the wages explosion of its first two years in office, which it had actively encouraged, which stripped industry of its profits, and which contributed to a rate of inflation of 25 per cent, with every prospect of rising. In these circumstances the prospect for planning agreements, even on a voluntary basis, looked dim; the future seemed too uncertain to bear the precision of forecasting which was implicit in the concept.

Given a need to rethink, the industrial strategy of the Labour government emerged slowly, largely to be overtaken by political and industrial events. It involved a considerable switch of emphasis from the concept of a National Enterprise Board to the well-tried and long-suffering NEDC, which was revitalized in 1975–9, with a welcome emphasis on an inductive development of a growth and modernization policy which for once seemed to have got the problem the right way round. The strategy – somewhat of a misnomer since it was not imposed but emerged from the initially disaggregated work of analysis sector by industrial sector – was based on information gathered from the needs of a large area of industry; the EDCs were supplemented by thirty-nine working parties, which between them covered about 40 per cent of manufacturing output.[19] The staffing of the NEDC was improved, and the government seemed set to give political backing to the strategy which emerged and to support it by direct intervention. But the process of analysis was lengthy – the sector working-parties were not set up until the end of 1978, and the final NEDC report was only presented in 1979, when the parliamentary situation had deteriorated to a point where the continued existence of the government for its full term was in doubt. The Industrial Strategy remained, as Budd remarks, a slogan, instead of being translated into practical measures; in the period after 1976, with its severe cuts in public expenditure and stringent control of the money supply, scope was limited both for industrial aid and for acquiring companies through the National Enterprise Board.

In so far as the industrial strategy of the Labour government had ultimately any substance, it was dependent on the operations of the NEB. The Board had been duly set up under the terms of the 1975 Industry Act, which also provided for the introduction of planning agreements. Its funding was far lower than had been envisaged by the NEC; there were no powers for compulsory purchase of companies by the Board, and planning agreements were made voluntary. Initially it seemed that the role of the NEB had been reduced to that of taking responsibility for state-owned industry; it was early identified with rescue operations, such as that of British Leyland which initially absorbed the bulk of its investment funds, rather than with successful enterprise. Yet a creative role was developed for it, following the replacement of the first chairman, Mr Don Ryder, an orthodox industrialist, probably chosen to sell the concept to industry, by Sir Leslie Murphy, under whose chairmanship the Board adopted a wider and more creative role, more analogous to, although free from the accompanying ideological commitments, the original conception of a state holding-company. Sir Leslie Murphy designated five roles which the Board ultimately came to have: as an industrial holding-company for the strategic direction of state-owned companies, a role he thought better performed by senior industrialists and trade unionists than by ministers and administrators; as support for regional initiatives; as support for exports; as support for small companies; and, what evidently Murphy saw as the most important role, as responsible for the development of a pragmatic industrial strategy determined by commercial criteria – ultimately, the function which the theologians of the new Conservative government after 1979 could not tolerate.

So far as the first role was concerned, there seems little substance in the remark of Sir Leslie Murphy's more complaisant successor as chairman, in the Board's 1979 Report, to the effect that the role of the NEB in relation to British Leyland in particular, had been minor and largely illusory. It was the NEB which stopped BL's £150m. foundry programme, because it could not be justified. Similarly it stopped plans to build a new £65m. centralized engineering centre, and cut BL's 1979 funds from the government. And although government approval was needed, it was the NEB which removed the chairman and chief executive of BL and appointed Sir Michael Edwardes. As Sir Leslie Murphy remarked after his resignation from the NEB, 'Had it not been for the decisiveness of the Board, I do not think that ministers and civil servants would have made the management changes in BL that were essential for its future'. It was the reluctance of the government to take similar action in the case of Rolls-Royce which was the immediate cause of the resignation of Murphy and the rest of the Board in November 1979.

In regard to the NEB's wider function of acting as the agent of an industrial strategy, it had made some considerable and rapid progress before the change of government in 1979. Illustrative of this was the NEB's 1978 Annual Report, published in May 1979, in which Sir Leslie Murphy, in detailing the Board's achievements, made a strong but in the event unavailing plea for it to be protected from 'political dogma'. Essentially the Report was couched in the form of a major justification of the NEB and a vigorous defence of its record, and, written just when the 1979 election campaign had started, was a plea for some degree of continuity of approach to industrial policy, asking that the NEB should be allowed to continue with its work 'free from doctrinal hostility'. In a much fuller Report than was usual, the Board spelled out its philosophy of intervention, as being, primarily, 'a catalyst of risk'. Explaining why he believed that the NEB's entrepreneurial activities should not be cut back, the chairman wrote: 'It may be asked why there is any need for the NEB to be involved, either as an investor or as a moving spirit, in profitable centres in which there is major market promise. It is a feature of the western world that governments of almost every major manufacturing country respond to public pressures to try to stimulate the pace and direction of industrial development. If we stand aside in this country and allow market forces alone to operate we shall be overtaken and displaced by those of our competitors who have learned the skills of forcing the pace of development and seizing the market opportunity by reinforcing commercial drive with the impetus of public financial support. If the UK is to respond, it is right to find the institutions appropriate to the task. I believe that in the NEB this country has created such an institution.'[20] Illustrating this central role of the Board was its function in relation to Alfred Herbert, the machine-tool subsidiary, which, with problems inherited from the previous government, the NEB took in hand with an investment and direction programme designed, over a five-year period, to transform the company from a low-technology to a high-technology machine-tool manufacturer. Inevitable temporary losses on this project depressed the Board's profit figures for 1978, but illustrated the need for state aid to underwrite such transformations in the industrial structure, which, in a period of practically non-existent profits, market mechanisms cannot ensure.

But the record of the NEB, as it probably knew by 1979, was to carry little weight in the decision regarding its ultimate fate. Even as the NEB was developing and implementing a largely successful strategy of industrial intervention, the right wing of the Conservative party was planning a quick death for it should the party be returned to power. The task of preparing the case against the Board was undertaken by the Centre for Policy Studies, founded by Sir Keith Joseph and Mrs Thatcher to provide the detailed underpinnings for a free-market philosophy. The establishment of the NEB under the 1975 Industry Act had been bitterly opposed by the Conservatives, not surprisingly given the initial ideological loading of the concept. But hostility had persisted, despite the pragmatic style which the NEB quickly adopted. The Centre for Policy Studies began work on a project designed to provide a timetable for the winding-up of the NEB before the 1979 general election. The authors were John Redwood, a merchant banker, and Mr Michael Grylls, a Tory back-bencher of committed free-market views and the then vice-chairman of the Conservative industry committee. A contributor to the project was Mr Nicholas Goodison, at the time chairman of the Stock Exchange, who made the remarkable claim that the NEB had at best been irrelevant to the country's economic ills, and that it 'had gone for symptoms and failed to attack the underlying disease'. The ensuing pamphlet of the Centre was not published until May 1980, when most of the major decisions concerning the running down of the NEB in its wider capacities had been put in hand by Sir Keith Joseph. Its borrowing powers were reduced, cash was stopped to a number of companies, including Alfred Herbert, others like Ferranti earmarked for disposal to the private sector, and the Board merged with the National Research Development Corporation to form the British Technology Group, with the reduced if still important task of promoting high-technology industry. But the plans put forward by the Centre for Policy Studies for further reduction in the Boards's functions have supplied a blueprint for its total demise, should it fail to gain sufficient industrial and financial backing for its new role.

Sir Leslie Murphy and his entire Board resigned in November 1979 over the decision to switch responsibility for monitoring Roll-Royce from the NEB to the Department of Industry. In January 1981, in a bitter speech to the Royal Institute of Public Administration, Sir Leslie launched a swingeing attack on both main political parties and on Sir Keith Joseph, still at that time Secretary of State for Industry, for their treatment of the NEB. In the context of this chapter his remarks are worth noting at some length. The main burden of his speech was that the NEB had become yet another victim of the continuous strife between the two main parties on how to deal with industry:

In this strife the merits of the case are ignored. The Left wing of the Labour Party continues to press for more and more public ownership, ignoring the very mixed record of the publicly-owned corporations over the last thirty years . . . The Right wing of the Conservative Party sees no merit in anything except private enterprise and market forces, ignoring the failures of the first and the gaps in the second . . . I must confess that I have become sick and tired of this sterile confrontation. What a relief it would be to have a government that addressed itself objectively to find the best solution of each problem, and put away dogma and prejudice. If the debate about a Centre Party were to take us along this road, I for one would be an enthusiastic supporter.

What Sir Leslie called 'the Right-wing bigots of the Conservative party' had refused to recognize the importance of the role of the NEB, which, overcoming 'the ideological handicaps with which we were lumbered initially', had approached its tasks in a commercial fashion; had kept away from involvement with planning agreements; had not acquired shares in profitable companies as an ideological end in itself; or used its financial strength to acquire companies against the wishes of the shareholders. It is not surprising in these circumstances that Sir Leslie Murphy became one of the first industrialists to join the Social Democrat party when it was formed, and is now a leading member of the party's Industry committee, co-author with the former Labour minister Edmund Dell and Professor John Heath of the party's Green Paper on industrial strategy which appeared in June 1982.

If the demise of the NEB in its broad conception was one result of a new Conservative government, it might well have been that, but for the 1981 Cabinet reshuffle, in which Sir Keith Joseph was moved from Industry to Education, the Department of Industry itself would have lost its separate existence, having too much of a history of industrial intervention, and too many civil service personalities who exemplified this tradition, to suit the tastes of its minister. With less and less to do there was an increasing case for the department to be merged back into the Department of Trade, with the inevitable destruction of the collective institutional knowledge and experience of industrial policy which it had painfully built up in its dealings with the governments and industry in the 1970s, and which, at some stage, would have had to be relearnt and reassembled. Evidence of a growing *malaise* in the department was the resignation of two of its leading civil servants, for jobs in the Post Office and GEC, in particular that of the Deputy Secretary in charge of industrial and economic issues, the strongest departmental proponent of industrial aid and intervention. If this further change in the machinery of economic government had taken place, the department would have become the coping-stone of the wreckage of institutions with which, as has been said earlier, the post-war administrative and economic landscape of Britain is littered.[21]

It was stated at the beginning of this chapter that the political arrangements which have dominated post-war Britain can fairly be described as a system in which both the mechanics of two-party domination and the consistent ethos and doctrines of the parties and their closest groups of support produce a style of politics which has largely predictable results. A pattern of events is thus likely to repeat itself, unless an extraneous and unbargained-for factor intervenes. The history of the decade of the 1970s, when compared with that of the 1960s, brings some support to this hypothesis, although the dominant economic factor of the 1970s was inflation, and less the balance of external payments. But once again in the early years of the decade a Conservative government was converted to policies of economic intervention; its successor, hardly concerned initially with consensus, began with an ideologically inspired blueprint for large-scale planning, which although diluted as time wore on succeeded in alienating the private sector. Again the emerging strategy, as in the mid-1960s, turned out to be largely formal, as much concerned with politics as with economics, and was largely abandoned, in 1976, as a result of a financial crisis, again as it had been ten years earlier. A central institution, the NEB, like its predecessor, the IRC, fell victim to the same process of politicization. To continue the cycle, a neo-liberal Conservative government took over at the beginning of the new decade, this time armed with more powerful ideological arguments. But the election of June 1983 showed clearly that a large proportion of the electorate had become aware of the increasing dysfunctionality of the two-party political process. Although this awareness failed to register in Parliament, its impact in terms of votes was considerable, and would have been greater had it not been for the purely fortuitous factor of the Falklands war, an instance of Machiavelli's *fortuna* in politics which is unlikely to be repeated.

Some comments, mainly from abroad

Jaques Leruez, writing in 1975, remarked about the planning movement in Britain: 'one can scarcely speak of a crisis in British planning, if only because it has never been more than a succession of isolated efforts which have led to nothing, and which have been temporary expedients rather than thoroughgoing reforms . . . [but] while its economic impact may have been no more than marginal, one cannot say the same of its influence on British political life and institutions.' (Leruez, p. 297.) It is worth noting that in Britain – if we set aside the immediate post-war emergency period – as in France, planning emerged from the centre and right of the political spectrum, rather than from the Labour party which is more ideologically inclined in this direction. This being so, as Stephen Blank, the American political economist has noted, its collapse 'destroyed the opportunity to gain the support of a substantial segment of British industry (and, more important, to mobilise a cadre of Britain's brightest young businessmen) for the planning experiment'.[22] Neither Macmillan nor Wilson could substitute for a Monnet, and support lost in the 1960s could scarcely have been expected to be won by the more ideologically motivated initiatives of the 1970s.

In assessing the reasons for failure, there is some congruence of views between outside observers such as Leruez and Blank, to take two of the more percipient writers. Both level some primary criticism at the administration, Leruez in particular, with a customary readiness to point up British failures by reference to French successes. He makes the obvious point, stressed much earlier by British writers such as Andrew Shonfield and Jack Hayward, that the varied and heterogeneous lobby which called indicative planning into being in the late 1950s and early 1960s was not a permanent and established pressure group, and, as is now obvious, was, with a few exceptions, deficient in its assessment of the political system and its capacities. 'Indeed, in this field of planning the celebrated realism of the British has been largely conspicuous by its absence.' (Leruez, p. 280.) Leruez goes on to lament the lack of a British equivalent to the French *grands corps*, whose permeation of the major economic institutions of France provided a constant means of assessment and co-ordination of economic policy. The DEA, an attempt in British terms to provide an alternative civil service for planning and to avoid the departmentalism of the major economic ministries, signally failed in this same task. Far from co-ordinating the relevant parts of the administration into a common endeavour, it succeeded in alienating them, and the philosophy of its creation virtually guaranteed this result.

But Leruez goes deeper into the motivation of the British administration, alleging that those qualities of the civil service which emphasize the preservation of departmental interests, the resolution of conflicts, and the maintenance of continuity, all of which have been apparent in the narrative of this chapter, whilst having some considerable political value, are not those qualities nor aims which meet the exigencies of economic management, and indeed can also be a source of difficulties themselves. Much the same points are taken up and made the subject of a fundamental critique of the British political and administrative ethos by Professor Hayward, another Francophile, in an article published in 1976.[23] It is difficult to quarrel with the analysis, except that, like Leruez, Hayward hardly advances solutions to the British problems. To condense a complex argument, Hayward is concerned with the problem of immobility, of government stalemates in both France and Britain, and in the case of Britain this is analysed largely in terms of institutional inertia, on the part of the civil service in particular, and a traditional reliance on pluralism and incrementalism as the overriding characteristics of government. He believes that France has shown a superior capacity to mobilize essential consent and to overcome dissent, and that French *étatisme* has worked more successfully than British voluntary tripartitism between government, business, and trade unions. The addiction of the British administration to crisis avoidance has prevented 'the emergence of new men and methods' and fostered a foredoomed reliance on salvation through attempted imitations of continental institutions. Like Leruez, he underscores the value of the role of the French 'techno-bureaucratic elite', with its self-confident assertiveness as opposed to 'the self-effacing British bureaucracy', and stresses its effectiveness in breaking down resistance to innovation on the part of traditional French institutions.

Whilst Professor Hayward is careful to distinquish between basic British and French culture, British liberalism and pluralism in practice on the one hand, the relatively integrated and monolithic French state on the other, and also to bring in other considerations which have in France had a positive effect, such as a weak Parliament and parties, and an undeveloped trade union movement, neither he nor Leruez have a formula for Britain, and as a result their analyses, whilst useful in emphasizing characteristics of British decision-making which tend to be taken for granted, are essentially barren of prescription. It is perhaps only right in such an analysis that the profound deficiencies of the French style of economic government should be given equal weight in the argument, which both authors to their credit briefly attempt. Although participation in Britain by both sides of public and private industry has been widespread, there is no doubt that it has been inadequate in making some genuine impact on economic development. On the other hand, the restricted dialogue which has accompanied French planning has demonstrated its weakness in the mobilizing of democratic consent. The occasional debate on planning policy in the French Parliament has seldom been more than lip-service to popular choice and opinion. This restricted degree of participation has produced its own alienations, especially on the Left. There is a sense in which the troubled events of May 1968 were a verdict on a particular style of French economic management. Professor Hayward makes the same point in a more generalized way – he quotes de Gaulle's view that

'France only undertakes reforms in the wake of revolution', and direct action is usually needed to correct the inadequacies of what Hayward calls a predilection towards 'government by a techno-bureaucracy'. In striking a balance between respective national achievements, more than indices of comparative economic growth needs to be taken into account.

Stephen Blank, with more of a cultural affinity with Britain, is on the whole more sympathetic in his comments than either Leruez or Hayward. His analysis of the characteristics of the British administration, whilst very similar, displays some sensitivity to the constitutional position of the civil service, and the extent to which its general ethos and practical approach have been determined both by the political culture in which they operate, and also, crucially, by the consistent shortcomings of the party political system which directs them. Blank admits that the civil service has been the governmental institution with the key responsibility in an era of changing party control for maintaining a degree of continuity of policy, and that it has been a master of crisis avoidance. For the most part its perceived political neutrality has helped in its dealings with the powerful interests in British society. But as Blank remarks, 'in many cases the excess of its virtues is the source of its vices'. The civil service has never constituted itself as a French *grands corps*; it tends to have a strong departmental view except at the highest levels; and has difficulty in dealing with the long as opposed to the short term. But given the nature of British party politics it is difficult to see how it could be otherwise. In a situation where constitutional attitudes and institutional characteristics derive largely from the political system the civil service can only be a reactive agency. The allegation, often made, that the administration has connived at, or at least acquiesced in, every development which has contributed to the post-war decline of Britain, whilst maintaining intact its organization, practices, and general ethos, may be largely true, but then there is scarcely a British political institution to which the same criticism cannot be directed. Parliament is surely a prime target for the accusations. Uniquely in Britain, institutions reflect and focus the characteristics of the political system in which they are located. If, as Blank asserts, the British administration has failed to meet the needs of the present environment of British politics, the need for discretionary policies and 'the need to operate in environments in which the border between the public and private sectors is increasingly unclear', then it can be said that the parties themselves have seldom provided the stable policy-frameworks and institutions, or created the appropriate patterns of political thought to which the administration could respond.

As it is, the civil service has related to political failure in its own fashion, directed by a basic concern with continuity and stability. Its job has not been to initiate, but to constantly evaluate and repair, where it can, the failure of the larger policies. That this is no substitute for consistent and effective political government, Blank, for all his criticisms, readily admits. There have now been sufficient examples of this particular civil service reaction in relation to economic policy for generalized conclusions to be drawn. As Blank says, regarding Treasury influence over policy: 'In retrospect it seems that the Treasury never wished to take over the helm. On the one hand, it sought some fixed point, such as the state of sterling in the world economy, against which direction could be determined automatically. On the other hand its officials worked dutifully, even heroically, in the bilges, manning the pumps to ensure that the ship stayed on an even keel, no matter where it was sailing. But no one steered.'[24] A damning, but correct analysis of relations between the British political and administrative systems in the post-war years.

Blank ultimately arrives at the fundamental determining factor which were sketched at the beginning of this book – the overwhelming importance in Britain of the party political process, which is still basically manifesting a nineteenth-century political culture in twentieth-century circumstances. He admits, with Samuel Beer, that in Britain, 'party is indeed king', and he agrees that the difficulty of the civil service in adapting to an environment characterized by a blurring of the distinction between public and private powers has been compounded by the intellectual weaknesses of the major parties, which are still basically imbued with the nineteenth-century notion of a rigid separation between politics and economics, which contributes to the inability to evolve lasting institutions appropriate to an advanced industrial society and a diversified economy.

Blank does not analyse in any detail the process of politicization which has been the leitmotiv of this chapter, nor extend his commentary to the effect of the basic and enduring doctrines of the parties. But at the risk of repetition his views are worth recording at some length, if only to show how the phenomenon strikes an outside observer. He remarks that 'Since the early 1960s the British government has undergone more reorganization than at any other period in modern history. But the general impression is of indecision and failure . . . From

Neddy and all the little Neddies to the DEA, the IRC, and MinTech and the ups and downs of ten more years of alphabet soup, institution creation can easily be perceived as a substitute for significant change and development.'[25] And again:

The British have been terribly willing to jettison programmes, plans and institutions long before there has been an opportunity to see what will work and what will not. Both political parties seem impressively ignorant of the conditions and requirements of institutional development. Achievements in institution-building were in fact not neglible. The development of the NEDC from 1961 to 1965 and the experiments with the Prices and Incomes Board remain impressive. But their long-term impact was limited . . . The result was to degrade the policies, demoralise the participants, and strengthen the position of those institutions, especially the Treasury, traditionally responsible for the conduct of economic affairs and the policies with which they were identified.[26]

In seeking an explanation for this marked failure, weight needs to be given to the received culture of the parties and the administration, still in some degree an expression of nineteenth-century assumptions. Blank points to the fact that the British system seems happy when dealing with a strict and well-demarcated division between public and private sectors; but the messy and complex political business of devising and operating forms of flexible and discretionary intervention is not a process which either party, or the civil service, has found particularly appealing. Essentially this reluctance to engage in the politics of pluralism and diversity in the economic sphere derives from a related liberal assumption – the strict conceptual separation of economics and politics. This manifests itself in numerous ways, as interpreted through each party's ideology. On the Labour side, the historian E. H. Carr makes the point [27] that Marxism and socialist thought in general were as much a reflection of nineteenth-century assumptions as the most extreme manifestation of *laissez-faire* liberalism, inasmuch as they were predicated on an economic system with laws and imperatives of its own, working independently of the state and of the process of politics as here defined. This economic system has also provided an inheritance of thought and feeling which has always been powerfully present in the Conservative party, and which the failures of the last two decades have tended to bring to the surface. It is depressing to note the marked retreat from the politics of pluralism by both parties which has been a feature of the 1970s and early 1980s. So far as Labour is concerned, there have been developments on the Left which deny the potential of the British voluntary tradition, with a constant movement, occasionally diverted but always gaining ground, towards statutory compulsion – 'planning with teeth' – as a major step towards the permanent socialist goal of a planned society, with politics turned into administration. On the Conservative side the movement has been towards the disengagement of politics from economics, to the point where Conservative political economy has been reduced to the technical control of the main money aggregates in the economy and little else.

Indicative of these broad philosophical positions is the reaction of the parties to corporate agencies in the economy, and their necessary concertation in any positive policy of economic intervention. Not excluding the massive integration of the unions into the polity in the inter-war period, as an essential condition of political stability, which Keith Middlemas has so ably chronicled, the 'corporate bias' of British politics has never been whole-hearted, despite increasing evidence of its indispensability. All too often, except perhaps for the brief episode of the early 1960s, it has been a feature of negative crisis-avoidance rather than a positive commitment. Corporatism as a style of politics is as much resented on the Left as on the Right, either due to a belief that it blurs and attempts to modify an essential class antagonism or as a result of an instinctive regard for liberal individualism. Trevor Smith, in his *Politics of the Corporate Economy*, puts only an extreme manifestation of this distaste; his views have a wide currency. In such attitudes, however, there is usually an element of realism as well as ideology. As Professor Hayward remarks, close contacts between government and their clienteles have in Britian all too often put weak governments at the mercy of powerful groups which are guaranteed access to power and 'capable of commanding more loyalty from their members than the government can secure from its citizens'. Whereas the same consultative process in France has usually worked to the benefit of government. Too often in Britain vested economic interest have been used to bring about changes to which the interests themselves have proved to be the main obstacles. It is a severe criticism of the underdevelopment of British political thought that until recently little attention has been given to the relations of interests with government, or to the means whereby a political and parliamentary context might be developed stable and powerful enough to undertake reform and to require, more successfully than can the present system that corporate interests relate to public purposes. Most reformist writers have contented themselves, in the characteristic fashion of British political science, with purely institutional analysis and innovation. The problem, as indicated at the outset of this section, is inevitably one of party politics. Devising political structures which can integrate sectional interests without perpetuating a restrictive and retrograde corporatism is now the central task of contemporary statecraft in Britain, and is one which would ultimately face any government, neo-liberal, social democratic or socialist. Current political arrangements have failed dismally to integrate corporate interests permanently into the public choice process. Interest groups have been accommodated largely through private negotiations and private settlements. Although the current party system is supposed to produce 'strong' government, British administrations have demonstrated in practice little power to determine the outcomes of public policies. The current Conservative administration has temporarily solved this problem by just not governing, but on any detached view, apart from that of the convinced neo-liberal, the problems are merely being postponed and are mounting. Before giving up the struggle, and concluding that Britain is in the long run inherently ungovernable, it would be worth attempting constitutional change, especially in the electoral arrangements which largely determine the shape and capacity of the basic political process.

5

CONCLUSION

Part A

S. A. WALKLAND

It has become more difficult in recent years to gain a clear perspective on the adversary politics thesis in so far as it affects economic policy, since this issue, like most others in current British political discourse, is now heavily politicized. The arguments tend to reflect the political stances of the protagonists rather than rest on detailed analysis. It is probably correct that no simple theory of the operation of party politics can satisfactorily explain the economic decline of Britain, but an argument predicated on the dysfunctionality of the party system for the optimum management of the post-war economy would appear to rest on considerable evidence. But on the part of the governing parties in Britain there is now a marked reluctance to accept this thesis, and this for political ends.

The Left of the Labour party is anxious to dub the period from 1945 up to and including the Labour administrations of the 1970s as one in which the essential aims of socialism were consistently betrayed by right-wing parliamentarians, an analysis which sees a generation of such parliamentary leaders, stretching back to Attlee, as crypto-Tories. Such an argument is dialectically needed to buttress the Left's arguments for constitutional changes in the party, changes which would make the Parliamentary Labour Party the creature of Conference and produce detailed accountability of Labour MPs to the activists in the constituency parties. In such as argument the evidence of the results of adversarial politics is discounted to serve a wider ideological need. Much the same can be said of the present Conservative economic theoreticians, equally anxious to dub the period before 1979 as some sort of agreed and unquestioned Keynesian inflationary swamp, totally responsible for the present ills of the economy and representing thirty years of a consensus which refused to treat the economy according to monetarist and social market formulas. And. of course, a simplistic portrayal of the ills of two-party confrontational politics constitutes the basis on which the Social Democrat/Liberal Alliance constructs its main appeal to the electorate. All three scenarios are over-simplified – those of the main parties especially – as this book attempts to demonstrate, but that they have some political value which bears only a coincidental relation to the truth has been demonstrated beyond question in the recent history of all three parties. Hagiography is still a powerful force in British political argument. There have also been some non-political arguments, notably those of Richard Rose,[1] which have denied that the political process has had much significance in determining the post-war course of the British economy, identifying the determinants as economic cycles and other non-political forces which governments of whatever persuasion are unable to control. This is both true and a truism – there are those, for example, who are churlish enough to assert that the comparatively rapid economic growth of the 1950s and 1960s was based on cheap energy rather than on any success of Keynesian economics. But this still does not explain the laggardly performance of Britain compared with her international competitors who shared the same advantage, Rose's further denial of discountinuity in national policies attributable to the party system, his assertion that party government in Britain is characterized by the 'dynamics of a moving consensus', whereby an Opposition party usually only opposes a small proportion of the Bills introduced by the government and when returned to power accepts most of the measures which it opposed in Opposition, whilst decreasingly true, is hardly relevant to the formation and implementation of economic policy. Parliament, and the primary forms of parliamentary procedures, have played little if any major part in this process. In Britain perhaps only the areas of consumer protection and monopoly control have called Parliament and its legislative function into play.[2] In economic affairs the increasing specificity of government decisions entails wide discretionary powers and inevitably detracts from the functions of Parliament. Much of the economic activity of British government resembles foreign policy in that it is conducted under what John Locke called 'federative' powers, based on prerogative and involving negotiation and decision-making with interests essentially outside Parliament.

To do justice to this thesis, that there have been periods of 'good' government in post-war Britain in the sense of being attentive to prevailing economic circumstances, either international or inherited, which might be dubbed 'centrist' in the sense that it is difficult to imagine the Opposition doing otherwise, is adequately borne out by the facts. The best Keynesian expansionist government of the 1960s was that of Macmillan and Maudling form 1962; the most successful and effective monetarist regime, with public expenditure well in control, that of Wilson and Jenkins from 1967; the best post-OPEC oil-price rises regime that of Callaghan and Healey after 1976. But these were emergency administrations attempting to come to terms with the results of former indulgence. It would seem that governments in Britain, like many people, only act reasonably when all other courses of action have been exhausted. This analysis is supported by a thesis put forward by the American political economist, Douglas Ashford; that despite the generally adversarial nature of British politics, in times of stress the system has reacted to produce what he calls 'an elite consensus', which has concentrated decision-making in the Cabinet and the higher reaches of the civil service, acting independently of party pressure, excluding Parliament from the process, and in general dampening down the system. But this has been done at the expense of wider examinations of the deeper weaknesses and complexities of economic policy, in favour of creating a minimum degree of stability and continuity in government. That this sort of politics is now coming to an end so far as the Labour party is concerned (and there is considerable evidence of dissatisfaction with this style in the Conservative party) cast doubts on the possible continuance of agreements forced by circumstances and applied through independent leaderships in collaboration with the civil service.

The consequence of the almost total exclusion of Parliament from the processes of economic management will be touched on later. But since there has been a general tendency to shuffle off responsibility for failure on to the administration, it is worth while taking up some space to comment on the broad relations of the civil service with the system of adversary politics, and its general role in the management of the economy. The two lines of argument need to be separated.

So far as the first relationship is concerned, again it is difficult to gain a perspective, since this subject has also and inevitably become politicized. Politicians on all sides, as Professor H. A. Turner has commented[3] have demonstrated their dissatisfaction with the civil service as it exists. Devices, including the Fulton reorganization, have been numerous. Labour governments in the 1960s brought in a number of sympathetic economists. Mr Heath in 1970 set up the CPRS and Programme Analysis Review (PAR); Labour after 1974 attempted to reinforce political control by appointing 40 special advisers to ministers. Mrs Thatcher has brought in independent policy advisers and efficiency experts, and is in the process of adapting the Treasury to a monetarist economic view by a policy of selective promotion and in general taking tighter control of the First Division hierarchy. The civil service has not been insensitive to the lines of criticism, and has responded in a number of ways – accepting tighter control of public expenditure in the 1970s and new techniques of performance appraisal. But the general broad relations of the Service to the political process, and particularly to adversary politics, are complex. The imaginings of the Left of the Labour party, as exemplified by Mr Tony Benn and Mr Michael Meacher, who see First Division civil servants as natural class enemies, and accuse them of conspiracies to deradicalize Labour programmes and impede socialist policies, are easily dimissed. If anything, the contrary is the case, and the argument can be sustained that the civil service has been altogether too sensitive to the demands of adversary politics and has done too little to educate their political masters. One witness to this thesis is Sir Leo Pliatzky, who by virtue of his career as a leading Treasury official might be accused of *parti pris*. But he notes[4] that although civil servants rightly try to influence ministerial policy if they think it necessary, they do not attempt to mislead or obstruct, and that 'least of all do they attempt to argue against the carrying out of a clear political commitment'. But, as Pliatzky intimates, the civil service is inherently cautious, and scepticism has been reinforced by the evidence, briefly chronicled in this volume, of the relentless collapse of politically inspired policies which did not take account of real and unavoidable constraints on political action. It is all too predictable that the administration will be sceptical about new policies which are generated primarily by the essentially confrontational nature of British two-party politics. But as Pliatzky observes, 'It has sometimes seemed to me that in the early days of a new government, which has a mandate for such policies, Civil Servants are more liable, for constitutional reasons, to soft-pedal their doubts than to exaggerate the difficulties.' Pliatzky also states in defence of his view that the civil service is only too sensitive to party political direction, that U-turns in economic policy, some of them spectacular, can be explained always in the first instance by factors external to Whitehall, and only after that by reference to Whitehall's response to them. 'To believe otherwise seems to me to take a Berkeleyan view of events as depending on ideas, whereas the contrary is nearer to what happens.'

Pliatzky's thesis is echoed by David Shapiro of Brunel University, who states in a recent article, 'returning to the charge that the British Civil Service is notably unresponsive both to politicians nominally in control and to the general public, we need to balance this criticism against the opposite charge. Those who believe that many of Britain's ills stem from adversary politics must obviously argue that in practice the British Civil Service has been only too responsive to political direction. . . .There is a fairly obvious thesis that Britain's ills stem from the swings of the political pendulum.[5] He concludes, after a brief review of the U-turns and discontinuities in post-war British government, that 'what Britain has suffered from has been the confrontational nature of the political battle; and the Civil Service, so far from being too unresponsive to the politicians, would have done better in the general public interest to try to educate incoming governments about the merits of their predecessors' achievements . . . If the process of adversary politics has been so damaging to the country over a twenty-year period then it is fair to ask why the British Civil Service has shown so few signs of taking any initiative to try to damp down the effects of adversary politics. Could the Civil Service have tried more energetically to educate Oppositions?' Pliatzky warms to the same theme, pointing out that constitutionally at election time the process of policy-making is taken out of the government machine and handed over to the party machine, His contempt for the results is only thinly veiled. He also points out that an election in Britain is sudden death – there is no prolonged and educative hand-over period as in US Presidential elections. His conclusion is that whatever the faults of the Service, and the need for a greater diversification of experience amongst top officials, the achievement of which would be a long and difficult process, 'I do not believe that (training and career development) is in any way central to the present problems of the government of the United Kingdom. Whether we are to have another decade or two of discontinuity in government policy seems to me a much more serious matter.'

There is, however, a more fundamental criticism of the administration than the politically inspired one, which has little direct connection with the process of adversary politics. It requires attention, since it is an integral if not developed part of the arguments which have been deployed in Chapters 3 and 4 of this book. It has of late been most forcefully put by Professor Sidney Pollard in his *The Wasting of the British Economy*,[6] although it has run for some time as a strand in much of the criticism of post-war economic policy. It focuses on the Treasury, and the critique has already been touched on in Chapter 4. It has little to do with the politicization of institutions in Britain, but alleges a Treasury role in economic policy which draws on a too limited stock of responses, and particularizes the emphasis on the British inherited liberal political culture, which has been a marked feature of twentieth-century government. Major responsibility for Britain's economic decline is firmly traced by Pollard to the politician's preoccupation with the short term, a view which supports those of Hayward and Blank. It is, however, a fault which is not only traceable to the exigencies of the two-party system but to some basic predilection on the part of the political parties and the civil service, which has been reinforced by an odd attachment to macroeconomic theories. It has produced, in Pollard's view, a stagnation which has not arisen from any initial reluctance of industry to invest, or from resistance on the part of the unions. It is not surprising that this view has been confirmed by a number of otherwise unrelated observers, including John Eatwell from Britain and Douglas Ashford from the USA. It is an attitude which Pollard alleges has been maintained by governments in combination with the policies of the Treasury, supported by the Bank of England, and effectively acquiesced in by most professional economists, with their obsession with the larger macroeconomic parameters and their neglect of the micro-problems of industrial development and production. Preoccupation with the balance of payments, the rate of inflation, and latterly the money supply and the PSBR have led politicians and the Treasury essentially to solve successive crises in similar deflationary ways, neglecting the crucial long-term solution of expanding the national industrial base. All the devices with which we are familiar – the customary battery of measures used by successive governments: credit restrictions, cuts in public spending (usually at the expense of capital rather than current expenditure), direct controls, high interest rates – have cut down demand and production, with their greatest impact on investment. The process of deflation has been persistent, and in the long term has produced a vicious downwards spiral.

Yet to stay with the civil service, it is difficult not to conclude that Pollard is too scathing in his location of much of this process in the attitudes of the Treasury. It is true that the British higher civil service has been more receptive to macroeconomic arguments than many of its European counterparts – a phenomenon which this author finds difficult to explain. But to blame the Treasury exclusively for a reaction to circumstances which are largely political in origin is to some extent to misplace blame. For example, what created the conditions of the 1950s and the 1960s to which domestic deflation seemed to hard-pressed governments to be the only answer, the continuing external deficit induced by high overseas spending on defence, and the imperial nostalgia behind this deficit, shared by both parties, can hardly be blamed on the administration. Professor H. A. Turner has suggested, 'However much their continuity of restrictive policy contributed to the process of decay, the economic cycle created by the impact of the periodic pre- and post-electoral generosities demanded by politicians, and by their intervening withdrawal of these benevolences, combined with the disruptive pendulum of policy and counter-policy in such key areas as nationalisation, taxation, social insurance and labour law, have hardly created a stable climate for investment, collective bargaining and growth.'[7] Again it is the interplay of two-party politics on the British model which is discerned as a fundamental conditioning factor in the process of decline.

Yet doubts remain. Some basic antipathy in the British political and governmental system towards consistent and positive policies of state-led industrial investment and restructuring emerges from the analysis which has been made in this volume and elsewhere. John Eatwell, in his odd, gnomic, but penetrating analysis of what has gone wrong in Britain,[8] devotes a section to 'The Keynesian Ideology'. To summarize a complex argument, Eatwell traces the hold which Keynesianism has had on post-war politics and the administration alike, to an excessive reliance on the free market, which the nineteenth-century economic successes embedded in the political and economic culture of Britain. In Eatwell's words, whilst the power of the market can only be controlled by the state, inherited nineteenth-century attitudes have meant an abdication of economic power to the market. The state has never successfully and consistently impinged on the market organization of production. As Eatwell remarks, echoing Schonfield and Hayward, in France and Germany the role of the state has been quite different – in France through centralized authority, and in Germany through the power of the industrial banks. But Keynesianism, aided by the inability of the political parties in Britain to galvanize the liberal tradition into non-ideological modes of continuous state intervention, limited the role of government to the overall management of demand, leaving the industrial structure and the detailed composition of investment to the market. Not entirely, but the limited record of, say, the IRC or the NEB has been made apparent in Chapter 4 of this volume. It is in fact the case that the first Act of Parliament to authorize direct general intervention in the economy came in 1972 – Mr Heath's Industry Act, dangerously late in the post-war epoch and for which Mr Heath paid a large political penalty. The reliance on market mechanisms received a tremendous boost in 1979 from the onset of a superficial and misunderstood monetarism. On the face of it there is nothing in the doctrine of monetarism which precludes state intervention in the economy – it merely postulates a causal relationship over time between the money supply and the rate of inflation. Whilst admitting that most advocates of monetarism are free-market enthusiasts, the social market philosophy of the present administration derives more from an inherited strand of nineteenth-century ideology than from any macroeconomic theory. There is a case to be made, *à la* Eatwell, that during the war the Treasury was captured by Keynesian economists, and that this thinking predominated for the next twenty-five years or so. But it received massive support from political circles – largely, one suspects, because Keynesianism was the only doctrine which the political parties could agree upon without doing damage to their fundamental, and opposed, beliefs. Because they have not suffered to anything like the same extent from adversary politics in the economic sphere, Keynesian ideas and macroeconomic philosophies in general have had considerably less influence in France and Germany than in Britain. In both countries demand management has been fortified by policies designed to provide long-term protection against the short-term vicissitudes of the market. As Eatwell concludes, and as was indicated in more general terms in Chapter 1 of this book, 'The Keynesian ideology provided a comforting blanket into which the ideas and prejudices of 19th century Britain could snuggle. . . . More radical reforms to control and direct the market were unnecessary.'[9]

Much the same analysis, but one which, unlike Eatwell's, brings centrally into play the post-war political system, has been made by yet another American political economist, Douglas Ashford, in his analysis of *Politics and Policy in Britain: The Limits of Consensus*[10]. In his view, the Treasury's concentration on the larger parameters, in particular the control of public spending, has diverted it from the broader and more detailed examination of the economy that went on in most other West European countries in the 1960s and earlier. Until recently Keynesian doctrine prevailed and the Treasury's task was mainly to expand and contract aggregate demand. But Ashford goes on largely to exonerate the Treasury and to lay the charge where it always should lie, with the political system. About Keynesianism he remarks that all advanced industrial nations have had to devise monetary and fiscal instruments to stabilize prices and live in the interlinked world economy. 'What differentiates Britain from other European countries and Japan is how slowly changes in economic policy-making took place, and how reluctant political leaders were to re-examine the British economy. The temptation to place responsibility on the Treasury will not do even though there is evidence that the Treasury resisted proposals that might diminish its influence. From one perspective the Treasury has done a good job. But the more important questions concern ways of using public power to combat underlying economic and industrial weaknesses.'[11] He continues: 'The explanation goes much deeper than Treasury pride or even Ministerial competition. The political system does not create incentives to re-think economic policy. Ministers have their eye on the next election, and Treasury officials are pre-occupied, often with good reason, with the short-term. In this sense the pattern of economic policy-making and concentration on public spending fit well with the immediate political interests of Westminster and Whitehall.'

Few could doubt on the evidence that this analysis, and the similar judgements of Eatwell and Pollard, are correct. The damage to the economy in the post-war period which can be attributed to the factors which they note is incalculable but huge. But this is, in one sense, so much water under the bridge, were it not for the fact that the reasoning, and the system which underlies and conditions it, shows no sign of weakening – if anything it is intensifying. What is infinitely depressing is that the same deflationary policies were still largely followed in the 1970s and into the 1980s. And even in 1983, with North Sea oil on full stream, the payments side of the economy is still sensitive, with a massive adverse balance on non-oil exports. So feeble now is much of British industry that a rise of 2½ per cent in domestic demand in 1982, the result largely of wages rising faster than prices, was accompanied by a further fall in manufacturing output and a 5 per cent rise in imports – a result which ought to give the Labour Party pause, but manifestly doesn't. For this situation successive governments are largely to blame; their inability to prevent the de-industrialization of Britain by persistent and calculated programmes of investment and the diversion of resources to lame ducks and some state industries have produced a lack of competitiveness and a dependence on imports over a whole range of manufactures which should not have occurred, and which is quite impossible to reverse in the short term. It is frustrating however, to have had to watch a deliberate intensification of deflationary pressures over the last few years, brought about only partly as a result of economic constraints and embraced largely as a result of dependence on dubious macroeconomic theory. It is, in any case, time that the term monetarism ceased to be used in relation to the economic policy of the 1979 Conservative administration, since monetarism was never fully taken up and since 1981 has been progressively abandoned, in fact if not in rhetoric. The 1979 Conservative government's achievement has been drastically to reduce the rate of inflation, but whatever has caused the reduction it was not control of M_3 three years ago. On the mid-1983 state of the money supply, inflation, on monetarist theory, should be twice the present rate. Recent attempts to revise monetarist theory to accommodate this result appear to be rationalizations. Nevertheless initial money monomania gave Britain for some time ruinous interest rates and the resulting $2.40 pound. Together with the wages explosion of 1979–80, considered at the time economically irrelevant by the theoreticians, it is not surprising that much of industry either contracted or went to the wall.

It is now obvious that what we have been watching over the last few years is a classic deflationary phase of a Keynesian economic cycle, resting on restrictive monetary and fiscal policy and a reduction in the rate of growth of public spending, accompanied again, in fact if not in theory, by a covert incomes policy, the package mitigated after 1981 by large counter-cyclical expenditure, including maintaining the value of social benefits, allowing local councils to raise rates, and increasing expenditure to meet nationalized industry deficits. The unintended result, from the point of view of the neo-liberals, is that, as Samuel Beer has pointed out, the government 'has spent counter-cyclically with greater munificence than any since the war, including Labour ones'. There is little of monetarist theory at work here. There can be no doubt that a main factor in reducing inflation has been the relatively low level of wage settlements since 1981, especially in the public sector, and it is of course the sobering effect that high unemployment has had on claims in the private sector that has contributed to the fall. But to be fair to the government, if it has come to the case that many ministers see unemployment at the present level as the solution rather than the problem, it is justifiable to ask when it has been that the unions have ever admitted, or seem likely to admit, what is substantial responsibility for the growth in the money costs of industry which have helped to produce present unemployment levels.

But analysis is easier than prescription. It is fine to prescribe, as have many leading economists and politicians, that the rise of money costs to industry are to be restrained to the rate of possible growth in national output, and to ensure by budgetary and monetary control that demand rises at the same rate. This is merely to restate the aim of all post-war Western governments. But in few countries has the achievement of this aim been so mishandled as in Britain since the end of the 1950s, and the obstacles in the way of achievement, political, electoral, industrial, and social, have only grown more severe in Britain with the passage of time.

Whilst admitting the powerful nature of these constraints on policy, it is hard not to conclude that the 1979 Conservative administration over-reacted. Despite a few welcome signs of pragmatism, in the main a dogged adherence to simplistic macroeconomic and social market dogma still largely conditioned its responses. Given the proven difficulties of forecasting annual turn-outs, its attitude towards the PSBR has been unduly restrictive, and probably owed as much to anti-public sector prejudice as to economic calculation. To say this is not to endorse the Labour party's plans for the deficit, which are more seriously flawed. To adopt monetarist categories for the moment, given the massive excess of current unemployment over any Friedmanite 'natural level', it is highly unlikely that moderate reflation would bring about a wages explosion in the short to medium term, whilst the exchange rate could be relied on to absorb the impact of increased import costs. Yet the Treasury attitude appears to be that approvingly set out in a leader in *The Times* in 1983, a view which wholeheartedly supports a crude monetarist approach, to the effect that economic expansion is not worth risking, that any improved prospects for the economy 'should not be a cause of particular jubilation', and that (*sic*) 'since the Government cannot in the long-run do anything, except by improving the working of the labour market, to promote full employment anyway, it would be best if ministerial statements continue to emphasise that the main official economic responsibility is the provision of a sound currency'.[12] When such gross simplifications become the staple of economic argument there seems little that can be done. The raising of inaction to the status of a major virtue has had other effects on policy. There is the affront to intelligence and decency of an expensive unemployment pool at the same time that the national infrastructure deteriorates for want of an investment programme which would cost a fraction of the figure, and which would also benefit the private sector in the classic Keynesian manner and significantly reduce unemployment. The official argument against this, resting on a dubious theory of the crowding out of private by public investment, and fortified by an imprecise distinction between capital and revenue spending within the framework of the so-called PSBR rules, does not convince.

But if overkill has been the Conservative government's reaction, then not surprisingly, given the symbiotic relationships of the parties in the British adversary system, overkill in the opposite direction has been the response of the Labour party, which in the run-up to the June 1983 general election began to exhibit all the symptoms of the 'during the lifetime of one Parliament' syndrome which seems inseparable from the post-war conduct of British politics. The deficiencies of Labour's spending plans have been well aired, and need little discussion. Their highly inflationary implications in the absence of a rigorous incomes policy (discussion of which in the Labour movement having reached the status of the higher metaphysics) is established beyond argument, and admitted by some Labour leaders. It is not necessary to accept monetarist theory on the money supply before observing the marked contradiction between a massively expanded PSBR on the one hand and continuing low interest levels and competitive exchange rates on the other. Yet to expect caution and moderation from the Labour party, except in times of crisis, is, as this volume has shown, virtually to ask the impossible. The recent economic history of France should in any case emphasize the unwisdom of expansionary policies of this magnitude in the absence of corresponding initiatives by main trading partners. The TUC has realistically accepted this; so far it has not registered with the Labour party.

At present most economic discussion is concentrated on the demand side of the economy, how to increase demand in recessionary circumstances without increasing inflation, constituting further evidence of the British predilection for macroeconomic argument. But all recent evidence suggests that countries in the economic vanguard are those who have adapted to change, and who have not suffered industrial arthritis. There is still and will continue to be a need for a concentration on the supply side of industry. It is not sufficient only to influence the level of activity in the economy; there is a greater need than ever before to improve performance by influencing technical change, levels of productivity, and levels of investment, through a continuous industrial strategy which will be largely unaffected by political fluctuations. There is a negative, depressing and dead-end feel about the Conservative government's effort to improve the performance of the economy by lowering the level of activity; this reduction more than offsets the gains in productivity which have resulted from the shake-out of British industry. Official prescriptions give no indication of how higher employment based on falling inflation rates will actually be managed; presumably the market will cope and produce the required adaptations in the economy. But in a period of historically low profitability and relatively high interest rates this is unlikely. The structural rigidity which is imposed on industry by an inability to finance radical change was recognized in the 1982 Report of the OECD as a general phenomenon, with Britain identified as the worst case. Innovation, except in the case of small items like some consumer goods cannot now be undertaken by industry. Large projects, especially in the high technology sphere, and extending in Britain into major industries, cannot be developed to the profitable stage without help from government. In this situation, as Graham Searjent has remarked, increased demand alone will not necessarily produce the expected results, 'We cannot reverse the film through the projector to get the unemployed back into jobs'. Britain is now suffering more from a chronic shortage of production rather than from a shortage of demand. The spare capacity, of which there is now plenty, would fit imperfectly with the detailed profile of any future expansion of demand.

If the supply-side policies currently in force or proposed by the Opposition parties are examined, those of the Conservative government have been highly restricted, capricious, and inadequate, although there were a few welcome signs of flexibility after the replacement of Sir Keith Joseph as Industry Minister. The government's attitude to public sector investment, although softened in 1983–4, remains unduly restrictive; cuts in taxes on business costs have been too little and late, and business rates not yet touched. There are no guarantees, except for the small business sector, of low and stabilized interest rates. Direct government aid is largely restricted to new technology projects, where its record is confused and inconsistent, influenced by social market dogma, and, overall, inadequate. In the case of the British Technology Group, formed from the slimmed-down National Enterprise Board and the NRDC, there was in early 1983 a typical and dogmatic retreat from the sponsoring of high technology, largely based on doctrinal opposition to the NEB's entrepreneurial role as a major equity investor, which led to an accelerated sale of its holding. The NEB was denied the £100m. funding which it needed to make it self-financing, yet, capriciously, only a few months later, a larger, yet still inadequate by international standards, £250m. package of technological aid was announced, after the Alvey Committee had reported. So far as the rest of the private sector is concerned, consistent action has only been taken in the small business sector, which has attracted a disproportionate share of interest from an essentially Poujadist administration; where the financial outlay is, in any case, in Budget terms, 'negligible', and where there seems little realization that the success of small enterprise depends almost wholly on large enterprise. With the problems of the latter, the Conservative administration seems to have little sympathy; it should be remarked that in 1983 the Department of Industry's cash spending was severely reduced in other directions as part of the Treasury's attack on the department, the reductions relating to regional investment, support for Rolls-Royce and BL, and export aid, The starting-point for this strain of Treasury thinking seems to be that manufacturing only accounts for a quarter of jobs and 30 per cent of output, a view which discounts the fact that invisible earnings depend fundamentally on basic manufacturing trade. Otherwise, industrial policy seems only responsive to crisis situations. It would be laughable, if not inherently tragic, to have had to watch in 1983 an expensive rescue operation being mounted for the bankrupt machine-tool firm Alfred Herbert and its suppliers, by a specially appointed Minister for the West Midlands, when, for ideological reasons, the NEB was forced to sell the firm in 1979 with a modernization programme only half completed.

But the alternative proposed by the Labour party in the run-up to the 1983 election inspired no confidence. The party had apparently learned so little from past experience as to make the Bourbons seem exemplars of adaptation and flexible innovation. The programme combined all the failed or rejected policies of the 1960s and 1970s, conflating the National Plan with all Stuart Holland's later prescriptions, the whole a towering edifice of Planning Ministries, Boards, five-year comprehensive Plans, statutory planning agreements, widepread nationalization, and detailed union participation at every level of economic and social activity, all a paradigm of a socialist corporate state. Whilst admitting that under-investment is the most critical feature of the British economy, the programme made no attempt to answer the questions, what sort? where? and at what return? Money, in large quantities, was to be thrown at everything in sight.

Britain needs to invent no new institutions – it needs a more stable political context to enable the successful instruments which have abounded in the past to function to capacity over a longer term than the two-party system has so far permitted. The NEDC is still a potentially powerful agency of industrial analysis; the NEB and the IRC in their former pragmatic roles are there as exemplars. Market-oriented intervention backed by new sources of investment funds, and free from ideological overtones, is what the economy cries out for. It is ironic that Professor Sir Douglas Hague has recently discovered some merit in the short-lived IRC of the late 1960s,[13] which apart form its main industrial thrust played a role in improving management standards and relationships between government, industry, and the City. Britain is the only country in Europe without some scheme for long-term and stable finance of industry, and there is a strong case for the concept of a state-funded industrial bank, along the lines the IRC was developing before it was disbanded for ideological reasons. Some control of financial markets for industrial purposes has been the key to much of the relative success of Britain's main industrial competitors, and need not imply nationalization, with all its accompanying political turmoil.[14]

The programme which most closely approximated this analysis in the the 1983 election was that of the Alliance, with an accompanying emphasis on the political change needed for longer-term stability. But the analysis has to withstand the criticism that it essentially looks backwards rather than forwards – that is is, in the words of Ralf Dahrendorf's jibe, seeking 'a better yesterday'. It has been said that the Alliance programme was the most intellectually conservative of the three parties in the last election – odd, when the Labour manifesto was a catalogue of antique grievances and its economic reasoning was suspect. But the Alliance proposals were more modest, pragmatic, and on their own terms more rigorous than the intellectual shoddiness of the era of the National Plan. They were in any case consistent – present Conservative policies are an intellectual mess, propped up by a social policy which owes more to class prejudice than any other factor. Criticism of Alliance polices rests on the mistaken assumption that there are further and as yet untried solutions to Britains's economic plight; the short answer is that they don't exist – the stock of responses provided by economic theory is very small. The only new policy on offer is that of the extreme Liberals, based on an innate mistrust of corporatism and centralism and a willing acceptance of a low- or no-growth economy, plus some vague sentiments concerning community rather than economic values. But for a trading nation such as Britain no-growth is not a stable option, nor is there much evidence of support for the social philosophy which accompanies this analysis.

That there is a need for a wider and more sophisticated debate on economic policy than the present political system can secure is self-evident. But this is not likely to come from the central institution of representative government, the House of Commons, which can only act as the focus and quintessence of the two-party system. Its deficiencies as a forum for economic debate have long been obvious, and its basic legitimacy and relevance are now bound to be called into question when it so inadequately reflects the wishes of voters. The secrecy and lack of public debate which surrounds the operation of government in Britain has been most noticeable in the sphere of economic policy. Post-war policies of demand management were formulated and asserted by technicians, largely the Treasury and the Bank of England. The change in macroeconomic policy in the 1970s to a qualified monetarism was achieved again largely without fundamental political debate, and certainly without any evidence of deep parliamentary understanding of what the changes entailed. Major micro-policies similarly have been the product of extra-parliamentary activity – the few instances of parliamentary involvement, of pre-presentation, have seldom resulted in thorough appraisal, partly through economic ignorance and partly since the policies required no legislative endorsement.[15] For economic planners, such as Andrew Shonfield, the problems presented themselves as essentially technical, and Parliament was an afterthought. The situation might be thought to have improved with the installation of the Commons' Select Committee system in 1979, which for the first time gave the House a specialized economic forum in the Treasury and Civil Service Committee. Yet a positive economic policy critique still has to emerge from this agency, although its work in the field of theoretical explanation is notable. But in common with other committees attempting to integrate their membership into a common approach in a period when two-party political attitudes have seldom been so polarized, its limitations have emerged clearly.[16] The committee has in any case confined itself to macroeconomic analysis – the more important supply side of the economy has been ignored, although the Trade and Industry Committee has now tentatively ventured into this field.

About the routine occasions which pass for economic debates on the floor of the House of Commons, the less said the better. Their infantile character has grown worse of late. The only mode of parliamentary economic discourse is now charge and countercharge, accusation and rebuttal. It reflects the degradation of politics which the economic crisis has produced – a general urge to find simplistic macro-systemic explanations and prescriptions, whether from the Marxist inheritance of the Left or the neo-Liberalism of the Right; a fruitless search for overarching theories which deny complexity, exalt simplicity, run counter to pluralism and diversity, deny the potential of other, richer traditions, and which in their language and metaphors degrade political and economic debate. But these characteristics have always been latent in the post-1945 political system. Constitutional change, especially a different electoral system, is needed not to facilitate a technocracy free from political control, but to revitalize the liberal tradition and make possible more genuine debate on the political requirements for economic regeneration.

These conclusions emerge smoothly from the analysis – too smoothly, since it has always underestimated the strength of the political power structure which it aims to change. The most regressive element in this structure has in the last generation been the Labour party and its trade union link, which has been a burden on the sinews of the economy. But there is now clear evidence that British society is recognizing that the world of the future, a world of weakening class loyalties and economic uncertainties, demands a different political structure to deal with it. But the realization is probably too late. The process of political realignment in Britain should have begun in the early 1960s, after the failure of Gaitskell's attempted reform of the Labour party. The secular decline of Labour, which has been masked by the operation of the electoral system, would have accelerated if the Conservatives had won the 1964 election, which, with a different leader, they might well have done. But the system was given a new lease of life, underpinned by the analyses of such writers as Samuel Beer, who signally failed to recognize the deeper movements in British society and the economy which were gathering pace. Their recantations have come too late – it seems in truth that the owl of Minerva flies at dusk.

Some concluding words on the British political structure and its economic implications. To hold the present much-touted view concerning a breakdown of consensus is to ignore a number of factors. In particular it is to fly in the face of the slow-moving mechanisms of social response and administration, which are subject to the inertia of tradition. The views of party activists look very different from the intimations of the man in the street. But Britain suffers from a closed political process, probably the most élitist and unresponsive in the West, whether one considers parliamentary candidate selection, the oligarchical structure of the unions, or the operation of an electoral system which guarantees unrepresentative government, grossly magnifies swings in electoral opinion, exaggerates class and regional divisions, facilitates access to political power of favoured but unrepresentative interest groups, and operates powerfully and viciously on popular consciousness. The counter-productiveness of such a system cannot be exaggerated – it signally fails to realize the potential of the British liberal tradition, which, despite the battering it has received in the post-war period, still survives as a basis for national revival. But it is not surprising that the peculiarly closed British political arrangements have produced poorer economic results than other, more open, if unruly, political societies.

That the system has long contained the seeds of economic failure has been obvious to this author for some considerable time. But the pace of decline is now accelerating. An American, Douglas Ashford, ends his survey of Britain, which is essentially a prolonged critique of the cramped character of British political processes, with the observation that Britain is faced with 'the painful process of rebuilding societal consensus or radically restructuring the nature of elite consensus'. Roughly translated into English, the choice is either electoral reform or an emergency national government produced by economic crisis. The former is postponed indefinitely. From the standpoint of 1983, the latter seems the more likely.

Part B

A. M. GAMBLE

During the 1970s two of the most prominent interpretations of British politics were the adversary politics thesis and the corporatist thesis. Their estimates of what was most important in determining the pattern of British politics contrasted sharply. The corporatist thesis suggested that institutional bases of power outside Parliament were now much more important than anything which occured within Parliament itself for the formulation and implementation of policy. On this view the adversary rituals and adversary rhetoric of Parliament only succeeded in diverting attention away from the process of bargaining between the central bureaucracy and the major producer groups and the highly organized management of public opinion which were now the cornerstones of modern government, and which ensured a high degree of continuity in practice between administrations, however much the parties threatened discontinuity in their manifestos and on the floor of the House.

The strength of corporatist institutions and techniques helped promote an extensive literature in the 1960s on the decline of Parliament and what was required to reform it. Many argued that MPs should play a much greater role in the dialogue between government and the producer interests. A corporatism with a parliamentary rather than a bureaucratic bias was the objective. Few argued against corporatism as such.

The adversary politics thesis, however, followed a quite different line. It drew attention to the time bomb at the heart of British democracy, which decades of developing corporatism had failed to remove. The British political system has long been praised for its record in producing strong governments. Since 1900 minority administrations have had to be formed after general elections only in 1910, 1923, 1929, and 1974. This has much to do with the British electoral system which provides a loose and at times highly erratic distribution of seats in relation to votes. Few governments have been formed with even a majority of the votes cast – only one government (the National Government in 1931) has had more than 60 per cent of the vote. Every government formed since 1945 has been elected on a minority of the votes cast and a still smaller minority of the electorate. And in recent elections the number of those failing to vote has often come near to exceeding the number of those voting for the winning party.

The system has long been justified on the grounds that electing a Parliament involves at the same time electing an executive. The organization of mass parties has ensured that the electorate is presented with a clear choice between two rival sets of leaders and policies. Since general elections are held to be about electing a government and not about reflecting opinion in the electorate, the occasionally huge disparity getween votes cast and seats won is considered a small price to pay for safeguarding the election of strong party governments, avoiding the necessity either for coalitions or for weak minority administrations.

For such a system to work, however, certain political conditions are necessary which are not spontaneously generated by the mechanisms of party politics. Since each new government's decisive parliamentary majority is only at best a bare electoral majority and usually a substantial minority, serious problems for political stability could arise if governments took full advantage of their position. The extraordinary concentration of powers in Britain gives overwhelming advantages to the party in government. Very few restrictions exist on the unfettered exercise of party rule. Apart from controls which the courts and the House of Lords may impose there are remarkably few checks on the government if it has a secure majority in the Commons. The major check is the holding of general elections every five years, which at least creates the prospect that those exercising the powers of the executive can be replaced.

It is precisely because general elections are the main constitutional check to unlimited power that the danger of adversary politics arises. For if the government were to change hands frequently the possibility clearly exists for a wild oscillation between the policies and style of successive administrations. For the British system to deliver political stability and reasonable continuity in policy, as well as strong government, it is neccessary either that the government never changes hands or that there is a substantial consensus in practice between the parties on the priorities of policy. If political stability is to be maintained then the electorate can be offered an effective choice between teams of leaders but not between policies. This is the paradox of the adversary system. In order to establish the credibility of their leaders the parties present themselves as adversaries on policies, but if these adversary positions were to be translated directly into policy then government could become chaotic. The degree of political conflict unleashed could make the country ungovernable.

This is the adversary nightmare. If the leadership groups in the main political parties were ever to begin taking their adversary rhetoric seriously, a real rather than a symbolic polarization would occur in British politics. The concentration of powers enjoyed by governments under the British constitution would be used to further 'narrow', 'partisan', 'ideological' programmes at the expense of continuity or consensus.

What the adversary politics thesis reminds us is that the maintenance of corporatist institutions and techniques as a way of handling problems of managing the economy, and defusing major social and political conflicts, depended upon the acceptance by the two main parties of a consensus on policy priorities and policy objectives – the acceptance therefore of constraints on their freedom to implement party policies. So long as parties were prepared to operate in this manner the British political system looked immensely strong and stable. But it was always dependent on certain special circumstances. If either of the two major parties ceased to behave within the constraints of the parliamentary conventions the consensus would collapse, incoming governments would seek to reverse major measures passed by their predecessor, and major social and political upheavals could occur. A potentially devastating cycle of adversary elections, adversary parliaments, and adversary governments might ensue.

This account conflicts markedly with the heroic view of democratic politics expressed so forcefully by Margaret Thatcher at the 1979 Conservative Party Conference: 'Those who voted Conservative know the principles we stand for. We have every right to carry them out and we shall.' This view, more common on left than right, sees parties uniting around a programme which reflects their basic values, campaigning on that programme, and having won popular endorsement, using the coercive machinery of the state to implement it. Parties are regarded as instruments of the popular will, translating the views and opinions of the majority into legislation. Without adversary conflict and a clear difference between parties the electorate would be disenfranchised, unable to influence the content of government policy.

The main problem with this account is that in a simple plurality voting system where governments are regularly elected on a minority of votes, and still smaller minorities of the electorate, the possibility arises that governments acquire the right to implement policies supported by only a minority, and strongly opposed by another minority, or even the majority of the electorate. If this occurs, a major threat to political stability might arise. The attempt to pursue a minority mandate backed by a parliamentary majority may produce extra-parliamentary resistance from the institutions and forces threatened by it. Even Governments backed by majority mandates cannot always secure the acceptance of legislative changes by those groups most affected by them. The theory of pure popular sovereignty would only apply if electoral verdicts were unanimous or were accepted by all citizens as binding. But they are neither. Instead the terrain on which any democratically elected government operates is structured by the institutional and social organization of the state and civil society. Elections never wipe the slate; they can, at best confirm trends and help change a particular balance of forces and create new opportunities for change and movement.

This is why an adversary cycle is potentially so destabilizing. Its potential for harm has been concealed in Britain for so long because of the time it took Labour to establish itself as an equal electoral force to the Conservatives. During the inter-war period Britain experienced not a true two-party system but a dominant-party system. The Conservatives polled more votes than any other party in every election and only the Conservatives were able to form majority governments. The two minority Labour adminstrations lasted only for short periods and were unable even if they had wished to implement radical measures. The continuity of policy over the period was certainly not hindered by the party system.

Since 1945, however, a true two-party system has been in operation. The strength of the two main parties between 1945 and 1983 was very evenly balanced and the government has changed hands after only small swings of electoral opinion. There was a prolonged political stalemate, which neither party succeeded in breaking until 1979, although both at times seemed on the brink of doing so. In the early phase between 1945 and 1959 only one change in government took place and the major changes in policy and institutions achieved during the 1940s were generally accepted. After 1959, however, this compromise between the parties weakened, the failure of key government policies was widely recognized and no government until 1983 managed to secure re-election after serving a normal term of office. The alternation of parties in government through the 1960s and 1970s began to reveal the hidden potentiality of the adversary system.

In the 1970s and particularly after the Heath government had lost the February 1974 election after fighting on a 'Who Governs?' platform there was an outburst of writing about the ills of the British political system. Much of it stemmed from panic about the growing strength of the Left in the Labour party and rising industrial militancy. The Labour movement no longer seemed prepared to play the role allotted to it in the two-party system. The adversary politics thesis was formulated at this time, often betraying a stong anti-Labour bias. Some of the converts to it and the associated remedy of electoral reform lost their enthusiasm once Conservative party fortunes were restored after 1979. Elective dictatorship was only a problem when the wrong dictatorship was elected. Nevertheless the adversary politics thesis deserves serious consideration because it draws attention to neglected effects of the party system on policy and on how democracy operates. At its core is the insistence that parties do make a difference to the way policies are formulated and still more to which policies are carried out. How well do its claims stand up?

It is clear that in many of its formulations the adversary politics thesis has suffered from the exaggerated rhetoric which it condemns in the adversary style of party politicians. When the whole field of economic policy is surveyed and not merely selective aspects then the evidence suggests more continuity than discontinuity in economic policy – overwhelmingly so in the period between 1945 and 1959, but also in the period 1959–83. The adversary politics thesis in its well-known version exaggerates the role of parties in policy formulation and implementation and underplays the role of other bodies and institutions, and still more the constraints which circumstances, administrative procedures, events, and outside forces impose on any government. The politics of power is very different from the politics of support and one of the main results of parliamentary democracy in Britain is to produce leadership groups in the main political parties which learn how to manage the pressures that stem from their parties and from interest groups in the light of their understanding of what is practicable in government. They work within the prevailing consensus. The operation of the British political system tends to select those who are willing to fill this role and to exclude those who are not. There have been major politicans such as Tony Benn and Enoch Powell who have refused in part to play this role. Both were forced to the margins of their parties. More typical of British politicians was Anthony Crosland who led the resistance in Cabinet to the 1976 cuts on the grounds of his ideological principles and of the opposition of the Labour party. But while he argued strongly against the Treasury case he was anxious his arguments should be considered serious and responsible by the Treasury since he wanted to be viewed as a future Chancellor. He was therefore gratified to learn that the Treasury did regard him as their most formidable opponent in Cabinet, and he achieved this because he was arguing within the circle of their own intellectual assumptions.[17] Such assumptions necessarily include calculations of what can and cannot be done based upon a knowledge of the reaction of the agents in key markets and key institutions to particular policies and decisions.

From the outside, British economic policy since the war appears to be shaped by a bipartisan consensus. On the crucial issues of foreign economic policy the debates occurred within the parties not between the parties. The rejection of imperial preference and a neutralist foreign policy ensured that both parties adhered to the post-war system of alliances, the linchpin of which was the alliance with the United States. Integration of the British economy into the new American-dominated world economy was the single most important development of post-war British economic policy and at no time did it become a contentious issue between the parties. The broad lines of policy on the movement of goods, of capital, and of labour have in practice not been challenged by the parties in government. The main exception would appear to be policy concerning the EEC, though here again on careful examination the major disputes occurred within the parties rather than between them. In government the party leaderships of both parties become firmly committed to the EEC. The only elections before 1983 in which the EEC appeared as an issue sharply dividing the parties was in 1974. Labour campaigned on a pledge to 'renegotiate' the terms of entry and put the result to a national referendum. This was much less than a straight pledge to withdraw. Only in 1983 was there a true adversary division on the issue, and in that election the adversary divide extended further than before.

The continuity of the main lines of foreign economic policy was a major factor shaping both stabilization policy and industrial policy. In an economy as open as the British and as dependent on world trade the basic choice as to the nature of integration into the world economy conditioned all other policies. It ensured the effective abandonment of full-employment policy as early as 1947. Full employment was maintained through the next twenty years though not primarily because of the government's policy stance but because world conditions facilitated it. Inflation and the balance of payments were the policy targets to which governments gave greatest attention. When the boom slackened and unemployment began to rise governments acquiesced in it. There is only one occasion when the economy was deliberately reflated to reduce unemployment. That was in 1972–3, but even then not higher employment but faster growth was the real purpose behind the budgetary measures.

Keynesianism as a style of policy belonged to the era of the long boom and fixed exchange rates. Stabilization policy in this period whichever party was in power was obsessed with keeping down domestic costs and maintaining a surplus on the balance of payments. The two were closely linked with one another as well as to policy on the exchange rate for sterling. The displacement of Keynesianism by monetarism as the preferred intellectual framework of stabilization policy for major national governments and for the international institutions has to be grasped in relation to the ending of the long boom and the collapse of the system of fixed exchange rates. The weakening of many of the factors that had made such a long period of expansion possible, in particular cheap and plentiful labour, major new investment opportunities, cheap raw material and energy costs, and a stable international financial and trading system, greatly increased inflationary pressure, and made a stabilization policy aimed at containing inflation while avoiding a major slump, the chief international concern. The enforcement of the new rules for international stabilization came primarily from the international financial markets. Governments were forced to adapt their internal policies to avoid currency collapse, and currency collapse had to be avoided if national economies were to remain integrated into the world economy.

When the rhetoric is stripped away the continuity of policies in most areas is what is striking, although at all times accompanied by ritual conflict over certain policies. This suggests a much more minor role for the parties in influencing policy than is claimed either by politicians or by some proponents of the adversary politics thesis. But it would be wrong to conclude that because the adversary politics thesis overstates the role of parties in policy-making that parties have no role at all. The adversary politics thesis is unsatisfactory because too often it strikes the wrong target. It generalizes from a few instances of flagrant discontinuity to the whole of policy-making. It reflects fears about the potential damage an unrestrained adversary system would unleash rather than the actual harm it does.

Even in its flawed form, however, it manages to highlight a number of features of policy-making in Britain. The indictment of adversary politics is greatly strengthened when the full effects of the party system on policy are considered. What is so characteristic of adversary politics in Britain is that so often it is a sham. The parties are not real adversaries at all and the choices they offer the electorate are imaginary. The adversary conflict is sharpest over a number of issues such as the rival merits of public and private ownership but almost non-existent in many other fields, particularly foreign economic policy. The issues which generate most adversary heat such as steel nationalization were often given quite disproportionate importance. They became ideological totems which concentrated debate into well-worn channels. The adversary politics system was certainly functional for holding together two monolithic, tightly disciplined party organizations in the House of Commons. It was much less adept at providing serious detailed opposition to government policy and exploration of alternatives. It helped to concentrate responsibility for policy-making in a tiny circle of top officials and the two rival cabinet teams of the political parties.

The main problem with this system was not that it destroyed continuity of policy but that it discouraged a wide-ranging debate about policy because of the fear that the two-party consensus might be undermined. An alternative to the adversary model of parliamentary politics and policy-making would have been a broader policy-making process which gave opportunities to a much wider range of groups, interests, and opinions to participate openly in the formulation of policy within a constitution safeguarding major political and social rights, and the formal separation of powers between branches and levels of government. The British policy-making machinery has always been highly secretive and confined to a small number of participants. Pressure groups have operated in this system but often covertly. The ability of Parliament to scrutinize civil service decisions and ministerial appointments has lagged far beyond their increasing scope and scale. There has been a steady drift to centralized control of local government. The leaderships of the two main parties have connived at protecting arrangements which give a monopoly of formal power to the party forming the government because under the adversarial system each has the expectation of forming the government at regular intervals.

External observers are often surprised at how centralized power is in democratic, pluralist Britain, and at how few individuals are expected to be legitimately involved in making policy. The élites in the civil service, in business, in politics, and in the universities are sealed from one another to a remarkable degree – interchange between different sectors remains very small. The civil service is permanent and has the specific task of advising on policy and drawing up options, while ministers tend to be extremely ill-prepared when they enter government, in part because they spend so much of their time in opposition engaged in the adversary rituals they find so diverting. Continuity of policy except in a few important instances has not suffered because the pressure for consensus is so strong, and because scrutiny and evaluation of policy have been consisitently weak, and major new initiatives such as the supply-side policies of the 1960s have foundered because the wider political conditions for ensuring success were neglected.

Adversary politics in Britain has helped to maintain a stalemate on policy. The two teams of leaders have engaged in ritual conflict over certain potent ideological symbols centred on the dividing line between the public and private sectors. Other issues have hardly been politicized at all although often they are of much greater importance for determining the direction of economic policy.

The strength of the adversary system in the past was that while the ideological differences between the parties were deep-seated, both parties were prepared to co-operate in making the constitution work and ensuring reasonable stability and continuity of policy. Churchill expressed this after the Conservatives' narrow election victory in 1951:

> We meet together here with an apparent gulf between us as great as any I have known in fifty years of House of Commons life. What the nation needs is several years of quiet steady administration, if only to allow socialist legislation to reach its full fruition. What the House needs is a period of tolerant and constructive debating on the merits of the questions before us without every speech on either side being distorted by the passions on one Election or the preparation of another . . . Controversy there must be on some of the issues before us, but this will be a small part of the work and interests we have in common.[18]

This idea that each government was bound by the major decisions of its predecessor and that the Conservatives in 1951 had a duty not to reverse socialist legislation but to allow it to come to full fruition, was the essential restraint necessary to allow the system to function. Even in the 1950s when the two main parties were receiving over 90 per cent of the vote, no party was securing on its own even a bare majority of the votes – shares of the electorate were still smaller.

The decline in electoral support for the two major parties and in the authority of the party leaders over their parliamentary followers, and in the case of the Labour party over their supporters in the constituencies, underlined just how important were the conventions that led the party leaders voluntarily to produce the constraints that the constitution did not supply. At the same time the repeated failures of government after 1959 to attain their objectives helped make voters less partisan in their attachment to either of the two main parties and highlighted the arbitrary character of the mandates which each party government claimed.

The *potential* for a dramatic polarization of the parties on major issues and the pursuit of radical programmes which were supported even formally by only a minority of voters, emerged starkly.

Complaints about the effects of adversary politics have come from democratic as well as antidemocratic opinion. The antidemocratic argument reiterates the traditional fear of what may ensue if governments are no longer elected by a restricted franchise – the plundering of the rich by the poor. The entry of the masses remains a disturbing spectre for many antidemocrats and the idea that the procedures of democracy might legitimately produce a government committed to radical change is anathema. The containment of the 'masses' and more particularly the masses as represented by and organized in the Labour movement has long been a central objective of Conservative statecraft, an objective which has been substantially achieved.

There is also, however, a powerful democratic critique of adversary politics. Here the objection is not to political conflict and radical challenge, but to the narrow way in which political power is won, policies formulated, and mandates claimed for particular courses of action. The problem with the two-party adversary system in Britain is that it gives a monopoly of the right to formulate and initiate policy to the party which wins a majority of the parliamentary seats. This is dangerous for democracy when the party that forms the government enjoys only minority support in the electorate. The legitimacy of government is eroded and resort to extra-parliamentary action from those adversely affected by the government's policies becomes more likely. Governments committed to radical policies are certain to meet such resistance. The conditions under which radical changes may nevertheless be accepted peacefully are complex and cannot be explored here, but they certainly require as a minimum that the building of consent to a programme of radical change has gone beyond the active members of the governing political party and has created a coalition of interests, actively involved in its formulation.

In modern democracies, extra-parliamentary resistance to government policies is commonplace but it rarely reaches the point of open defiance of the law and the authority of the government. The system of adversary politics makes such challenges more likely because it tends to produce governments elected on a minority vote who nevertheless monopolize the authority of government and claim a mandate for policies whose formulation had generally involved a tiny fraction of the community. In this way adversary politics can contribute to a social and political polarization which might lead ultimately to the destruction of democratic institutions. Many feared that Britain in the 1970s was locked into such a cycle.

The 1983 election has interrupted this cycle, at least temporarily. It is the first time since 1959 that a government has been re-elected after serving a full term. The pattern of the parties alternating in government every five years has been broken. Furthermore the two-party system has been decisively weakened because of the electoral gap between the two main parties. The Conservatives had a final lead over Labour of fifteen percentage points, the largest gap at any election since the war.

This election result removes any reason for discontinuity in policy stemming from the party system. It is possible that as in the inter-war period the opposition to the Conservatives may remain fragmented and this may allow the Conservatives to rule uninterruptedly. A new dominant-party system would replace the two-party system of the post-war years and worries about adversary politics causing arbitrary shifts in policy and creating a climate of uncertainty for business investment would disappear. It has always seemed self-evident to partisans of one party that the best way to ensure continuity in policy is to have rule by their party.

The drawbacks of the adversary two-party system however would not disappear. Its more flagrant disadvantages would no longer be on display but the underlying problems of British government – the narrowness of policy-making and the lack of regular and effective review and assessment of policy – would remain and would probably be exacerbated. Dominant-party systems are often insulated from effective criticism and become inert and unresponsive to new problems.

The result may be to encourage a much sharper polarization of politics in the future. A foretaste of this was provided by the 1983 election itself. The gulf between the parties' programmes was wider than at any election since the war. In all three areas of economic policy – foreign economic policy, stabilization policy, and industrial policy – there were major divergences. If Labour had won the 1983 election and carried through its programme there would have been a major break in economic policy – much more profound than the minor adjustment carried through in 1979. Since the Conservatives and their allies were completely opposed to many of the items of Labour's alternative economic strategy extra-parliamentary resistance would have been particularly fierce.

Labour did not however win the 1983 election, so whether it would have provided a more radical government than previously cannot be known. But the capacity of the adversary system under certain conditions to promote not consensus, stability, and continuity, but conflict, instability, and discontinuity has been abundantly demonstrated. Such special conditions were created in Britain in the 1960s and 1970s by the failure of successive governments to arrest economic decline. Despite extremely favourable circumstances the British parties failed to create the conditions for a successful modernization strategy. This failure permitted the polarization of opinion within and eventually between the parties to develop, and this weakened the legitimacy of government and of the two major parties.

The operation of the adversary system certainly contributed to this failure, both because initiatives were not sustained over long enough periods and because policies in some fields were too frequently reversed, but more fundamentally because the assumptions underlying so much of British economic policy and in particular the proper relations between state and industry were never challenged politically. The reforms that were needed were understood in a mechanical technocratic manner as changes to be introduced and imposed by governments, rather than as reforms which simultaneously altered forms of social organization. The attempt at modernization failed because the wider political and social conditions essential for its success were never created. There was a cruel mismatch between the expectations politicians aroused and what they were able to deliver.

The dashing of hopes of modernization encouraged new thinking on both right and left and radical programmes emerged which questioned the whole pattern of post-war state intervention and welfare spending.

Both Left and Right became antistatist in their thinking and strategy. So far the Right has accomplished this task with much greater success, since the post-war consensus on state management of the economy and welfare was always more strongly identified with Labour than with the Conservatives. With the growing ascendancy of the New Right in the party the Conservatives have learnt how to detach themselves from the old consensus with the result that it is the New Right which has so far won the battle to determine the agenda and the criteria for handling the severe problems of world recession and economic restructuring in Britain.

The dilemma for the Labour Left is that it owed its growing strength in the 1970s to the evident failings of Labourism and its critique of the statism of post-war social democracy, but its own alternative economic strategy as diluted in party policy documents often appeared little more than a restatement and extension of traditional statist Labour policies. The circumstances in which the modernization strategy failed revealed the weakening of Labourism and of the cohesion and solidarity of the traditional Labour movement. The profound restructuring of the British economy in process in the 1970s and 1980s ensured that the traditional bases of the Labour movement would no longer be enough to achieve a Labour electoral majority. This was confirmed in stark terms by the 1983 election result.

The future shape of British politics will depend on whether the Conservative government can continue to manage the process of economic decline with the skill and good fortune it enjoyed in its first term of office, but also on the state of the oppostion to its policies. Under the present electoral system the most likely outcome of the continued fragmentation of the opposition to Conservatism is Conservative domination of British politics for a long period, as occurred between 1886 and 1906 and between 1919 and 1940.

Two other electoral alternatives are however possible. If the Alliance maintains its challenge as a third party and begins to erode the Conservative vote while the Labour vote does not decline further then one or perhaps a series of hung parliaments become likely at some stage. This would create a very different political terrain. It might lead after a short period of instability and minority government to renewed Conservative hegemony, or it might create new parliamentary cross-party alliances, able to carry through major constitutional changes and leading to further political realignment.

A third possiblity is that one of the opposition parties emerges as the clear and undisputed focus of opposition to the government. If the Alliance were to achieve this and if it gained a parlimentary majority then it would be able to introduce constitutional reforms and the two-party system of adversarial politics would be destroyed. If the Labour party, however, re-establishes itself as a credible challenger for government office again then the two-party adversarial system may well gain new life.

The pressures on the Labour party after the 1983 election to reorganize itself as a moderate centre party resuming its traditional adversarial role as HM Opposition were considerable. This is because playing the adversary two-party game remains the easiest route for Labour to return to government office. Since the present electoral system rewards electoral minorities with parliamentary majorities and a monopoly of executive power it fosters the illusion that if only Labour had the right leaders and the right policies the election of a Labour government would ensure the first steps in the establishment of socialism.

There are many on the Labour Left who now argue on grounds of democratic principle that the electoral system should be reformed because it has become unfair and unrepresentative. But such arguments lack force because Labour has acquired a vested interest in perpetuating the present system. Those who justify the present electoral system argue, sometimes in terms reminiscent of the opponents of the 1832 Reform Bill, that there is no perfect electoral system because every electoral system must perform different functions – the election of a government, the representation of the electorate, and the representation of particular communities and interests. Proportional representation it is claimed can produce a less democratic result than the two-party system because it allows politicians rather than the electorate the freedom to negotiate which parties should form the government and what its policies should be. But this only highlights the fact that reforming the electoral system is only one of a number of reforms which would need to be introduced if democracy in Britain is to be strengthened and extended. The present two-party system does not prevent policy bargaining between politicians – it merely confines it normally to the secret and informal processes within the two major parties which out of electoral necessity are broad coalitions, only loosely united on principles and objectives.

The precedent of the Thatcher Government is often used in praise of the two-party adversary system. Here is a government, it is said, which has not indulged in sham but real adversary politics. After a leader sympathetic to the New Right in the party had been elected in 1975, the party committed itself to a radical programme which it then proceeded to act upon once it was returned to government in 1979. What Labour needs, it is sometimes argued, is a conviction politics to rival that of Margaret Thatcher.

Such a view seriously mistakes the terrain on which Labour operates. If the two main parties ever became genuine adversaries the system would cease to be workable. It is only workable so long as both parties are prepared to maintain a 'consensus' over most areas of policies. The need for such a consensus which is not genuine agreement but a practical accommodation to the realities of governing is a fundamental requirement of the way the British system works. It is sustained by many public institutions especially the political parties and the media. It constantly narrows debate, conferring legitimacy on a very narrow band of opinion, and labelling everything which falls outside this band extremist.

In this closed and elitist political system the Labour Left faces an immense task in being accepted as a legitimate government on its own terms. The freedom and the space available to the right to redraw the post-war consensus does not exist for the Left. This is because the complex British political system is in part a product of Conservative statecraft stretching back over sixty years, a primary purpose of which has been to contain the socialist wing of the Labour movement and foster the emergence of a responsible and moderate political and industrial labour leadership. By attacking the post-war consensus and reopening many long-settled questions about the scope of public responsibility for the economy and for welfare and about the rights of trade unions, the Thatcher leadership has indeed threatened the traditional interests and the dominant priorities of the Conservative party. It has done so because it judged the moment to be right for a decisive attack on the political and institutional strength of the Labour movement, as part of a coherent strategy to deal with the problems of British economic decline and the world recession. The restructuring it proposes is not just economic but political and means establishing over a period new priorities for policy, a new consensus. If this new Thatcherite consensus becomes consolidated then readmission to the adversarial two-party game can be offered to any opposition party or grouping that is prepared to play under the new rules.

The Conservatives despite a long-term weakening of their position[19] remain the dominant party in British politics, not merely in electoral terms, but also overwhelmingly as the party of the dominant institutions of the British state and society. The two-party adversary system has always been lopsided, never a struggle between equals, except in the narrow electoral sense discussed above. The terms of the conflict have always been weighted in the Conservatives' favour. This means it is much harder for a radical Labour than for a radical Conservative government firstly to be elected at all, and, if elected, to carry through a radical programme. Only once before in the 1940s was the Labour party actively involved in developing a new consensus. For the most part it has played a subordinate role in British politics.

The problem for the Labour party is to recognize the difficulties of being a party of reform in a two-party adversary system. These difficulties do not originate in the adversary system but they are exacerbated by it, because the system encourages illusions among Labour supporters about the scope which Labour governments have to effect radical change. The Labour governments that have been elected in Britain with the partial exception of the Attlee government, have been elected by means which have made them unwilling prisoners of the assumptions and priorities of the existing state, unable to deploy any countervailing forces of their own. The politics of the Labour movement in Britain have been built around industrial and community struggles to preserve jobs and services and to fight for new social and political rights. These have then been linked to efforts to elect Labour governments to initiate legislation that could protect and extend rights already won and gradually alter the balance of power in society in favour of the interests of the Labour movement.

The Labour movement was in such disarray in the 1980s because the two parts of the formula had come into violent contradiction. Labour governments administering the centralized machinery of the state to manage the national economy and the huge programmes of public expenditure clashed repeatedly with the industrial power of the trade unions. The Labour movement proved incapable of establishing the kind of social democracy successfully practised in several European countries. In so failing the political initiative has passed in Britain not to the Left but to the Right. It is this new situation which Labour has to confront.

The Labour party has a number of choices open to it in its bid to secure a future for itself in British politics. The party could seek to be readmitted as a respectable and trustworthy opposition, within the new

Thatcherite consensus. Many doubt the ability or the will of the party to perform such a feat without the expulsion of the bulk of the Left.

Alternatively the party could move decisively to the Left, facilitating further defections to the Alliance and reconstructing the party as a focus for extra-parliamentary struggle against the Conservative government. Such a party would necessarily be a party awaiting an economic and political catastrophe to befall the British state. In the short run, deprived of legitimacy, it could expect to be marginalized in electoral terms, though possibly holding on to a bloc of seats in the traditional Labour heartland.

A third path would be for Labour to reorganize itself as a socialist party seeking to develop a long-term strategy for socialist advance. A priority for such a strategy would be remedying the long-standing weaknesses that have restricted Labour's popular appeal and consequent effectiveness as a party of reform. Among the other things this would oblige Labour to seek the permanent destruction of the adversary two-party system with its sham conflicts and sham consensus, and would make the party support the creation of a more open and diversified political system.

Such a system would be likely to produce more conflict not less, a greater range of policy alternatives and debate, and above all greater popular participation in policy making. Major changes of direction in policy would be harder to achieve than under the present system, but once achieved they would be more durable because the political system would become geared to creating the political conditions necessary to ensure their success.

Whether the Labour party will emerge as such a party is not yet clear. There is some new thinking in the Labour movement and a new sense of political strategy. The prospects, however, for any party of reform ultimately rest on a political balance shaped by actions and events which the party itself does not control. Whether it can make use of these opportunities depends on how responsive it is to the demands and interests of those it seeks to represent and those it needs to persuade. Such a Labour party has a deep interest in constitutional reform to end bogus adversary politics, to free debate, to reform the system of patronage, to alter the character of the civil service, to make the process of government less secret, to make the media more accountable, and to introduce in Britain the kind of political and social rights which are commonplace in many other European countries. Such measures would improve the working of British democracy and help to widen political participation and political understanding in an electorate in which neither is widespread. It is one of the paradoxes of the adversary politics thesis that when it was first formulated many of its adherents argued that adversary politics must be halted to prevent socialism being foisted on an unwilling people. But the system of adversary politics as it has been developed and perfected in the last sixty years was actually one of the most successful creations of Conservative statecraft and helped to prevent the emergence of a truly radical alternative to Conservatism. The rituals of adversary politics have been an essential buttress to conservative political hegemony and to the maintenance of economic policies which have prevented any sustained assault on the root causes of Britains's economic decline and the new inequalities which now disfigure British society. Sweeping away adversarial politics in the traditional sense will be an essential part of any serious attempt to create either a radical or a socialist alternative to Conservatism. The Alliance parties had clearly grasped that crucial fact even before the 1983 election. Labour however even after its most serious defeat in the last sixty years still seemed to doubt it.

NOTES

PREFACE

1. See Andrew Gamble, 'Explanations of Economic Decline', Paper for the Annual Conference of the Political Studies Association, University of Newcastle, Apr. 1983.
2. S. E. Finer, *The Changing British Party System, 1945–1979*, Washington, American Enterprise Institute for Public Policy Research, 1980. See especially pp. 225 *et seq.*, 'A personal Post-script.

CHAPTER 1

1. Alan Cawson, *Corporatism and Welfare*, London, Heinemann, 1982, p. 39.
2. Tom Nairn, *The Breakup of Britain*, London, NLB, 1981.
3. H. S. Morrison, *Government and Parliament*, London, OUP, 1954.
4. M. Pinto-Duschinsky, *British Political Finance, 1830–1980*, Washington, American Enterprise Institute, 1981.
5. See Andrew Gamble, 'Liberals and the economy', in Vernon Bogdanor. (ed.), *Liberal party politics*, Oxford, OUP, 1983, pp. 191–216.
6. Keith Middlemas, *Politics in Industrial Society*, London, André Deutsch, 1979.
7. Middlemas, op. cit., p. 27.
8. R. T. McKenzie, 'Policy Decision in Opposition: A rejoinder', *Political Studies*, 5. 2 June 1957, 177.
9. *Parliamentary Affairs*, xix. 3, Summer 1966, 379.
10. Tom Nairn, *The Breakup of Britain*, London, NLB, 1981; Perry Anderson, 'Origins of the present crisis', *New Left Review*, No. 23, Jan.–Feb., 1964.

CHAPTER 2

1. C. D. Cohen, *British Economic Policy, 1960–69*, London, Butterworths, 1971, p. 269.
2. See C. J. F. Brown and T. D. Sheriff, *De-Industrialisation in the UK: Background Statistics* (Discussion Paper No. 23), London, National Institute of Economic and Social Research (NIESR), 1979.

3. See particularly Bo Särlvik and Ivor Crewe, *Decade of Dealignment*, Cambridge, CUP, 1983. See also H. M. Drucker, *Multi-party Britain*, London, Macmillan, 1979.
4. The idea of a hundred-year decline is not universally accepted. See S. Blank, 'Britain: The politics of Foreign Economic Policy, the Domestic Economy, and the Problem of Pluralistic Stagnation', *International Organization*, 31. 4, Autumn 1977, 673–722.
5. S. E. Finer (ed.), *Adversary Politics and Electoral Reform*, London, Wigram, 1975, p. 3.
6. N. Johnson, *In Search of the Constitution*, London Methuen, 1977, p. 66.
7. S. Beer, *Modern British Politics*, London, Faber, 1965, p. 357.
8. G. Sartori, 'European Political Parties', in J. La Palombara and M. Weiner (eds.), *Political Parties and Political Development*, Princeton University Press, 1966, p. 172.
9. Ionescu, 'How to Look, or Not to Look, at Modern British Politics', *Government and Opposition*, 18. 1, Winter 1983.
10. R. T. McKenzie, *British Political Parties*, London, Heinemann, 1965.
11. R. Rose, *Do Parties Make a Difference?*, London, Macmillan, 1980.
12. Formulations of this variant include M. Stewart, *The Jekyll and Hyde Years*, London, Dent, 1977; and a Hansard Society Report, *Politics and Industry*, London, 1979, p. 56.
13. See, for example, Samuel Brittan, *The Economic Consequences of Democracy*, London, Temple Smith, 1977.
14. See, for example, Douglas Ashford, *Policy and Politics in Britain*, Oxford, Blackwell, 1981.
15. T. Nairn, 'The Future of Britain's Crisis', *New Left Review*, Nos. 113–14, Jan.–Apr. 1979, 51.
16. See especially J. Alt, 'Political Business Cycles in Britain', in P. Whitely (ed.), *Models of Political Economy*, London, Sage, 1980, pp. 155–76.
17. Rose, op. cit., ch. 7.
18. See The Hansard Society, *Politics and Industry – the Great Mismatch*, London, Hansard Society, 1979, ch.2.
19. See, for example, S. Brittan and P. Lilley, *The Delusion of Incomes Policy*, London, Temple Smith, 1977.
20. See J. Alt, *The Politics of Economic Decline*, Cambridge, CUP. 1979.

CHAPTER 3

1. E. E. Schattschneider, *The Semi-Sovereign People*, New York, Holt, 1960, p. 141.
2. A. Cairncross (ed.), *Britain's Economic Prospects Reconsidered*, London, Allen & Unwin, 1971, p. 235.
3. Douglas Ashford, *Policy and Politics in Britain*, Oxford, Blackwell, 1981.

4. See J. Tomlinson, *Problems of British Economic Policy, 1870–1945*, London, Methuen, 1981, ch. 1.
5. J. M. Keynes, *Essays in Persuasion*, London, Macmillan, 1972, p. 75.
6. C. Lindblom, *Politics and Markets*, New York, Basic Books, 1977.
7. F. W. S. Craig, *British General Election Manifestos*, London, Macmillan, 1975, p. 115.
8. Craig, op. cit., p. 125.
9. Ibid., p. 125.
10. Ibid., p. 126.
11. J. Grimond, *Memoirs*, London, Heinemann, 1979, p. 132.
12. Craig, op. cit., p. 174.
13. Ibid., p. 171.
14. Ibid., p. 154.
15. Ibid., p. 191.
16. Ibid., p. 214.
17. Ibid., p. 154.
18. Ibid., p. 190.
19. Conservative Party Conference Report (CPCR), 1949, p. 89.
20. Ibid., p. 96.
21. Ibid., p. 50.
22. Ibid., p. 52.
23. Harold Macmillan, *The Middle Way*, London, Macmillan, 1938.
24. Harold Macmillan, *Winds of Change*, London, Macmillan, 1966, pp.223–4.
25. A. Crosland, *The Future of Socialism*, London, Cape, 1956.
26. Craig, op. cit., p. 223.
27. Ibid., p. 256.
28. CPCR 1963, p. 94.
29. Craig, op. cit., p. 378.
30. Quoted by J. M. Keynes, op. cit., p.115.
31. Ibid., pp. 90–1.
32. See S. Brittan, *Steering the Economy*, London, Secker and Warburg, 1969, ch. 5.
33. I. D. M. Little, in G. D. N. Worswick and P. H. Ady, *The British Economy in the 1950s*, Oxford, OUP, 1962, p. 274.
34. G. D. N. Worswick in Cairncross, op, cit., pp. 58–9.
35. 'The ideas of economists and political philosphers, both when they are right and when they are wrong, are more powerful than is commonly understood. Indeed the world is ruled by little else . . . I am sure that the power of vested interests is vastly exaggerated compared with the gradual encroachment of ideas.' J. M. Keynes *General Theory of Employment, Interest and Money*, London, Macmillan, 1973, p. 383.
36. Ian Gilmour, *Britain Can Work*, Oxford, Martin Robertson, 1983, p. 160.
37. R. C. O. Matthews, 'Why has Britain had full employment since the war?', *Economic Journal* 78, Sept. 1968, pp. 555–69. See also the

monetarist analysis by R. J. Ball, *Money and Employment*, London, Macmillan, 1982.
38. See E. Brett, *International Money and Capitalist Crisis*, London, Heinemann, 1983.
39. Harold Macmillan, *At the end of the day*, London, Macmillan, 1973, p. 89.

CHAPTER 4

1. London, Wigram, 1975.
2. S. Blank, 'Britain: the politics of foreign economic policy, the domestic economy, and the problem of pluralistic stagnation, Harvard University Centre for West European Studies, 1975.
3. London, Dent, 1977.
4. Oxford, Martin Robertson, 1979.
5. London, Allen & Unwin, 1945.
6. Oxford University Press, 1965.
7. In French planning an uncompromising use of executive power to which political persuasion is secondary; highly developed discrimination in favour of particular firms within industries; the instrumental use of fiscal means and direct financial inducements to facilitate compliance by industry; the central position of the state-owned Bank of France and other publicly owned financial institutions in supplying commercial credit; the close co-operation of the French Treasury; the detailed intervention in the capital market of the Commissariat du Plan; etc. See *Modern Capitalism*, pp. 163–71.
8. Op. cit., pp. 144–5.
9. Quoted in Smith, op. cit., p. 148.
10. David Judge, 'Specialists and Generalists in British Central Government: A Political Debate', *Public Administration* 59, Spring 1981.
11. Oxford, Martin Robertson, 1975.
12. Harold Macmillan, *The Middle Way*, London, Macmillan 1938.
13. London, Allen & Unwin, 1979.
14. See Shonfield, op. cit., pp. 96 *et seq.*; Leruez, op. cit., pp. 67 *et seq.;* P. D. Henderson, 'Government and Industry', in G. D. N. Worswick and P. H. Ady (eds.), *The British Economy in the 1950s*, Oxford, OUP, 1952.
15. Cambridge, CUP, 1964.
16. A. Lord, 'A Strategy for Industry', Sir Ellis Hunter Memorial Lecture, University of York, 1979.
17. London, Fontana, 1978.
18. 'The Sociology of Planning: Thought and Social Interaction', in M. Bornstein (ed.), *Economic Planning East and West*, Cambridge, Mass., Ballinger, 1975.
19. For this period, see David Coombes, *Representative Government and Economic Power*, London, Heinemann 1982, pp. 104 *et seq.*
20. NEB, *Annual Report and Accounts*, 1978, London, NEB Information Department, May 1979.

21. Since this chapter was written, the Department of Industry was merged back in early 1983 into the Department of Trade.
22. Stephen Blank, 'British Economic Problems: Lies and Damn Lies', Washington Centre of Foreign Policy Research, Johns Hopkins School on International Studies, 1979.
23. J. E. S. Hayward, 'Institutional Inertia and Political Impetus in France and Britain,' *European Journal of Political Research*, (Amsterdam) 4, 1976.
24. Blank, op. cit., pp. 76–7.
25. Ibid., p. 83.
26. Op. cit., p. 77.
27. E. H. Carr, *The Twenty Years' Crisis*, London, Macmillan 1962, p. 116.

CHAPTER 5

1. R. Rose, *Do Parties make a Difference?*, London, Macmillan, 1980.
2. See David Coombes and S. A. Walkland, *Parliaments and Economic Affairs*, London, Heinemann, 1980. See especially Part 11, 'Parliament and the Economy in Great Britain'.
3. Professor H. A. Turner, 'Sources of Decline', *The Times Higher Educational Supplement*, 4 June 1982, 16.
4. Sir Leo Pliatzky, 'Ministers and Officials', *London Review of Books* 2. 10 June 1980.
5. D. Shapiro, 'When in doubt, blame the bureaucracy', *The Times Higher Educational Supplement*, 12 June 1981, 11–12.
6. London, Croom Helm, 1982.
7. Turner, op. cit., 16.
8. J. Eatwell, *Whatever happened to Britain?*, London, BBC Publications, 1982.
9. Eatwell, op. cit., pp. 84–5.
10. Oxford, Blackwell, 1981.
11. Ashford, op. cit., p. 120.
12. *The Times*, 18 Mar. 1983.
13. Sir Douglas Hague and Geoffrey Wilkinson, *The IRC: an Experiment in Industrial Intervention*, London, Heinemann, 1983.
14. See J. C. Carrington and G. T. Edwards, *Reversing Economic Decline*, London, Macmillan, 1981.
15. See D. Coombes and S. A. Walkland, op. cit.,
16. See S. A. Walkland, 'Parliamentary Reform through Electoral Reform', in David Judge (ed.), *The Politics of Parliamentary Reform*, London, Heinemann, 1983.
17. See Joel Barnett, *Inside the Treasury*, London, André Deutsch, 1982, p. 77.
18. A. Seldon, *Churchill's Indian Summer*, London, Hodder & Stoughton, p. 437.
19. See the discussion by John Ross, *Thatcher and Friends*, London, Pluto, 1983.

SELECT BIBLIOGRAPHY

Alt, J., *The Politics of Economic Decline*, Cambridge, CUP, 1979.

Ashford, D., *Policy and Politics in Britain*, Oxford, Blackwell, 1981.

Beer, S., *Modern British Politics*, London, Faber, 1965.

Beer, S., *Britain Against Itself*, London, Norton, 1982.

Brittan, S., *Steering the Economy*, London, Secker and Warburg, 1969.

Brittan, S., *The Economic Consequences of Democracy*, London, Temple Smith, 1977.

Budd, A., *The Politics of Economic Planning*, Fontana, 1978.

Cairncross, F. (ed.), *Changing Perceptions of Economic Policy*, London, Methuen, 1981.

Cawson, A., *Corporatism and Welfare*, London, Heinemann, 1982

Coombes, D., *Representative Government and Economic Power*, London, Heinemann, 1982.

Coombes, D., and Walkland S. A. *Parliament and Economic Affairs*, London, Heinemann, 1980.

Crouch, C. (ed.), *State and Economy in Contemporary Capitalism*, Oxford, Martin Robertson, 1979.

Drucker, H. M. (ed.) *Developments in British Politics*, London, Macmillan, 1983.

Finer, S. E. *The Changing British Party System*, Washington, American Enterprise Institute, 1980.

Finer, S. E. (ed.), *Adversary Politics and Electoral Reform*, London, Wigram, 1975.

Johnson, N., *In search of the Constitution*, London, Methuen, 1977.

Keegan, W., and Pennant-Rea, R., *Who Runs the Economy?*, Oxford, Martin Robertson, 1981.

Leruez, J., *Economic Planning and Politics in Britain*, Oxford, Martin Robertson, 1975.

Middlemas, K., *Politics in Industrial Society*, London, André Deutsch, 1979.

Nairn, T., *The Breakup of Britain*, London, NLB, 1982.

Pollard. S., *The Wasting of the British Economy*, London, Croom Helm, 1982.

Rose, R., *Do Parties Make a Difference?*, London, Macmillan, 1980.

Smith, T., *The Politics of the Corporate Economy*, Oxford, Martin Robertson, 1979.

Stewart, M., *The Jekyll and Hyde Years*, London, Dent, 1977.

INDEX